LEADERSHIP
IN
HEALTHCARE

LEADERSHIP
IN
HEALTHCARE

Essential Values and Skills

FOURTH EDITION

Carson F. Dye

ACHE Management Series

Library of Congress Cataloging-in-Publication Data is on file at the Library of Congress, Washington, DC.

ISBN: 978-1-64055-361-3

The paper used in this publication meets the minimum requirements of American National Standard for Information Sciences—Permanence of Paper for Printed Library Materials, ANSI Z39.48-1984. ∞ ™

Acquisitions editor: Jennette McClain; Manuscript editor: DeAnna Burghart; Project manager: Andrew Baumann; Cover designer: Brad Norr; Layout: PerfectType

Found an error or a typo? We want to know! Please e-mail it to hapbooks@ache.org, mentioning the book's title and putting "Book Error" in the subject line.

For photocopying and copyright information, please contact Copyright Clearance Center at www.copyright.com or at (978) 750-8400.

Health Administration Press
A division of the Foundation of the American
    College of Healthcare Executives
300 S. Riverside Plaza, Suite 1900
Chicago, IL 60606–6698
(312) 424–2800

For Andrew—what a story and what a wonderful young man

Contents

Foreword

Brett D. Lee, PhD, FACHE
President, Texas Health Resources/University of Texas
Southwestern Medical Center, Frisco

THERE IS AN event in the life of every healthcare leader, likely further removed in our minds by time than by memory, that made each of us aspire to a career of guiding and inspiring those around us. It may have been the experience of witnessing a great leader in action that was the catalyst to attempt to emulate their influence, or for others it may have been a deeply personal healthcare journey that they or a loved one experienced that motivated them to pursue a life in service to others. In many cases, however, we can point to a book that we have read in our past that touched us personally and through which the author greatly influenced our thoughts and actions as a leader.

Leadership in Healthcare by Carson Dye (now in its fourth edition) has become one of the seminal guidebooks in our industry and has helped to shape the development of generations of healthcare leaders. The foundational elements of the original text are as relevant today as they were when they were first introduced over a decade ago, and the content in this latest edition has been updated to better prepare our emerging leaders for the unprecedented challenges we face in healthcare today.

I often think about my first boss, an incredibly talented healthcare CEO who began his leadership career in the early 1960s, and how the modern healthcare landscape would likely seem very foreign to him. Concepts such as value-based care, population health management, and virtual care delivery platforms were not even contemplated during his time in our industry, and the key strategies that he implemented so well to make his hospitals successful would prove to be liabilities today. No matter how much the industry evolves, however, there are certain traits, characteristics, and skills that will help to ensure leadership success regardless of the shifting sands of circumstance.

This latest edition of *Leadership in Healthcare* focuses on the importance of developing a core set of values that guide our behavior as leaders. At no time in the history of our industry have these values been so critical, as we are faced with situations, such as confronting a global pandemic, for which there is no experiential playbook. It is our values that serve as our guiding light as we navigate turbulent waters and that help to ensure the decisions we make in the face of difficult circumstances are grounded in a firm ethical foundation. As our organizations become more complex and we are placed in the position to manage teams and influence relationships across the continuum of care, understanding the lessons this book imparts on how values develop within teams and how they can affect behavior and outcomes is critical for anyone contemplating a career in healthcare leadership. Fundamentally, values drive behavior, and we must seek to understand our personal values and the values of those around us if we hope to lead them toward a common goal.

While the past several years have been some of the most disruptive in the history of our industry, I look to the future with great hope and anticipation. Every great challenge brings with it a set of new opportunities for those with the foresight to recognize them. In the wake of the worst pandemic in 100 years, we have seen a proliferation of new partnerships between healthcare organizations, rapid innovation in pharmaceutical development, and the proliferation of telemedicine, all of which will completely change the healthcare landscape for generations to come. In his historic inaugural address, Barack Obama said that "change will not come if we wait for some other time or some other place. We are the ones that we have been waiting for."* I challenge each of you who read this book to remember these words and to translate the lessons you will learn from *Leadership in Healthcare* into action, so that you make your own mark on our industry. *You* are the leaders we have been waiting for.

---

* Obama, Barack. 2008. Speech to supporters after nominating contests, delivered in Chicago, February 8, 2008.https://www.nytimes.com/2008/02/05/us/politics/05text-obama.html

Academic Foreword

Andrew N. Garman, PsyD
Professor, Rush University

I WRITE THIS foreword during a time of unprecedented evolution in both healthcare and higher education, with far-reaching implications for leaders' roles. The relationship between leaders and employees is shifting, with employees demanding a greater voice in their roles and expecting more from the organizations they choose to work for. Yet the business models healthcare and higher education were founded on are themselves unsustainable. The runaway costs of healthcare and tuition are contributing to levels of economic inequality not seen in this country in more than 80 years—trends the pandemic has only accelerated, with public mistrust growing right along with it. At the same time, scientists are painting us an ever-clearer picture of a planetary life support system in urgent need of much better maintenance, and a growing need to assess the impact of our decisions today on the well-being of many generations to come.

And yet there remain reasons for hope.

Healthcare professionals are coming together like never before, demanding meaningful progress toward better health for all. Across the country, health systems and universities are recognizing their important status—and responsibilities—as anchor institutions in their local economies. Health systems are widening their views about what it means to have a mission of health, by using both their expertise and purchasing power to strengthen communities and address root causes of health disparities. Universities are recognizing they need to ensure their students' debt burdens are sound long-term investments and are working with employers to strengthen these returns. Forward-thinking health systems are increasingly vertically integrating with university and private-sector learning programs, creating meaningful and accessible career pathways and improving the value proposition for students and employers alike. And the governments of 50 countries around the world—including the United States—have publicly committed to develop climate resilient and low-carbon health systems in support of the United Nations' decarbonization goals.

What will our future look like? Which path will we take? Those questions will be answered by the values we as leaders subscribe to, and how willing we are to take the bold actions needed.

This is where *Leadership in Healthcare* comes in. There are lots of good books out there on the *what* and the *how* of leadership, including *Exceptional Leadership: 16 Critical Competencies for Healthcare Executives*, which Carson and I coauthored. But there are far fewer books on the *why*. *Leadership in Healthcare* was written to address the *why* of leadership. After more than 20 years and four editions, its longevity is a testament to the importance of its contents.

As our understanding of values-based leadership has evolved, so too has this book. For the latest edition, Carson has developed many new resources to support applications within formal learning programs and higher education. He has also updated the references to emerging theory, in addition to the important foundational works this text cites.

I encourage you to read this important book at least twice during your career. On your first read, take special note of the passages that speak to your personal values or articulate things you know in your heart but find difficult to convey to others in words. Bookmark these for later.

Down the road, you will undoubtedly find yourself at your own crossroads in the choices you need to make. These could be times when what you think is right also seems most risky, or times when doing what's best for your community requires considerable sacrifice by the organization that employs you to look after its success. When you find yourself in this space, take out this book again and flip to the pages you bookmarked on your first read. Reflecting on these passages a second time can help you firm up your convictions while making difficult decisions.

Your values are there for a very important reason: to guide your actions when things get difficult. Now more than ever, we need value-driven leaders.

Like you.

Preface

Leadership remains a relatively mysterious concept despite having been studied for several decades.

—Atul Gupta, Jason C. McDaniel,
and S. Kanthi Herath (2005)

VALUES COME INTO play here.

I wrote *Leadership in Healthcare: Values at the Top*, the first edition of this book, at the turn of the new century. The second edition appeared in 2010 and the third edition in 2017. I continue to be amazed and humbled by its reception. Practitioners and students alike have used it and communicated with me about their reactions, thoughts, and suggestions. I remain humbled by the first edition's selection as the ACHE James Hamilton Book of the Year. I am struck by the power of the message of values in leadership. Yes—values come into play here.

Twenty-plus years after the publication of the first edition, much has changed in the world, in American society, and in the US healthcare system and its leadership. At the time of writing this fourth edition, our planet continues to face one of the greatest challenges of all time—the COVID-19 pandemic. Certainly healthcare will never be the same. Yet, despite critical challenges, many healthcare leaders continue to lead and lead successfully. Many realities face leadership, including the following:

1. *Effective leadership is difficult to define.* So many "definitive" leadership books exist, but so few articulate the principles underlying effective leadership.

2. *The ethics of leaders has been on the decline.* Power can corrupt, which is evident from the much-reported unethical and criminal activities of top executives in many industries. When inappropriate conduct is committed in healthcare, it not only erodes the public's trust but also threatens patients' safety and lives.

3. *The constant stresses in healthcare cause burnout and change of careers.* As a leadership and former search consultant, I am acutely aware of leaders' frustrations and uneasiness about the rapid pace of change in the field. Many of them leave the field as a result, while others struggle through these problems, tired, dejected, and pessimistic. COVID-19 has only intensified this challenge, with many healthcare employees choosing to leave entirely in an ongoing trend known as "The Great Resignation."

4. *Leadership development is still not a top priority.* Although many senior executives express an interest in professional growth and development, they devote little time or funds to this pursuit. This paradox is apparent when leadership development becomes the first to get cut from the organizational budget. The economic downturn became another excuse (next to limited time) for overlooking development opportunities.

5. *Effective leaders are almost always values driven.* Those who rely only on hard data and measurable standards often say that values are vague contributors to effectiveness because they cannot be quantified. However, a review of empirical research, coupled with my observations and constant contact with executives, reveals that values are cited by highly effective leaders as major factors of their success.

6. *Effective leadership can be learned.* Some people are "born" leaders. They possess and live by deep, unwavering values. They have a natural ability to interact with and lead others. However, these qualities can be learned by people who are not born with such talents. Becoming aware of the need for learning and practicing a sensitive, practical, and appropriate value system is the first step toward becoming a world-class leader.

In 2010, I wrote, "We now live in a more frenzied, Internet-driven culture, where technology gives to but also takes away from our daily lives." As trite as it may seem, that frenzy has grown, the Internet has more impact than ever before, and technology helps but also hurts us. And in the 2017 third edition, I wrote about new challenges of cost management and reimbursement, location of care, quality, the challenges of larger and more complex organizations, labor shortages, and physician/clinician burnout. Little did I know that COVID-19 would make all of this look simple for healthcare leaders. And while it is not the intent of this fourth edition to deeply delve into the issues of COVID-19, it cannot be ignored, and there are many new sections and resources that address this taxing challenge.

I argued then—and I argue even more strongly now—that while technology has allowed us instant access to other people and to enormous amounts of information, it has shrunk our chances for face-to-face communication. The human element is not what it once was. The COVID-19 pandemic has certainly changed that. And again, values come into play here.

And while social media—Twitter, Facebook, LinkedIn, and the like—have enabled us to network, stay in touch, and even make "friends" from distant locations, they have also introduced unique challenges in the workplace. Although the Internet age in healthcare has made some veteran executives say that interactions are "not as fun as they used to be," it does attract and excite the younger leaders among us. But once again, values come into play here.

We now live in a world that is very divisive, a country that is polarized, and we work in a healthcare world that has changed enormously. The political, social, and economic uncertainties we face manifest themselves in our healthcare facilities, exacerbating the crises that organizational leaders must solve every day. The pandemic forced many organizations to cope with an inability to provide care, greater labor shortages than ever before experienced, and a workforce that is exhausted and spent. Emergency departments continue to be the front door and often primary providers of healthcare. Telehealth, while a solution during the pandemic, provides new challenges. We continue to see a shortage in all kinds of workers, made much more serious as a result of the pandemic. Retail operators have now entered our world of service and care to others. Financial challenges continue to threaten the availability and quality of care, advances in medical technology and pharmaceuticals have been ramping up the cost of care, and the American public's scrutiny of the healthcare field has gotten closer and deeper. Although not entirely new or insurmountable, these challenges add even more pressure to the already-strained healthcare workforce and its leaders. But once again, values come into play here—and vividly—for our leaders.

Although much progress has been attained in the field, much still needs to be accomplished. This is the environment in which the fourth edition of *Leadership in Healthcare* is truly effective.

THE INTENT OF THIS BOOK

My goals for this edition are the same as the goals for the first three editions:

1. Raise leaders' awareness about values and their meaning and applicability to leadership.
2. Posit that values play a major role in leaders' effective performance.

3. Recommend practical strategies for living by those values at work and at home.

Judging by the strong reception to and enduring support for the earlier editions, this book has filled a latent hunger for discussion about values-based leadership, something that even I did not anticipate. The need for such a discussion is not confined to the healthcare executive world; it is also demanded by graduate and undergraduate programs as well as other providers of professional education. The following that the first three editions have garnered has prompted me to present an updated edition that reflects our drastically changed environment.

Changes in the Fourth Edition

This edition remains true to its original premise. However, to better illustrate and highlight the concepts, I have added new elements and expanded the discussions. These additions further facilitate teaching, dialogue, and self-reflection:

- Chapter 20, "Inclusive Leadership," written by Carla Jackie Sampson, PhD, FACHE
- Chapter 21, "Physician Leadership Issues," written by Margot Savoy, MD, FAAFP, FABC, FAAPL, CPE, CMQ
- Chapter 22, "Humans Working with Humans to Heal Humans," written by Katherine A. Meese, PhD, David A. Roger, MD, MHPE
- Chapter 23, "Leadership Matters—For Healthcare's Present and Future," written by Patrick D. Shay, PhD
- Chapter 24, "Post-COVID Leadership"
- New treatment of the impact of COVID-19 on healthcare leadership
- New or revised strategies and examples

This edition retains many of the elements of the previous editions:

- Opening vignettes that reflect workplace situations
- Sidebars that support the discussions
- Cases and exercises that stimulate reader response
- Additional readings that can provide an expanded understanding of chapter content

Content Overview

The book has two forewords—one by Brett D. Lee, PhD, FACHE, and another by Andrew N. Garman, PsyD. The rationale here is to represent the perspectives of the book's main audience, which is composed of both healthcare executives and health administration educators and students.

The book is divided into five parts. Part I—Leadership in Healthcare—contains chapters 1 through 5 and sets the stage on which the field and its leaders perform their roles. Part II—Personal Values—includes chapters 6 through 12 and catalogs the key values that influence the leader's behaviors, priorities, thought processes, and actions. Part III—Team Values—comprises chapters 13 through 16 and explores the values that guide a leadership team. Part IV—Evaluation—encompasses chapters 17 through 19 and provides guidance for assessing team values and effectiveness and careers at all stages.

Part V—Additional Perspectives on Leadership—contains chapters 20 through 24.

Chapter 20 is written by Carla Jackie Sampson, PhD, FACHE, clinical associate professor of healthcare management and director of health programs at New York University's Robert F. Wagner Graduate School of Public Service. Dr. Sampson also serves as the editor of *Frontiers in Health Services Management*. Dr. Sampson's chapter, "Inclusive Leadership," provides unique insight into the

Mary C. Gentile. AZQuotes.com, Wind and Fly LTD, 2022. https://www.azquotes.com/quote/1608956, accessed July 07, 2022.

Ortega y Gasset, J. 1958. *Man and Crisis*. Translated by Mildred Adams. New York: W. W. Norton & Co.

INSTRUCTOR RESOURCES

This book's Instructor Resources include PowerPoint slides for each chapter, additional discussion questions, and web links.

For the most up-to-date information about this book and its Instructor Resources, go to ache.org/HAP and browse for the book's title or author name.

This book's Instructor Resources are available to instructors who adopt this book for use in their course. For access information, please e-mail hapbooks@ache.org.

Acknowledgments

AFTER WORKING IN healthcare for more than 40 years, I thought I had seen it all. Then COVID-19 hit—truly hit. And I pondered the future of healthcare leadership. I have worked—no, lived, really lived—in healthcare for most of my life. (They say once you move past 40 years, you shouldn't be quite so precise.) My entire career has been marked by interaction with leaders. From Sister Mary George, RSM, first CEO of Clermont Mercy Hospital, and my first boss in healthcare, to the wide-ranging group of leaders participating in my last ACHE workshop, my career has focused on identifying strong leaders, coaching and counseling leaders at all levels, guiding physicians as they begin their own leadership journeys, and serving clients in hundreds of executive searches. I have learned so much from all of these people. And all of these thousands of individuals should be acknowledged—but alas, they are too numerous to be listed.

My good fortune has been compounded by working for and with some exemplary leaders. While that list would also be too lengthy to include in this preface, I do think of Sister Mary George, Michael Covert, Donald Cramp, and the late Dr. Lonnie Wright and Sy Sokatch from Children's Hospital in Cincinnati. Michael Covert was a great leader to work for and expanded my viewpoint of what was possible in healthcare leadership. Other leaders have given me the chance to recruit them, recruit for them, counsel them, help them on board, and work with their boards and senior teams. All of these leaders have had a significant influence on my thinking:

Dr. Scott Ransom, Michael Ugwueke, Chip Hubbs, Kris Hoce, Dr. Scot Remick, Dr. Kathleen Forbes, Brett Lee, Tim Putnam, Larry Gumina, Scott Malaney, Bill Linesch, Dr. Greg Taylor, Dr. Akram Boutros, Dr. John Byrnes, Dr. David James, Dr. John Paris, Dr. Doug Spotts, Dr. Lily Jung Henson, and Dr. Jeremy Blanchard. Moreover, having the ability to work alongside Kam Sigafoos, Bill Sanger, the late Dr. Ed Pike, Mark Hannahan, Mark Elliott, Walter McLarty, Gretchen Patton, and Randy Schimmoeller gave me great day-to-day lessons in leadership.

It's all about values, and these individuals represent great values. I have watched them and learned much from them. Often, they were unaware that I was making mental notes on what they did and how effective they were in their leadership activities. But their behavior always came back to their inherent values. These are the leaders of our healthcare enterprises in America, and because of their values, we can stand confidently knowing our healthcare organizations are in their hands.

Over the years it has been an honor and a privilege to teach in the academy. My academic career began at the University of Cincinnati in the summer of 1977, continued with Xavier University from 1978 to 1981, and grew with Dr. Steve Strasser at the Ohio State University from 1985 to 2007. I have also been honored to teach at the University of Alabama, Birmingham. All this classroom time has given me the impetus to grow in my academic knowledge of leadership. I find myself always going to the scholarly articles section of Google before reading the popular literature. My hope is that more practitioners will turn to the evidence-based literature, and more frequently.

Appreciation also goes to the various faculty who have chosen this book for their leadership courses. I am honored that I can be of some assistance as they fulfill the calling of preparing tomorrow's healthcare leaders. Thank you all.

While waxing scholarly, I would like to acknowledge Andrew Garman, my friend, colleague, and occasional coauthor. Andy brings a true scholarly focus to his work and outlook, and I have benefited from my work with him. He was kind enough to provide the academic foreword for this book, and I am in his debt.

I am also very appreciative of several who have added to this leadership tome. Dr. Margot Savoy provided great insight into the special issues of physician leadership, and I salute her contribution. Dr. Carla Jackie Sampson has such vision and comprehension in the area of inclusive leadership; I cannot thank her enough for her gift of counsel. Dr. Katherine Meese, who has influenced me so much in my understanding of wellness, joined with Dr. David Rogers in creating an incredibly unique chapter about humans caring for humans caring for humans. UAB is fortunate to have these two healthcare leaders, and I am lucky they were able to help me. I so appreciate Dr. Patrick Shay, who is a thought leader in the area of organization theory. Once again, he provided a wonderful chapter on the critical importance of leadership in healthcare. The contributions of these professionals have made this book far stronger, and I cherish their offerings.

My counsel as a leadership consultant, my work as an executive search consultant, and my focus on leadership assessment give me exposure to exceptional leaders every day. These individuals practice values-based leadership, and I always gain from my exposure to them. Each and every day is an exciting day of learning for me. I am so fortunate to have had this career.

Finally, conducting workshops, training sessions, and webinars for healthcare associations and other organizations continues to expand my understanding of leadership concepts. I have had the good fortune of teaching for ACHE for longer than I can remember, and every one of those opportunities has taught me much.

Again—Health Administration Press (HAP) is *our* publisher for our industry. We are quite lucky to have them. They dedicate their hours and days to finding authors who can expand our understanding and help us do more effective work and service. Their publications are timely and high in quality. I want to acknowledge and praise them.

Specifically, I am grateful for the leadership of Michael Cunningham and Jennette McClain. Jennette helps scour the horizon and is quite tuned in to contemporary issues in healthcare management and leadership. Although she transitioned to another role before publication of this edition, her many contributions to the HAP program are much appreciated. Thanks also to Sharon Sofinski, who helped see many small details and added greatly to this books' readability.

I said this in the third edition and I repeat it here: To work and serve in such a distinctive field as healthcare is a calling and a blessing. Healthcare has so many devoted, values-driven leaders who deserve much credit and acknowledgment. Again, I also acknowledge those many men and women in uniform with whom I work so often—the Army, Air Force, Navy Medical Service Corps, Medical Corps, and Nursing Corps. Many of them gave me great leadership lessons, including David Rubenstein, Paul Williamson, Kathy Van Der Linden, Steve Wooldridge, Kyle Campbell, Patrick Misnick, and Mark Wilhite. I salute and thank them.

My most important acknowledgment always goes to my family. They have missed me often as I traveled the country working with leaders, and yet they are always my greatest sources of support and love. So I acknowledge my four wonderful daughters, Carly, Emily, Liesl, and Blakely; a great son-in-law, Jeremy; three grandsons, Carson, Benjamin, and Andrew; a second great son-in-law, Philippe Larouche, and granddaughter, Celine; and a third great son-in-law, Nick Brandon, and grandson, Henry. My wife, Joaquina, has always supported my writing and many, many times, has often made it much more logical.

This book has been a very special one for me. I was greatly honored with its selection in 2001 as the ACHE James A. Hamilton Book of the Year. While this fourth edition marks my fifteenth book, *Leadership in Healthcare* maintains its unique position. The book represents my belief in values-driven leadership and how each of us carries part of those with whom we work and interact into our own leadership styles. In the musical *Wicked*, the story of the witches in *The Wizard of Oz*, these words are shared between Glinda, the "good" witch, and Elphaba, the "bad" witch:

> I've heard it said
> That people come into our lives for a reason
> Bringing something we must learn
> And we are led
> To those who help us most to grow
> If we let them
> And we help them in return
> Well, I don't know if I believe that's true
> But I know I'm who I am today
> Because I knew you.

Thanks to you leaders out there—because I knew you, I have greatly grown in my understanding of leadership.

Carson F. Dye, FACHE

PART I

LEADERSHIP IN HEALTHCARE

The Leadership Imperative

*We are crossing a line into a territory with unpredictable
turmoil and exponentially growing change—
change for which we are not prepared.*

—John Kotter (2014)

UNIVERSITY **M**EDICAL **C**ENTER is hosting an annual reception for its retired employees. Jonathan Sneed, the medical center's CEO in the 1990s, is one of the special guests. Now in his 80s, Jonathan remains sharp as he sits at a table with Elizabeth Jankowski, the current CEO. The two are discussing the evolution of healthcare management.

JONATHAN. Elizabeth, your challenges are more complex than ours were years ago. Back then, we thought our issues were insurmountable! And I know that COVID has been a real challenge. But I suspect that 25 years from now, you'll think your problems now are simple. There's one constant necessity for leaders through the years, however. Leaders have to be constantly learning and adjusting their skills and knowledge. They always have to anticipate what's coming just past the horizon. This leadership quality has kept this academic medical center at the forefront and contributed to its great reputation as a learning organization.

ELIZABETH. Great point! I do get concerned sometimes about some of our leaders. In fact, last week at our senior council meeting, we talked about how so many of us have become so consumed with the COVID crisis that we haven't been able to invest time in leadership education. There are days we just put out fires. COVID has taken a real toll on our leaders. We have not had the chance to think about any future strategy.

JONATHAN. Watch out for that. I know this pandemic has been tough, but if you do not keep up with trends and the new realities that will come out of this crisis—well, it is like not changing the oil in your car often enough. You won't see the negative effects until it's too late.

"IT WAS THE best of times, it was the worst of times," writes Charles Dickens in his classic book *A Tale of Two Cities*. The same can be said of constantly evolving healthcare. Consider some of the realities (both good and bad) in the field that confront healthcare leaders today:

- COVID-19
- Shift from volume to value
- Clinical integration
- Transparency
- Population health management
- Management of the continuum of care—and care moving out of the acute care setting

- Telehealth
- Consolidation, alliances, affiliations, and consortiums among providers
- Professional shortages and decreasing recruitment pools
- Diversity, equity, and inclusion
- Retail healthcare (Walmart, Amazon, CVS)
- Continuing information technology (IT) pressures—artificial intelligence, electronic health record systems, and other clinical and information technologies
- Aging population
- Changes in worker and patient ethnic and cultural demographics
- Higher expectations from consumers; consumerism
- Loss of public respect and declining trust for the healthcare field

These challenges, and those yet to come, are exactly why the leadership imperative exists. The leadership imperative is the need for healthcare executives to enhance their understanding of the forces at play in the field and the way they manage through these changes. Leaders must now build judicious forecasts by thinking in the long term and changing these forecasts more frequently than every three years (the current traditional strategic plan cycle). The imperative demands planning that goes past the current work-day or budget year. Simply put, the healthcare field, its work-ers, and the people it serves need leaders who can rebuild trust; restore efficient processes; and ensure quality through uncertain environmental trends and practices, societal and economic flux, and organizational transitions. While COVID-19 has had an enormous impact, there are many other factors that also require skilled leadership.

EVOLVING ENVIRONMENT

Healthcare's evolution has brought not just improvements. In fact, it has created inefficiencies and disorganization. However, it has also ushered in more jobs, better operating standards and clinical outcomes, lifesaving advances, a focus on patients and disease management, improved services, and new sources of revenue (among other things).

Current trends (listed in exhibit 1.1) and common obstacles (discussed later in the chapter) shape the healthcare environment in which workers function and services are provided. In this landscape, physician–organization relations continue to be among the most challenging issues, along with strategic conflicts that could result from mergers or other steps to gain economies of scale or increase market share. Such conflicts may derail the flow of decisions and disrupt patient services.

Amid changes and problems, healthcare leaders plow through. Some are weary and doubtful of their ability to rebuild trust and

Exhibit 1.1 Current Trends in Healthcare

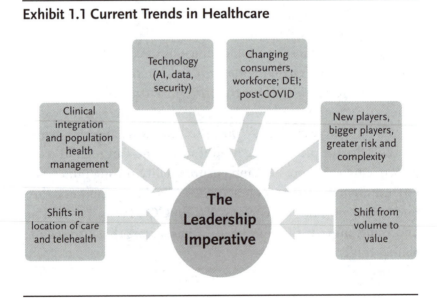

continue to guide their organizations. Some, however, are energized by the challenges. When I have asked about the current state of the field, several healthcare executives make the following comments:

- "These are very tough times to be a healthcare leader, but I would not have it any other way. This is a good test of my leadership."
- "Frankly, I wish some of my managers would leave healthcare. They are not up for the challenges we face. And they are bringing down our good leaders."
- "After 35 years in this field, I thought I had seen it all, but COVID caught me off guard. am just tired. But we have very important work to do, and we must be up for it."
- "I realize that at my level at the top of my organization, I have a better view and sense of direction. But I am concerned about my middle managers down in the trenches. I need to do whatever I can to help them keep holding on."

As these responses articulate, this era is both an exhausting and an exciting time to be a leader in healthcare.

COMMON OBSTACLES AND IMPERATIVE ACTIONS

Aside from coping with the current realities of the field, healthcare leaders also navigate the common obstacles of running multifaceted operations. In this section, these obstacles are listed along with an appropriate imperative action. An imperative action is a step that a leader may take to overcome the obstacle.

Obstacle 1: Organizations Today Are More Complex

> The problems of making healthcare work are large. The complexities are overwhelming governments, economies, and societies around the world. We have every indication, however, that where people in medicine combine their talents and efforts to design organized service to patients and local communities, extraordinary change can result.
>
> —Atul Gawande (2011)

Historically, healthcare organizations were structured in a relatively simple manner. Freestanding hospitals, private doctor's offices, nursing homes, and local pharmacies were the most ubiquitous embodiments of organizations. Healthcare *systems* did not exist, nor did integrated delivery networks and nursing home chains, and few mergers and acquisitions took place. Physicians were not employed by health systems; instead, they ran small, independent practices.

A hospital was not a conglomerate; it existed solely to provide care for the hospitalized patient. Therefore, its leaders were not mired in the politics of multiple business partners or the bureaucracy of multiple service lines. A hospital's mission and vision were clear.

"The more complex the system, the less efficient its operation" is an adage that is true of today's healthcare systems. Decreased efficiency results in less satisfaction not only for the system's patients but also for its workers. Complex systems exhaust leaders and resources because they require more attention and focus.

Imperative action: Restore the simplicity of the healthcare organization by clarifying its structure, mission and vision, and future direction. Work to minimize the complexities of intricate organizational structures.

Obstacle 2: Employee Engagement and Loyalty Are Low

Opinion surveys continue to reveal that employee commitment and engagement are low. Harter (2021) reports on recent Gallup surveys that show "employee quit rates are reaching record highs." In the same Gallup report, Harter (2021) also reports that "the percentage of actively disengaged employees is up slightly in the U.S., from 14% in 2020 to 15% through June 2021. Actively disengaged employees report miserable work experiences and are generally poorly managed."

> Is the US healthcare system expensive, complicated, dysfunctional, or broken? The simple answer is yes to all.
>
> —**Robert H. Shmerling (2021)**

Job security is one of the most important elements of a high-performance work environment. For a long time, healthcare offered just that: job security. Employees, in turn, showed their appreciation for this security by being loyal to the organization. Employees stayed at their jobs longer, performed harder and better, recommended family members and friends to apply for open positions, missed fewer workdays, and participated more in the activities of the organization. Gallup reports that "engaged employees are more enthusiastic, energetic and positive, feel better about their work and workplace, and have better physical health. Highly engaged workplaces can claim 41% lower absenteeism, 40% fewer quality defects, and 21% higher profitability" (Hickman and Robison 2020).

Today, even the hardiest healthcare systems cannot ensure jobs for their employees. One CEO suggests that the high levels of trust between management and staff that once existed in the healthcare field may never return: "I remember the first time I faced a room full of hospital employees who were to be laid off. That was 15 years ago, and I personally talked to all of them. However, the last three times my organization has laid employees off, I did not even go to the sessions. I was told that it was legally risky and that it could be better handled by our human resources staff. We handed the laid-off employees to an outplacement firm. I feel like I abandoned them and feel really bad, but I don't know what to do about it."

Imperative action: Enlist the engagement of strong employees by boosting trust levels and encouraging their participation in organizational initiatives, such as by giving them increased personal control and decision-making roles.

Obstacle 3: Physicians Are Increasingly Disengaged, Dissatisfied with the Field, and Burned Out

Physicians aged 55 or older have different expectations from those who are just beginning medical practice. Older physicians have witnessed the growth of managed care and eventual drops in reimbursement. They have experienced financial and legal challenges to their role as the "captain of the ship" in patient care. They mourn the disappearance of the club-like atmosphere of medicine, filled with people with the same concerns and priorities. The transition to electronic health records has tried the patience of many. Some physicians even regret having entered the profession.

Younger physicians, on the other hand, have different expectations. Most, if not all, of them begin their careers with enormous student loan debts (some estimates suggest an average of $241,600—see Association of American Medical Colleges 2021), so they desire stable employment with set hours and salary. In addition, younger physicians believe that medicine is only one part of their life, while older physicians put most of their lives' focus on medicine. These divergent perspectives and work styles have caused tension between these two groups.

> The world is now changing at a rate at which the basic systems, structures, and cultures built over the past century cannot keep up with the demands being placed on them. Incremental adjustments to how you manage and strategize, no matter how clever, are not up to the job.
>
> —John Kotter (2014)

Shryock (2021, 23) writes that "Four out of five physicians say they are burned out right now. Physician burnout in recent years has gone from a taboo topic to one of great concern in the health care industry."

The practice of employing physicians is a significant trend. According to the American Medical Association (2021), "With the steady decline since 2012 in the share of physicians working in private practices, there has been a concurrent increase in the share of physicians working directly for a hospital or for a practice at least partially owned by a hospital or health system. Almost 40% of patient care physicians worked either directly for a hospital or for a practice with at least partial hospital or health system ownership in 2020, up from 34.7% in 2018 and 29% in 2012."

Although physician employment can help align common interests and goals, it may also reduce the physicians' autonomy and complicate their decision-making. As a result, physicians, even employed ones, may end up losing faith in and loyalty to the organization. If given a choice, many physicians would rather have another physician as the leader of the organization, as this actual sentiment from a hospital physician board member underscores: "We seem to have forgotten our patients in our drive to build a bigger, more comprehensive healthcare system. At least having a physician as our CEO would bring back that patient focus."

The many significant changes within the field are enticing many physicians to move into leadership. Bisordi and Abouljoud (2015) report that "from payors and providers to facilities such as hospitals where services are delivered, healthcare reform has ushered in an era where physician leadership is, quite simply, essential for long-term success." Graduate schools throughout the country have developed management programs targeted at physicians. Multiple healthcare organizations have created physician leadership development academies. Many physicians enrolled in these courses are motivated by their dissatisfaction with how healthcare organizations are managed. These doctors seek to improve these facilities' operations and services as well as gain more influence over the strategic directions of their organizations.

Imperative action: Improve relations with the physician collective. Handle physician employment skillfully. Recognize—and address— physician burnout. Consider the fact that more and more physicians are needed in leadership roles. Build robust physician leadership development programs. Make room for the increasing number of part-time physician leaders who will remain in some clinical practice.

Obstacle 4: Pay for Value and Clinical Integration

Healthcare provision has been built on the concept of volume. It is a very simple-to-understand business in one respect: Bring more patients in the door, get paid for it, and business is good. "More heads in beds" was the mantra. Yet the reimbursement methodology is in the process of being turned upon its head. While talking about the so-called shift to a value-based reimbursement scheme is easy, guiding a real institution through the enormous changes it brought about—managing across that chasm—is almost frightening in its complexity. Coloton (2021) states, "The cost and complexity of updating operations in healthcare practices of today are extreme."

Clinical integration will create benefits for patients but massive changes for the field. Improvements include "the elimination of duplicate clinical and administrative work, a common patient record that ensures that the status of the patient is tracked throughout the entire course of care with no continuity-of-care gaps, a reduced chance of errors, systematic support of best practices and evidence-based care, and full alignment of the goals of all providers" (Dye and Sokolov 2013, 104). Yet, organizational complexity makes the move toward clinical integration quite difficult.

> **Imperative action:** Carefully craft logical strategic and tactical initiatives to shift toward value-based reimbursement and clinical integration without harming the care enterprise.

Obstacle 5: Patients Are Dissatisfied with Healthcare

Staggering healthcare costs, high insurance premiums or narrow-network insurance plans, poor quality of care, limited access to care, and lack of attention or information from providers are just some concerns that cause patient dissatisfaction. The COVID-19 pandemic further eroded trust in the healthcare sector.

Moreover, despite calls for improvement, quality and patient safety remain a serious challenge in the United States. Many patient safety advocates, including the Institute for Healthcare Improvement, have raised the level of awareness about dissatisfaction and have pushed various quality practices. The field has made some progress in this regard, but unfortunately, quality is just one of the many areas that need to be addressed.

Many healthcare systems have grown so large that patients report a lack of responsiveness similar to that experienced with large corporations. One educated patient compares her experiences with her health system to "calling an 800 customer service number in the middle of the night on Sunday." In a consumer-driven healthcare market, this type of treatment could lead to loss of revenue, at best, and loss of patient trust, at worst.

Imperative action: Make quality of care and patient safety your number-one priority. Pay attention to consumer service, and establish good relationships with the communities you serve.

Obstacle 6: Succession Planning Is Not a Priority for Some Retiring Leaders

An increasing number of baby boomer executives will retire in the next few years. Despite these retirement plans, many leaders have not developed succession plans to ensure that their transitions are handled effectively.

Next-generation leaders are ready and waiting for their opportunity to learn and grow in these management roles. Many are aware of the leadership imperative and are confident and excited about the future, although some are fearful of current trends.

Imperative action: Invest time and resources in succession planning and leadership development programs to ensure that the new generation of leaders will make the significant inroads and positive contributions needed for high-quality patient care and service to their communities.

CONCLUSION

The title of this chapter, "The Leadership Imperative," stems from two of the most urgent issues in healthcare today. First, leadership in healthcare is undeniably important, so the field needs a leadership book solely dedicated to healthcare. Healthcare is, in fact, different from other fields. As Gawande (2014, 6) writes, "Scientific advances have turned the process of aging and dying into medical experiments, matters to be managed by health care professionals. And we in the medical world have proved alarmingly unprepared for it." Leadership must walk side by side with healers and help remove barriers to success. Second, massive changes are transpiring in healthcare. Again, Gawande (2011) says it best: "You are the generation on the precipice of a transformation medicine has no choice but to undergo, the riders in the front car of the roller coaster clack-clack-clacking its way up to the drop. The revolution that remade how other fields handle complexity is coming to health care, and I think you sense it." Heeding the leadership imperative and taking up this mantle is what is required of leaders in healthcare today. Are you ready and willing?

But while the challenges facing healthcare are exceptional, some problems of leadership are classic. Root, a firm that helps organizations bridge the gaps in strategy and foster employees' understanding of that strategy and willingness to engage in it, presents a very unusual visual called *The Canyon* (see exhibit 1.2). Jim Haudan (2021), CEO of Root, describes it: "*The Canyon* reflects the reality of people's day-to-day jobs at all levels and functions of an organization. Dealing with those realities is the first step toward creating engaged employees and executing strategies like superstars. When leaders don't face reality head-on, it does not bode well for goal achievement."

Haudan (2021) further explains:

> What the image really shows are these canyons between the leaders of an organization who can see what needs to be done but don't have their hands on the levers of change every day, the managers stuck somewhere between the leaders and the doers so that they must balance a lack of full information with a need for employee guidance, and the doers who have their hands on change every day but can't see what needs to be done. So what you find, and maybe even metaphorically, is that everybody is at a different altitude, and everybody sees the problems that we face very differently.
>
> You know we have this wonderful saying: "People will tolerate the conclusions of their leaders, but they will act on their own." But if you are going to change the dynamic of that, which means that everybody is in a different corner, and that our conclusions are similar, then what we see in terms of our businesses must be explored equally. So everybody—leaders, managers, and individuals—must be able to see all the drama in the business and given the decency to compare and contrast, to check and recheck, to unlearn and to relearn, and when they are given that opportunity 99.9 percent of people come to very similar conclusions.
>
> The problem is what each of us sees is so different, our conclusions are so different, that again these canyons get perpetuated. And after the experiences that people have had with the COVID pandemic, the need to reach everyone in the organization is even more imperative.

Building bridges across the Canyon is, I think, the leadership imperative.

Exhibit 1.2 Root's *The Canyon*

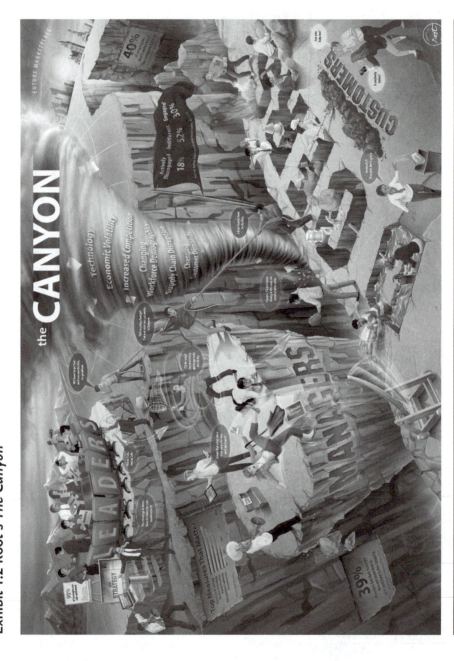

Source: The Canyon® is reprinted with permission of Root Inc. and Accenture. See more at https://www.rootinc.com/.

Self-Evaluation Questions

❑ Do I view myself as a leader? If so, is my goal to bring about needed change or, in the words of one CEO, "to build palaces and monuments to my legacy"?

❑ Do I view leadership as an act, a process, or a skill?

❑ Do I, and other leaders I know, think that a leadership imperative exists today?

❑ Have I observed any significant shifts and trends in the field and popular culture that affect leadership in my organization?

❑ Does it seem more difficult to lead and manage change today?

❑ What does the illustration of the Canyon mean to you as a leader?

Exercise

Exercise 1.1

Read and reflect on the following article concerning leadership following the COVID-19 pandemic. Suggest specific steps that leaders could take to reduce the problems created by COVID-19.

Geerts J. M., D. Kinnair, P. Taheri, A. Abraham, J. Ahn, R. Atun, L. Barberia, N. J. Best, R. Dandona, A. A. Dhahri, L. Emilsson, J. R. Free, M. Gardam, W. H. Geerts, C. Ihekweazu, S. Johnson, A. Kooijman, A. T. Lafontaine, E. Leshem, C. Lidstone-Jones, E. Loh, O. Lyons, K. A. F. Neel, P. S. Nyasulu,

(continued)

(continued from previous page)

O. Razum, H. Sabourin, J. S. Taylor, H. Sharifi, V. Stergio-poulos, B. Sutton, Z. Wu, and M. Bilodeau. 2021. "Guidance for Health Care Leaders During the Recovery Stage of the COVID-19 Pandemic: A Consensus Statement." *JAMA Network Open* 4 (7): e2120295.

REFERENCES

American Medical Association. 2021. *AMA Analysis Shows Most Physicians Work Outside of Private Practice.* May 5, 2021. https://www.ama-assn.org/press-center/press-releases/ama-analysis-shows-most-physicians-work-outside-private-practice.

Association of American Medical Colleges. 2021. *Average Medical Student Debt.* Published July. https://educationdata.org/average-medical-school-debt.

Bisordi, J., and M. Abouljoud. 2015. "Physician Leadership Initiatives at Small or Mid-size Organizations." *Healthcare.* Published October 20. http://dx.doi.org/10J016/j.hjdsi.2015.08.008.

Coloton, K. 2021. "How the Healthcare Industry Can Drive Change Through Value-Based Care." Forbes *Innovation,* July 1, 2021. https://www.forbes.com/sites/forbestechcouncil/2021/07/01/how-the-healthcare-industry-can-drive-change-through-value-based-care/?sh=5f38a4425e64

Dickens, Charles (1859) *A Tale of Two Cities,* Para.1, Line 1, 1859

Dye, C. F., and J. J. Sokolov. 2013. *Developing Physician Leaders for Successful Clinical Integration.* Chicago: Health Administration Press.

Gawande, A. 2014. *Being Mortal*. New York: Metropolitan Books.

————. 2011. "Cowboys and Pit Crews." *New Yorker*. Published May 26. www.newyorker.com/news/news-desk/cowboys-and-pit-crews.

Harter, J. 2021. "U.S. Employee Engagement Holds Steady in First Half of 2021." Gallup Workplace, July 29, 2021. Retrieved November 15, 2021, from https://www.gallup.com/workplace/352949/employee-engagement-holds-steady-first-half-2021.aspx

Haudan, J. 2021. Interview with author, November 3.

Hickman, A. and Robison, J. 2020. "Is Working Remotely Effective? Gallup Research Says Yes." Gallup Workplace, January 24, 2020. https://www.gallup.com/workplace/283985/working-remotely-effective-gallup-research-says-yes.aspx

Kotter, J. 2014. *Accelerate: Building Strategic Agility for a Faster-Moving World*. Boston: Harvard Business Review Press.

Shmerling, R. H. 2021. "Is Our Healthcare System Broken?" Harvard Health Publishing, July 13, 2021. https://www.health.harvard.edu/blog/is-our-healthcare-system-broken-202107132542.

Shryock, T. 2021. "The True Cost of Physician Burnout." *Medical Economics* 98 (9): 24–26.

SUGGESTED READINGS

Ardebil, M. E., M. Naserbakht, C. Bernstein, F. A. Noodeh, H. Hakimi, and H. Ranjbar. 2021. "Healthcare Providers Experience of Working During the COVID-19 Pandemic: A Qualitative Study." *American Journal of Infection Control* 49 (5): 547–54.

Chen, J. K. C., and T. Sriphon. 2021. "Perspective on COVID-19 Pandemic Factors Impacting Organizational Leadership." *Sustainability* 13 (6): 3230.

Inouye, S. K. 2021. "Creating an Anti-ageist Healthcare System to Improve Care for Our Current and Future Selves." *Nature Aging* 1: 150–52.

Kamar, K., D. Novitasari, M. Asbari, Winanti, and F. S. Goestjahjanti. 2021. "Enhancing Employee Performance During the Covid-19 Pandemic: The Role of Readiness for Change Mentality." *JDM (Jurnal Dinamika Manajemen)* 11 (2): 154–166.

Kraus, S., F. Schiavone, A. Pluzhnikova, and A. C. Ivernizzi. 2021. "Digital Transformation in Healthcare: Analyzing the Current State-of-Research." *Journal of Business Research* 123: 557–67.

Lee, D., and S. N. Yoon 2021. "Application of Artificial Intelligence-Based Technologies in the Healthcare Industry: Opportunities and Challenges." *International Journal of Environmental Research and Public Health* 18 (1): 271.

Martinussen, P. E., and T. Davidsen. 2021. "'Professional-Supportive' versus 'Economic-Operational' Management: The Relationship Between Leadership Style and Hospital Physicians' Organisational Climate." *BMC Health Services Research* 21: 825.

Taylor, K. B. 2021. "Leadership Effectiveness, Employee Job Satisfaction, and Organizational Performance in the Healthcare Industry." *Walden Dissertations and Doctoral Studies* 10612. https://scholarworks.waldenu.edu/dissertations/10612.

CHAPTER 2

A Review of Academic Leadership Theories and Concepts

Leadership is a complex and diverse topic, and trying to make sense of leadership research can be an intimidating endeavor.

—David V. Day and John Antonakis (2012)

DR. MALCOLM LEARNED of Somewhere State University opened a health administration lecture with the question, "What is leadership?" Students offered the following responses:

- Getting groups of people to follow you.
- Using power appropriately to meet organizational objectives.
- The process of uniting individuals into groups to serve a vision or a mission.
- In the past, leadership was all about power, but today it's about influence.
- Understanding the global purpose of an organization and giving direction to subordinates to ensure their work is serving that purpose.
- It is engagement.
- It stands for the position and the activity of making change and moving toward a goal.

- Leadership comes down to having interpersonal skills, and it really is something that you are born with. Some people are just leaders, and others are just followers.
- Using a set of skills to make improvements in society or in organizations.
- Getting results. In instances when the leader abuses his or her power, the results may not be good. But in other cases, the results are beneficial to all those concerned.
- Although it may not be politically correct to say, leadership is all about power. This power can be used to coerce people into doing things they would not do otherwise.

Dr. Learned closed the discussion by asking, "Did you hear how disparate the answers to my question were? If we all have different definitions, how can we study leadership, and how can we improve ourselves as leaders?"

Guide to the Reader
Academic theories of leadership, though they sometimes seem opaque and confusing, can provide a great foundation for better understanding how to enhance one's leadership skills and competencies. Each theory has some piece of wisdom and some grain of significant truth.

LEADERSHIP IS ONE of the most discussed and, ultimately, the most misunderstood concepts in management. Is it an art, a science, or both? Is leadership defined by the act, the process, or the skill? Is a person a leader because she is in charge of moving a team from Point A to Point B? Is someone a leader because he has followers? What is the mark of a good leader, and does it matter how a leader achieves greatness? Are leaders born or are they made? Or both?

As a long-time leadership consultant, teacher, and executive recruiter, I have noticed that "you know what I mean" is one of the most repeated phrases during my discussions with employers about what qualities they are looking for in a leader. Although employers offer their favorite general descriptors of a qualified leader—for example, "an outstanding communicator" who has "integrity and high energy" and is "a people person, a team player, and results oriented"—they are hard-pressed to provide specific details of what they mean. As a result, these employers resort to replying with the statement, "Well, you know what I mean—I just want a strong leader." After all the publications, seminars, speeches, and casual banter about leadership, few leaders can actually articulate a comprehensive definition of leadership.

Leadership is a living phenomenon; therefore, it is expected to change shape according to its purpose and the demands of its followers and the environment. This adaptability is probably why a definition is so elusive.

It is most unfortunate that few practitioners in healthcare leadership are familiar with the rich academic history of leadership theory. Most had some exposure in prior graduate courses, but ever since they typically only read the popular literature. (Popular literature is targeted at mostly a practitioner audience and does not provide the amount of in-depth research done by scholarly or academic literature.) An examination of academic literature, though, is important for the multiple purposes of this book. Because the book is used significantly in health administration programs (graduate and undergraduate), a more inclusive examination will enhance students' understanding of leadership as they prepare to enter leadership roles in healthcare. In addition, the study of leadership in higher education has grown substantively over the past several years. Many colleges and universities now offer majors in leadership. Perhaps most important, looking first to research-based (or evidence-based) studies is vital to better understanding what leadership is and how it is practiced. While there is likely some art to leadership, there is also science. That science should be studied and understood. Clinical care relies on evidence-based practice, which is the process of collecting, processing, and using research to ensure that clinical practice is safe and effective. Leadership should be no different.

Currently, many books and articles on leadership are, in fact, *not* based on any credible evidence. Instead, they contain anecdotal observations and are based only on the subjective and often one-sided notions of the authors. This problem will become more apparent to the reader after finishing chapter 3, which examines popular leadership literature—comprising many books that, frankly, are not supported by evidence.

CHRONOLOGICAL REVIEW OF LEADERSHIP

One common way to study academic leadership theories is through a chronological historical review. Although the concept of leadership has probably been around since prehistoric days, the discussion in this chapter begins in the late 1800s. As the changes brought about by the Industrial Revolution became a more significant part of society, the German sociologist Max Weber wrote about bureaucracy and the benefits of organizing people into groups. He focused on the use of structure and power, viewing people largely as cogs in the overall production machine. Management theorists Henri Fayol and Frederick Taylor examined span of control and scientific management, respectively. While neither Fayol nor Taylor was an academic or thinking of the topic of leadership, their thoughts have long-term impact on the study of leadership.

Great Man Theory (1900 Through the 1940s)

As the Industrial Revolution gained full force, attention began to focus on how leaders (often called *managers* at this time) were identified. Essentially, the question facing the owners of factories was, "How can I pinpoint the person in the workforce who has the best ability to control the others?" The first major group of theories assumed that the best leaders were born that way and were thus "great men." Note that a feature of the great man theory continues to have great popular support (as opposed to evidence-based validation) because many individuals today believe that strong leaders possess charisma, intelligence, or inborn talent that makes them effective. However, evidence did not support this view for long—not all great leaders are men, and not all individuals with the identified inborn characteristics become great leaders. Leadership was shown to be more complex, and success hinged on many other factors.

> Until an "academy of leadership" establishes an accepted standard definition [of leadership], we must continue to live with both broad and narrow definitions, making sure we understand which kind is being used in any particular analysis.
>
> —**Bernard M. Bass (2008)**

Trait Theory (1920s Through the Present)

The great man theory morphed into the study and categorization of the characteristics of leaders and became known as trait theory. The two world wars provided impetus to this study. Faced with a critical challenge of determining who should be officers and lead other soldiers, sailors, and airmen, the US armed forces decided that if they could simply come up with a list of the qualities, attributes, or talents inherent in leaders, they could make effective decisions in selecting officers. Trait theory essentially attempts to identify those personality factors, characteristics, or qualities that effective leaders possess. Some examples include confidence, high energy, initiative, drive, decision-making ability, and creativity. A more recent example is emotional intelligence.

Great man theory and trait theory, although not well supported by long-term research findings, still form the foundation of many contemporary popular views of leadership. Many participants in leadership workshops answer the question, "What is a leader?" with descriptions related to traits or inborn characteristics. Exhibit 2.1 provides a visual picture of both theories and their common critiques.

Contingency and Situational Leadership Theories (1940s Through the Present)

In the 1930s and 1940s, interest in the academic study of leadership began in earnest. Perhaps the harbinger of this was Chester Barnard, author of the well-known *The Functions of the Executive* (1938). Although not an academic but rather an executive at AT&T and later chair of the National Science Foundation, Barnard (1938, 87) wrote that leadership was the "ability of a superior to influence

---

Exhibit 2.1 Early Leadership Theories: Great Man Theory and Trait Theory

GREAT MAN THEORY	TRAIT THEORY

CENTRAL IDEAS

- Heredity plays a significant role in who is a leader.
- Leaders are born, not made.

- Intelligence, personal drive, and extraversion are inborn and mark great leaders.
- Knowing the traits of effective leaders makes it easier to identify them.

CRITIQUES

- Leadership skills can be developed through proper education and experience.
- No scientific evidence exists showing why leaders become effective.

- No exclusive set of traits is appropriate across differing situations.
- Theory is inward-looking and ignores followers and situational tasks.

---

the behavior of a subordinate or group and persuade them to follow a particular course of action." In contrast to earlier leadership theories, Gabor and Mahoney (2013, 136) note that Barnard "viewed the organization as a complex social system."

This concept of the organizational context and its complexity gave birth to many diverse viewpoints on leadership and spurred pivotal studies of leadership. One of the more important advances was evidentiary support for the idea that multiple styles, approaches, and methods could provide effective leadership. Contingency or situational leadership theories, which postulate that there is not one single best way to lead and that good leadership depends on the situation, began to flourish. While the most significant theories surfaced in the 1960s, the full impact of the relevance of contingency and situational leadership continues to be felt today.

Stogdill (1975, 5) goes further in suggesting that leaders are "not self-made and not a product of personality, drive, or ability." Bass (2008, 85) states it simply: "The leader is a product of the situation and circumstances." Hughes, Ginnett, and Curphy (2015, 15) suggest an *interactional framework* approach to leadership. Essentially, this approach suggests that leadership is a function of three factors—the leader, the followers, and the situation they both face. Exhibit 2.2 provides a visual look at this concept.

Leadership style theories also began to surface during this time. The first variation of this theory, developed by Blake and Mouton (1964), is a simple two-factor concept of leadership that tried to identify what behaviors distinguished leaders from followers. They argue that leaders emphasize either people or tasks and results.

Similar to but more complex than the interactional framework view are contingency leadership theories, which gained a following through the work of Hersey and Blanchard (1969) and Fiedler (1986). These theories contend that different types of leaders are needed for different types of people and situations. As Hughes, Ginnett, and Curphy (2015, 525) explain, "In contingency leadership, leadership effectiveness is maximized when leaders correctly make their behaviors *contingent* on certain situational and follower characteristics."

Another way to view the fact that there is *not* "one best approach" to leading is to consider that the most effective leaders are those who can adapt. In our book, Garman and I list adaptability as one of our critical leadership competencies (Dye and Garman 2015, 185). We posit that being adaptable "requires leaders to take a more active role in planning for their interactions, reflecting on how they went, and doing so on a consistent basis." Note also that this often means that leaders who lack the adaptability competency may be quite effective in certain situations but fail in different situations. And in his well-known article in *Harvard Business Review*, Goleman (2000) states that "research suggests that the most effective executives use a collection of distinct leadership styles each in the right measure, at just the right time. Such flexibility is tough to put into action, but it pays off in performance."

Because the foundation and essentials of situational and contingency theories still have great applicability today, exploring them in depth is useful. By using the framework of the leader, the followers, and the situation, the complexities of leadership can be fully examined.

Exhibit 2.2 Interactive Framework of Leadership

The Leader

Much of leadership understanding and thought concentrates on the leader. To grow and develop, leaders ask these questions: "What should I be, what do I need to know, and what must I be able to do?" This principle is well illustrated through the US Army leadership paradigm (Hesselbein and Shinseki 2004). Certainly, the concept of traits from trait theory has logical applicability here. Essentially, the question to be answered is, "What does the leader need to be able to do (as a result of what she is and knows)?"

The Followers

The reality is that much of leadership depends on the followers. This idea is even more true today, given the nature of the work-force. What are the capabilities of the followers? How personally motivated are they to work toward the leader's vision? What is the complexity of the tasks to be handled by the followers? What are the interpersonal relationships between the followers and the leader? What are the power and ability of the leader to reward and reinforce their behavior?

A growing body of research suggests that the way to influence—and to lead—begins with being warm. Cuddy, Kohut, and Neffinger (2013, 56) argue for the importance of using warmth as a starting point in enhancing leadership and state that "warmth is the conduit of influence: It facilitates trust and the communication and absorption of ideas." Many believe that trust is a prerequisite of effective leadership and, essentially, requires the leader to connect with the followers. Building trust requires a demonstration of caring for others and a willingness and ability to help them.

A secondary but important consideration is that practically everyone who is a leader is also a follower. Almost every leader has a boss, including CEOs who report to boards of trustees. Thus, all leaders have the chance to reflect on followership. Moreover, many leaders view leadership from the perspective of how *they* themselves react and behave toward their leaders.

The Situation

Though Hersey, Blanchard, and Natemeyer (1979) built the foundations of the theory early on, Hersey, Blanchard, and Johnson (2007) further developed a model called situational leadership, which proposes four styles of leadership often labeled *telling, selling, participating,* and *delegating*.

This model suggests that leaders react to both tasks and people relationships. Moreover, leaders exhibit one of four styles of leadership:

1. *High emphasis on tasks and low emphasis on relationships*— often called a "telling" style; taken to extremes, represents an autocratic leader

2. *High emphasis on tasks and high emphasis on relationships*—a "selling" style; involves persuasion

3. *High emphasis on relationships and low emphasis on tasks*—a participative style; little direction given to followers

4. *Low emphasis on relationships and low emphasis on tasks*—a delegating style

Note that all four styles may have their place in leadership. For example, if the followers are resistant or unskilled, the leader may need to be much more directive in style. If the followers are highly motivated, capable, and skilled, the leader's style should be much more delegating in nature. A better understanding of their employees and the nature of the work to be accomplished will help leaders better adapt their styles of leadership to fit the situation.

Along these lines, Northouse (2021, 113) suggests that for a leader to be effective, he must determine the best course of action by evaluating his "followers and assessing how competent and committed they are to perform a given goal." In addition, according to Kaifi and colleagues (2014, 30), the "three core competencies of a situational leader are: diagnosing, flexibility, and partnering." Perhaps the most important learning point of this idea is the necessity of leaders being skilled and perceptive listeners who are constantly scanning the environment to discern the issues and concerns of the organization and its people.

From a practical viewpoint, the situational approach to leadership indicates that (1) leaders need to know themselves well through self-awareness, (2) leaders need to know their followers through listening and perception, and (3) leaders need to know conditions and circumstances by surveying and understanding their organizations.

Transformational (1970s Through the Present)

Burns (1978) and Bass (2008) presented the theory of *transformational leadership*. Much of the theory reflects the belief that followers want to be engaged in the vision for the organization. They need to understand—and subscribe to—a path for the future. Through what some describe as charismatic leadership, the leader motivates or influences followers to work toward strategic changes. Although no direct linkage is made in the literature, transformational leadership theory may have played some role in the development of the employee engagement movement.

Some would posit that transformational leadership stands in contrast to *transactional leadership*, an older style in which leaders use rewards and punishments to get followers to work toward goals. According to Burns (1978, 26), transactional leadership is simply a situation in which "one person takes the initiative in making contact with others for the purpose of an exchange of valued things." For example, though the notion retains little empirical support, many leaders today believe that pay is one of the prime factors in convincing followers to follow. In contrast, transformational leadership is not based on the idea of power, authoritarian approaches, or command-and-control styles of leadership.

OTHER APPROACHES TO UNDERSTANDING LEADERSHIP THEORIES

Though the popularity of many theories has come and gone, several ideas have proven applicable beyond their eras. The next few theories have solid academic support and are also quite usable by practitioners on a day-by-day basis.

Defining Leadership as a Process

In *Organizational Behavior*, Kreitner and Kinicki (2012, 31) describe leadership as "a social influence process in which the leader seeks the voluntary participation of subordinates in an effort to reach organizational goals."

This definition is true in three ways:

1. Leadership is a process because it takes place over a period, with a beginning and an end. Usually, the end is the point when leadership's effectiveness may be ascertained.
2. Leadership does not mean intimidation of followers into participation. Some healthcare "leaders" coerce "volunteers" to help them accomplish goals, but this technique is never acceptable and is highly unethical.
3. Leadership moves toward achievement or is progress driven, which is another symbol of effectiveness.

Uhl-Bien (2006, 655) expands on the process approach by suggesting that "relationships—rather than authority, superiority, or dominance—appear to be key to new forms of leadership." She further indicates that the study of leadership needs to "consider processes that are not just about the quality of the relationship or even the type of relationship, but rather about the social dynamics by which leadership relationships form and evolve in the workplace."

Path-Goal Theory

This school of thought purports that leaders must have versatility and be adaptable to various types of followers, organizations, and occurrences and view leadership as a process that moves along a path toward a goal. It has great merit and is one of the most validated theories of leadership. Vroom (1964) originated the idea with the *expectancy theory* of leadership, which, not unlike transactional leadership theory, posits that followers act in certain ways because they expect a certain outcome. House (1971) expanded the expectancy theory, and it became known as *path-goal leadership*. Exhibit 2.3 shows the simplicity of this model.

House (1971, 326) states that supervisors have influence over such factors as "financial increases, promotion, assignment of more interesting tasks, or opportunities for personal growth and development." Not surprisingly, many leaders view their oversight of these factors as critical in their ability to lead by "control."

Exhibit 2.3 Factors Influencing Goal Achievement: Path-Goal Theory of Leadership

---

Defining Leadership Comprehensively

Ralph Stogdill (1984) wrote what may be the most comprehensive treatise on leadership, *Stogdill's Handbook of Leadership*. In the book, he argues that leadership is any of the following:

- A focus on team processes
- Personality and its effects
- The art of inducing compliance
- The exercise of influence
- An act that results in others acting or responding in a shared direction
- A form of persuasion
- A power relation
- An instrument of goal achievement
- An emerging effect of interaction
- A differentiated role
- The initiation of structure

Furthermore, Stogdill believes that interaction between members of a team occurs when one team member modifies the motivation or competencies of others in the team. Leaders are "agents of change, persons whose acts affect other people more than other people's acts affect them" (Stogdill 1984, 86).

This comprehensive catalog of definitions serves as a checklist, pointing leaders to areas for improvement. Although the comprehensive theory explains the technical aspects of leadership, it ignores its art and spirituality. Doing so makes leadership seem mechanical.

Leadership Versus Management

The two terms *leadership* and *management* are often used interchangeably. Strictly speaking, this is an error. It leads to confusion, and many popular books today suggest that all workers should aspire to be leaders. In his book *A Force for Change*, John Kotter (1990) proposes that leadership is different from management because leadership is a process that focuses on making organizational changes, while management is primarily concerned with control and results. In contrasting leadership with management, Kotter (2001) notes that "both are necessary for success in an increasingly complex and volatile environment."

Although Kotter agrees that both responsibilities are important, he views leaders as the stimuli behind their organization's adoption of—and adaptation to—improved processes. As a result, many of his readers are convinced that being a leader is preferable to being a manager. But a full analysis of leadership and management should clearly show that organizations do need both to be successful. Moreover, most leaders manage and most managers lead.

COMPETENCY-BASED LEADERSHIP

The various definitions under Stogdill's comprehensive theory support the view that leadership is enabled by a set of competencies. The *competency theory*, which has gained a significant following in the past decade, suggests that leaders must demonstrate knowledge, skills, and abilities in several areas, such as communications and business. Competency-based leadership also means that the key competencies required for specific roles in a corporate culture are identified and prioritized by organizations when they engage in recruitment, make decisions regarding promotions, and develop leaders. Northouse (2021, 70) suggests that the competency approach "makes leadership available to everyone. Unlike personality traits, skills are competencies that people can learn or develop."

For example, a chief financial officer will require competencies different from those of a chief medical officer. A formal, structured organization requires different competencies than does a more laid-back environment. In *Exceptional Leadership*, Garman and I contend that "competencies work so well [because] they are so practical" (Dye and Garman 2015, xxiv). We further state that the competency theory leads to "a better understanding of the key qualities that drive highly effective leadership."

The Institute of Medicine's (2003) report *Health Professions Education: A Bridge to Quality* gave impetus to the competency movement in healthcare. The report observes the insufficient number of tools for assessing the proficiency of healthcare professionals and suggests a set of core competencies designed to improve quality of care. In addition, the Healthcare Leadership Alliance—a collaboration among five healthcare professional associations—issued a competency tool with 300 competencies (for more information, see www.healthcareleadershipalliance.org). In the past several years, many other competency frameworks have been developed for both healthcare management practice and education (Stefl 2008).

By providing specific examples, competency theory enables leaders to "see" the behaviors ideal for competent leadership. For instance, it describes and explains the traits or competencies of an effective communicator. Moreover, the competency approach promotes the development and use of indicators that can measure the strength or weakness of a given competency.

Because many models include 80 or more competencies, picking out the competencies critical for effective leadership becomes a challenge. The book *Exceptional Leadership* lays out the 16 key competencies that distinguish great leadership from good leadership. See exhibit 2.4 for the Dye–Garman Leadership Competency Model.

Exhibit 2.4 Dye–Garman Leadership Competency Model

Source: Reprinted from Dye and Garman (2015).

LEADERSHIP VIEWED BY PSYCHOLOGY

While some leadership books and articles steer clear of the field of psychology, I believe that approach is quite short-sighted. Psychology provides much research-based literature on and support for the principles of leadership. Hogan (2009, slide 3) sums up the issue quite effectively, stating, "The fundamental problems in life concern 'getting along' and 'getting ahead'—developing relationships and developing a career. These themes exist in a state of tension. We resolve these problems during social interaction. Some people are better at this than others, and they tend to move into leadership positions."

Effective leaders consider their own personalities and the impact they have on their followers.

The Five-Factor Model of Personality

The *five-factor model of personality* has great similarities to some traditional trait theories. Using the acronym OCEAN (O = Openness to experience, C = Conscientiousness, E = Extraversion, A = Agreeableness, N = Neuroticism), the model purports to describe personality holistically. Likely profiles of highly effective and less effective leaders might look like those in exhibit 2.5. Applied to leadership, the model implies that effective leaders have broad interests and knowledge, are orderly and task focused, are extraverts who get along well with people, are positive in outlook, and have good emotional intelligence. While the five-factor model can be a great tool for enhancing self-awareness, Sokolov and I note that it is "not invincible. For example, many people who are naturally introverted are able to behaviorally exhibit strong extraverted skills that allow them to function as effective leaders" (Dye and Sokolov 2013, 153). Regarding the introverted-extraverted part of the model, Grant, Gino, and Hofmann (2011, 528) write that "scholars have begun to question whether this conclusion [that extraverts have advantages as leaders] overstates the benefits of extraversion in leadership roles and overlooks the costs." It is interesting to note how so many discussions of leadership ultimately return to the situational or contingency theory viewpoint.

A grounded understanding of personality through the evidence presented in the field of psychology is critical. Hughes, Ginnett, and Curphy

> Collectively, the research findings on leadership from all of these areas provide a picture of a process that is far more sophisticated and complex than the often simplistic view presented in some of the popular books on leadership.
>
> —Peter G. Northouse (2021)

Exhibit 2.5 Leader Profiles Using the Five-Factor Model

Highly Effective Leader

- Openness: very open to experiences
- Conscientiousness: very conscientious
- Extraversion: extraverted
- Agreeableness: agreeable, easy to get along with
- Neuroticism: calm and emotionally resilient

Less Effective Leader

- Openness: reserved and quiet, not comfortable out in front
- Conscientiousness: disorganized
- Extraversion: introverted
- Agreeableness: lacks warmth, can be hostile
- Neuroticism: Anxious, impatient

(2015, 189) state, "Given the accelerated pace of change in most organizations today, leaders will likely have even more unfamiliar and ambiguous situations in the future. Therefore, personality traits may play an increasingly important role in a leader's behavior." And Wallington (2003, 12) argues, "The dictionary definition of personality is the collection of emotional and behavioral traits that characterize a person. That is, your personality is how you present yourself to the world. It is how others see you. Is that important for leadership effectiveness? I think so. Your public persona is the catalyst for enrolling followers."

A FINAL QUESTION—ASKED AND ANSWERED

Are leaders born or are leaders made? This question is posed throughout this book. Exhibit 2.6 summarizes the issue from an academic perspective.

Exhibit 2.6 Are Leaders Born or Made?

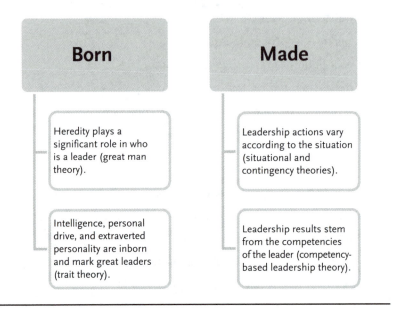

Born	Made
Heredity plays a significant role in who is a leader (great man theory).	Leadership actions vary according to the situation (situational and contingency theories).
Intelligence, personal drive, and extraverted personality are inborn and mark great leaders (trait theory).	Leadership results stem from the competencies of the leader (competency-based leadership theory).

CONCLUSION

The study of leadership from an academic perspective may often cause readers to feel as though they are going in circles. Yet the models and hypotheses provide great insight. The theories of contingency or situational leadership have great applicability to the practice of leadership today. With great changes occurring in society and the workplace, leaders must be able to interpret situations and deduce the best approach to take. Critical to this process are managing effectively (planning, organizing, staffing, controlling), having a firm understanding of the tasks or work to be completed, discerning how much guidance to provide to followers, and developing and leading teams. Understanding some of the research foundations of personality as it applies to leadership also gives leaders an enhanced self-awareness of their effectiveness.

Hogan, R. 2009. "Personality, Leadership and Organizational Effectiveness." Presentation at the International Personnel Assessment Council Annual Conference on Personnel Assessment, Nashville, TN, September. http://annex.ipacweb.org/library/conf/09/hogan.pdf.

House, R. J. 1971. "A Path Goal Theory of Leader Effectiveness." *Administrative Science Quarterly* 16 (3): 321–39.

Hughes, R. L., R. C. Ginnett, and G. J. Curphy. 2015. *Leadership: Enhancing the Lessons of Experience*, 8th ed. Burr Ridge, IL: McGraw-Hill Education.

Institute of Medicine. 2003. *Health Professions Education: A Bridge to Quality*. Washington, DC: National Academies Press.

Kaifi, B. A., A. O. Noor, N.-L. Nguyen, W. Aslami, and N. M. Khanfar. 2014. "The Importance of Situational Leadership in the Workforce: A Study Based on Gender, Place of Birth, and Generational Affiliation." *Journal of Contemporary Management* 3 (2): 29–40.

Kotter, J. 2001. "What Leaders Really Do." *Harvard Business Review*. Published December. https://hbr.org/2001/12/what-leaders-really-do.

———. 1990. *A Force for Change: How Leadership Differs from Management*. New York: Free Press.

Kreitner, R., and A. Kinicki. 2012. *Organizational Behavior*, 10th ed. Burr Ridge, IL: McGraw-Hill Education.

Northouse, P. G. 2021. *Leadership: Theory and Practice*, 9th ed. Los Angeles: SAGE Publications.

Stefl, M. 2008. "Common Competencies for All Healthcare Managers: The Healthcare Leadership Alliance Model." *Journal of Healthcare Management* 53 (6): 360–74.

Stogdill, R. 1984. *Stogdill's Handbook of Leadership: A Survey of Theory and Research*. New York: Free Press.

———. 1975. "The Evolution of Leadership Theory." *Academy of Management Proceedings* 1: 4–6.

Uhl-Bien, M. 2006. "Relational Leadership Theory: Exploring the Social Processes of Leadership and Organizing." *Leadership Quarterly* 17 (6): 654–76.

Vroom, V. H. 1964. *Work and Motivation*. San Francisco: Jossey-Bass.

Wallington, P. 2003. "How Personality Plays into Leadership." *CIO*. Published January 15. www.cio.com/article/2440255 /careers-staffing/how-personality-plays-into-leadership.html.

SUGGESTED READINGS

Crosby G. 2021. "Lewin's Democratic Style of Situational Leadership: A Fresh Look at a Powerful OD Model." *Journal of Applied Behavioral Science* 57 (3): 398–401.

Mirčetić, V., and M. Čudanov. 2021. "Revalidating Blanchard's Situational Leadership Model: Induction of the Unproductive Follower." *International Scientific Conference Strategic Management and Decision Support Systems in Strategic Management*, 225–34. https://doi.org/10.46541/978-86-7233-397-8_167.

Wuryani, E., A. Rodlib, S. Sutarsib, N. Dewib, and D. Arifb. 2021. "Analysis of Decision Support System on Situational Leadership Styles on Work Motivation and Employee Performance." *Management Science Letters* 11 (2): 365–72.

CHAPTER 3

Is the Popular Leadership Literature Worthless?

Management books and commentaries often oversimplify, seldom providing useful guidance about the skills and behavior needed to get things done.

—Jeffrey Pfeffer (2016)

THREE **CEO**S WERE discussing their investments in leadership development. The first said, "We've really turned the heat up this year. All our leaders are going through the 'Lead Like a Rock Star' development program. I know the title sounds off, but we found that rock stars shared several principles with strong leaders. They're very focused, they practice a lot, they're accustomed to being under the bright lights, and they're always preparing for the next big show. According to our consultant, leadership is a lot like that. He has assessments and modules built around the idea, and our leaders are really loving the program."

The second CEO replied, "Sounds odd, but I guess I'll give you the benefit of the doubt! Four years ago we started our 'Journey to Change' program. It's based on the book by Fred Futures, *Be Prepared for Your Journey*. There's a lot of reflective meditation in the various exercises, and our leaders are asked to do a lot of journaling and reflective work."

The third CEO replied, "Well, I guess our program is pretty different. It doesn't sound as jazzy as both of yours. We use several faculty members from the local university, and we have some of the National Hospital Association keynote speakers come to us. We built the program around a lot of academic literature and use real-world projects that we assign to our leaders. They work in teams and function a lot like internal consultants. We started a similar program for our physician leaders last year."

ANY STUDY OF leadership that neglects or overlooks the popular literature on the subject is doing a disservice to students of leadership. For purposes of our discussion in this chapter, the phrase *popular leadership literature* comprises books that are read zealously by practitioners of leadership. Many of their readers become staunch followers—fans of a sort.

Bookstores are filled with leadership texts that become so celebrated that many practicing leaders fail to challenge the soundness and logic of their premises. I often think of these titles as "airport leadership books." Many individuals purchase them in airports, apparently hoping that they are only a plane ride away from leadership perfection.

Simply put, some of the popular leadership literature is full of holes, lacking substantiation or evidence for the assertions made.

On the other hand, much of the academic literature reviewed in chapter 2 is, admittedly, hard to read and often full of tedious and mind-numbing statistics. Many of these articles appear in refereed professional journals and are not read by—or even available to—the average person in the C-suite. This literature does not appear in the airport bookstores or on Amazon.com and may be difficult to find, and its largest group of readers is currently in graduate school. Moreover, Hogan and Kaiser (2005, 171) state that the "academic tradition is a collection of dependable empirical nuggets, but it is also a collection of decontextualized facts that do not add up to a persuasive account of leadership." Simply put, it cannot compete successfully with the popular literature.

What leader has not heard of *Leaders Eat Last* (Sinek 2017), *The 7 Habits of Highly Successful People* (Covey 2013), *Good to Great* (Collins 2001), *The Five Dysfunctions of a Team: A Leadership Fable* (Lencioni 2002), *Who Moved My Cheese?* (Johnson and Blanchard 1998), or *Crucial Conversations* (Patterson et al. 2011)?

While commercial books may offer excellent lessons and great suggestions, the true student of leadership should always exercise caution and thoughtfulness when reading them. Look for evidence backing the assertions made in these publications. Are their ideas logical? Are they based on documented facts? Look to the questions posed in the next sections to challenge the premises of the popular leadership literature. The primary intent of this chapter is to get readers to be more judicious with the material they read, study, and adopt.

> The consuming interest in leadership and how to make it better has spawned a plethora of books, blogs, TED talks, and commentary. Unfortunately, these materials are often wonderfully disconnected from organizational reality and, as a consequence, useless for sparking improvement. Maybe that's one reason the enormous resources invested in leadership development have produced so few results.
>
> —Jeffrey Pfeffer (2016)

Is It Supported by Evidence?

Hogan and Kaiser (2005, 171) describe many commercial books as part of the "troubadour tradition." They state that "despite its popularity, the troubadour tradition is a vast collection of opinions with very little supporting evidence; it is entertaining but unreliable." Are the books filled with anecdotal observations? How reliable—and statistically valid—are their claims? What is the academic background or professional experience of the author(s)?

While it is not in the purview of this book to expound extensively on evidence-based practice, doing so has become common in healthcare. The medical profession has profoundly changed in response to A. L. Cochrane's 1972 book *Effectiveness and Efficiency*, which condemns the lack of reliable evidence behind many widely accepted healthcare interventions.

The business world has caught up with this trend. Pfeffer and Sutton (2006) wrote an excellent *Harvard Business Review* article titled "Evidence-Based Management." It discusses the problem of "repeatedly adopting, then abandoning, one ill-supported business fad after another." Moreover, they point out the existence of "a huge body of peer-reviewed studies—literally thousands . . . that although routinely ignored, provide simple and powerful advice about how to run organizations." And Rousseau (2006, 256) writes about "the failure of organizations and managers to base practices on best available evidence."

Readers should be mindful that solid evidence excludes such things as opinion, bias, hearsay, and fallacy.

Is It Applicable?

After determining that there is valid support for its premise, perhaps the next best way to evaluate popular leadership literature is to test its applicability—for example, by asking if Covey's (2013) seven habits support effective leadership. Most practicing leaders would argue that these principles do.

Consider one theory that has been broadly questioned in practice: strengths-based leadership, popularized by the Rath and Conchie (2013) book *Strengths Based Leadership*. Although the book is allegedly supported by research from Gallup, Kaplan and Kaiser (2009) argue that "it turns out you can take strengths too far" by failing to recognize and work on weaknesses. They suggest that the strengths-based approach can be overused and can greatly harm a leader. Chamorro-Premuzic (2016) also shows that the strengths approach means that "people get feedback on their relative strengths and weaknesses but cannot tell how they stack up against the competition—i.e., other people."

How to Deal with Academic Literature

Readers are encouraged to try a blend of both popular and academic literature. Although it can be dry, Brenner (2004, 99) explains that "scholarly discourse, especially written scholarly discourse, has a certain format. It is supposed to be factual and dry, 'objective,' or at least relatively clean of personal influence. It is supposed to contain extensive references to previous and current chains of learning." In other words, academic literature is dry by design, in an effort to avoid the very trendiness that seems to characterize popular literature.

Be mindful, when reading the academic literature, that its focus can be quite narrow. Many leaders prefer to read broader and more all-encompassing material on leadership. Much of the academic literature provides a deep, drill-down analysis of one aspect of leadership. This exhaustive nature makes it arduous and mind-numbing to read.

The Benefits of Popular Leadership Books

So, should students of leadership and practitioner leaders ignore the popular literature? Simply stated, no. In fact, some of the popular literature is actually supported by academic literature—the writers simply do not provide a large amount of scholarly content to avoid becoming dull and uninteresting. Many readers who would otherwise be bored to tears by typical journal articles and research-heavy books tend to be enthusiastically inspired by the precepts in the popular leadership literature. These readers then put the principles to work

> Being an expert on leadership research is neither necessary nor sufficient for being a good leader.
>
> —Richard L. Hughes, Robert C. Ginnett, and Gordon J. Curphy (2015)

and often become more effective leaders as a result. Healthcare organizations sometimes build programs around these books, such as a communication program based on Patterson and colleagues' *Crucial Conversations* (2011).

The pros and cons of academic literature and popular literature are summarized in exhibit 3.1.

Leadership Skill Theories and Competency Models

Skills-based leadership is one theory of leadership that has its roots in both academic and popular literature. Recently this theory has partially morphed into a competency-based view of leadership.

Mumford and colleagues (2000) write that, rather than emphasize what leaders do, the skills approach regards capabilities as what make effective leadership possible. Essentially, this means that leadership can be developed over time—it can be learned. Moreover, it suggests that if individuals are capable of learning, they can be leaders.

As Avolio, Walumbwa, and Weber (2009, 426) note, "Another very promising area of research that has not received sufficient attention in the leadership literature focuses on understanding what constitutes an individual's level of developmental readiness or one's capacity or motivational orientation to develop to one's full potential."

Garman and I propose in our book that the "answer to 'What makes a leader exceptional?' is simple: competencies. . . . We present a basic definition here. Leadership competencies are a set of professional and personal skills, knowledge, values, and traits that guide a leader's performance, behavior, interaction, and decisions" (Dye and Garman 2015, xiii). The Dye–Garman Leadership Competency Model is shown in exhibit 2.4.

Exhibit 3.1 Pros and Cons of Academic and Popular Leadership Literature

| Popular Leadership Literature | | Academic Leadership Literature | |
Pros	Cons	Pros	Cons
Easy to read	Conclusions may not be supported by evidence	Discussion is focused	Tedious to read—can be boring, repetitive, and uninspiring
Some premises are actually supported by solid research (although not always clearly stated)	May not fit situation or group of followers	Information is supported by evidence	
Examples drawn from real experience	May grossly oversimplify the practice of leadership	Information is not tied to the popularity of an individual author	
Accessible to leadership audience			Not easily accessible to leadership audience

CONCLUSION

Chapters 2 and 3 cover material that can fill a semester of a typical graduate-level leadership class. Certainly, academic and popular literature each has a place in the study of leadership. Be sure to challenge the popular leadership literature and not fall prey to leadership ideas that are not supported by facts and evidence.

Self-Evaluation Questions

❑ Have I ever become so enthralled with a book that I did not thoroughly assess its logic?

❑ Have I initiated programs that may be viewed negatively as the next program du jour?

❑ Am I guilty of following the newest management or leadership trends?

❑ Do I occasionally review the academic literature on leadership, or do I typically dismiss it as dry and boring?

❑ Are my bookshelves filled with partially read, popular leadership books that were once "hot" but have now lost their luster?

Exercises

Exercise 3.1

Read "What We Know About Leadership" by Hogan and Kaiser (2005). What is your impression of Hogan and Kaiser's (p. 171) "troubadour tradition" literature? To what extent does this article encourage you to read the classic "academic tradition" literature?

Hogan, R., and R. B. Kaiser. 2005. "What We Know About Leadership." *Review of General Psychology* 9 (2): 169–80.

The article is available online at https://psychology.illinois-state.edu/ktschne/psy376/Hogan_Kaiser.pdf.

REFERENCES

Avolio, B. J., F. O. Walumbwa, and T. J. Weber. 2009. "Leadership: Current Theories, Research, and Future Directions." *Annual Review of Psychology* 60: 421–49.

Brenner, A. 2004. *I Am . . .: Biblical Women Tell Their Own Stories.* Minneapolis, MN: Augsburg Fortress Publishers.

Chamorro-Premuzic, T. 2016. "Strengths-Based Coaching Can Actually Weaken You." *Harvard Business Review.* Published January 4. https://hbr.org/2016/01/strengths-based -coaching-can-actually-weaken-you.

Cochrane, A. L. 1972. *Effectiveness and Efficiency: Random Reflections on Health Services.* London: Nuffield Provincial Hospitals Trust. www.nuffieldtrust.org.uk/sites/files/nuffield/publication /Effectiveness_and_Efficiency.pdf.

Collins, J. 2001. *Good to Great: Why Some Companies Make the Leap . . . and Others Don't.* New York: HarperCollins.

Covey, S. R. 2013. *The 7 Habits of Highly Successful People: Powerful Lessons in Personal Change,* 25th anniversary ed. New York: Simon and Schuster.

Dye, C. F., and A. N. Garman. 2015. *Exceptional Leadership: 16 Critical Competencies for Healthcare Executives,* 2nd ed. Chicago: Health Administration Press.

Hogan, R., and R. B. Kaiser. 2005. "What We Know About Leadership." *Review of General Psychology* 9 (2): 169–80.

Hughes, R. L., R. C. Ginnett, and G. J. Curphy. 2015. *Leadership: Enhancing the Lessons of Experience*, 8th ed. Burr Ridge, IL: McGraw-Hill Education.

Johnson, S., and K. Blanchard. 1998. *Who Moved My Cheese? An A-Mazing Way to Deal with Change in Your Work and in Your Life*. New York: Putnam.

Kaplan, R. E., and R. B. Kaiser. 2009. "Stop Overdoing Your Strengths." *Harvard Business Review*. Published February. https://hbr.org/2009/02/stop-overdoing-your-strengths.

Lencioni, P. 2002. *The Five Dysfunctions of a Team: A Leadership Fable*. San Francisco: Jossey-Bass.

Mumford, M. D., S. J. Zaccaro, F. D. Harding, T. O. Jacobs, and E. A. Fleishman. 2000. "Leadership Skills for a Changing World: Solving Complex Social Problems." *Leadership Quarterly* 11 (1): 11–35.

Patterson, K., J. Grenny, R. McMillan, and A. Switzler. 2011. *Crucial Conversations: Tools for Talking When the Stakes Are High*, 2nd ed. New York: McGraw-Hill.

Pfeffer, J. 2016. "Getting Beyond the BS of Leadership Literature." *McKinsey Quarterly*. Published January. www.mckinsey.com/global-themes/leadership/getting-beyond-the-bs-of-leadership-literature.

Pfeffer, J., and R. I. Sutton. 2006. "Evidence-Based Management." *Harvard Business Review*. Published January. https://hbr.org/2006/01/evidence-based-management.

Rath, T., and B. Conchie. 2013. *Strengths Based Leadership: Great Leaders, Teams, and Why People Follow*. New York: Gallup Press.

Rousseau, D. M. 2006. "Is There Such a Thing as 'Evidence-Based Management'?" *Academy of Management Review* 31 (2): 256–69.

Sinek, S. 2017. *Leaders Eat Last*. London: Portfolio Penguin.

SUGGESTED READINGS

Rousseau, D. M. 2006. "Keeping an Open Mind About Evidence-Based Management: A Reply to Learmonth's Commentary." *Academy of Management Review* 31 (4): 1091–93.

Rousseau, D. M., and S. McCarthy. 2007. "Educating Managers from an Evidence-Based Perspective." *Academy of Management Learning and Education* 6 (1): 84–101.

CHAPTER 4

The Values-Based Definition

Leadership, simply put, is the ability to influence others.
Values-based leadership takes it to the next level. By word,
action, and example, values-based leaders seek to inspire and
motivate, using their influence to pursue what matters most.

—Harry Kraemer, Jr. (2011)

A HEALTH SYSTEM CEO led a discussion on leadership with second-year health administration graduate students. He posed the following questions: "Was Hitler an effective leader? Was Stalin an effective leader? And note that I did call them leaders. And before you answer, consider the fact that there's a leadership book called *Leadership Secrets of Attila the Hun* that's been popular since the 1980s. So I will add another question: Was Attila the Hun an effective leader?"

He went on to say, "If the primary goal of leadership is to get results, didn't Hitler and Stalin and Attila get results? Is it not evident that many, many people followed each of them?" He continued, "As leaders, are results all that matter? Is there something that makes us different from Hitler, Stalin, or Attila— or similar to them, for that matter? Does the concept of values come into play here? And can we even truly define values effectively when talking about leadership? Do some leaders have a set of values that is different from Hitler's? Is that a key deciding factor? If the answer is yes, then it would seem important—no, it would be *absolutely critical*—that as we study leadership, we must learn the role that values play in leadership."

AFTER LOOKING AT leadership from an academic perspective in chapter 2 and from a popular perspective in chapter 3, this chapter moves in a different direction. It provides the determinative foundation for the theme of this book—that is, internal values drive external behavior; effective leadership does, in fact, have a certain set of values; and those values drive the external behavior that helps make leaders effective. As stated in the preface, values come into play here.

But in establishing the definition of leadership for our purposes, we now add the requirement that effective leadership must have some beneficial good or purpose behind it. The vision must have a level of purity that benefits humankind.

For those of us who work in healthcare, serving in the field may be what many describe as the higher calling. The classic Robert Frost poem "The Road Not Taken" (see exhibit 4.1) underscores the conscious—and unusual—choice that exceptional leaders must make to live and lead according to their values. Their choices make all the difference, both in their lives and in the lives of those they serve.

External factors, such as changing regulations or pressure to meet financial goals, can threaten to move even the most ethical leaders on a perilous journey toward unethical decisions.

—Carson F. Dye and Brett D. Lee (2016)

BORN OR MADE? A VALUES-BASED RESPONSE

Chapter 2 reviews some theories that scholars have developed in response to the question, Are leaders born or made? I contend that

Exhibit 4.1 "The Road Not Taken" by Robert Frost

Two roads diverged in a yellow wood,
And sorry I could not travel both
And be one traveler, long I stood
And looked down one as far as I could
To where it bent in the undergrowth;

Then took the other, as just as fair,
And having perhaps the better claim,
Because it was grassy and wanted wear;
Though as for that the passing there
Had worn them really about the same,

And both that morning equally lay
In leaves no step had trodden black.
Oh, I kept the first for another day!
Yet knowing how way leads on to way,
I doubted if I should ever come back.

I shall be telling this with a sigh
Somewhere ages and ages hence:
Two roads diverged in a wood, and I—
I took the one less traveled by,
And that has made all the difference.

Source: Frost (2016).

1. leadership is both inherent and learned, and
2. leadership values and skills are interrelated. One cannot exist without the other.

Numerous studies suggest that many leadership skills and traits are the result of heredity (Hughes, Ginnett, and Curphy 2015). In this vein, so-called born leaders tend to develop certain values and exhibit strong leadership characteristics and skills *early* in life. Many managers, executives, and consultants—including me—hold the belief that those who are not born leaders must cultivate these values to enhance their leadership capabilities. Essentially, they have the possibility of learning behaviors or skills (read "competencies") that make them effective leaders.

What definitive characteristics differentiate strong leaders from weak leaders? What traits drive the behavior of effective leaders? What qualities do successful leaders possess that average leaders do not have? The only answer is having the appropriate leadership values.

WHAT ARE VALUES?

Values are ingrained principles that guide behaviors and thoughts. They are formed early in life and are likely correlated somewhat to heredity. They do develop more deeply with experiences and usually do not change much during a lifetime. As a moral framework, values help an individual analyze options, make decisions during times of stress, and rise above difficult or unexpected situations. Values are not necessarily all positive, however. Exhibit 4.2 provides an analogy for understanding how values are connected with and drive behaviors and thoughts.

Everyone has values, but those values differ from person to person. Some people have values that affect their leadership effectiveness. For example, Leader A highly regards being around other people, while Leader B highly regards being alone. Because Leader A spends time with others, she is more exposed to others' ideas and practices. She can learn from this exposure and, in the process, develop an appreciation for and openness to different experiences. Leader B's values, on the other hand, may not be as conducive to leadership improvement because he is isolated from the opinions and experiences of others. The real advantage of positive values depends on the degree to which a person allows these values to influence her development.

Sarros and Santora (2001, 7) state that "executives whose values are grounded in fundamental human virtues such as benevolence and honesty, but who also retain a need for personal gratification and success, are closely associated with transformational behaviors." And Zydziunaite (2018, 44) writes that "in organizations where leaders lead, the leadership values must be communicated by actions, mostly in the ways in which activities/actions are conducted on a day-to-day basis, and not so much in words directly spoken or written."

Personal and Team Values

One of the foundational precepts of this book is that there are both personal and team values that drive appropriate and effective

Exhibit 4.2 The Iceberg Analogy of Leadership Values

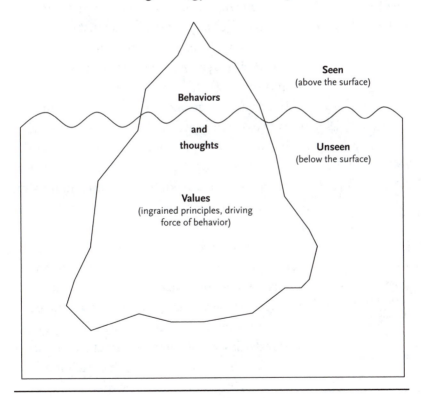

Behaviors

Seen
(above the surface)

and

thoughts

Unseen
(below the surface)

Values
(ingrained principles, driving
force of behavior)

leadership behavior. Learning these can make it easier to adopt effective leadership behavior.

Personal values affect how a leader perceives and is perceived by others. If leadership is a "social influence process," as Kreitner and Kinicki (2012, 34) suggest, then values can make an impact—negatively or positively—on this process. A leader is most influential when his followers know what he stands for because followers are clear on whether they can relate to the leader's ideals. This concept is illustrated whenever any new leader assumes a new leadership position. Practically all new leaders exert great effort to ensure that those in their new organizations know where they stand *personally*. One CEO remarks, "I spend much of my first 90 days helping people to learn—and understand—my personal history and style—this is who I am, why I am, and what I stand for. That way they will have a better understanding of the changes I will make." The same can be said of CEOs when they seek buy-in from organizational stakeholders. Lee and I state it clearly: "Executives must develop an understanding of leadership that includes a grasp of how their behavior influences the environment around them" (Dye and Lee 2016, 14).

The *influence* dimension of leadership requires the leader to have an impact on the lives of those being led. To make a change in other people carries with it an enormous ethical burden and responsibility. Because leaders usually have more power and control than [do their] followers, they also have more responsibility to be sensitive to how their leadership affects followers' lives.

—Peter G. Northouse (2016)

In addition, personal values guide the interactions between a leader and her followers, serving as the "fluid" of the social interchange. Under the contingency theory, in which a leader considers all variables before making a decision and moving forward, an effective leader relies on her values to steer her toward the most appropriate action.

Team values are commonly referred to using the French phrase *esprit de corps*, or *spirit of the group*. They serve as a bond that connects and links team members. These values guide the behaviors, decisions, and actions of team members. They also set the standards for how members interact with each other and work together, given that each member holds differing personal values that could cause conflicts in the group. In an organization, team values are often, if not always, tied to the mission of the enterprise. For example, if the mission is to serve those in need, regardless of their ability to pay, the team values will likely include community service, respect for diversity, accountability, and open communication—not pursuit of profits or one-upmanship.

Personal and team values contribute to leadership effectiveness. Exhibit 4.3 provides a distinction between these two types of values.

Values That Drive Behaviors

At the time of this writing, a Google search for "list of values" provided more than 5 billion results. Refining that to "list of leadership values" yielded 468 million results. Maggie Wooll (2021) offers a frequently used list of leadership values. They include the following:

- Empowerment and development
- Vision
- Communication
- Reinforcement and influence

Exhibit 4.3 Personal Values Versus Team Values

- Empathy
- Humility
- Passion and commitment
- Respect
- Patience
- Resilience
- Honesty and transparency
- Accountability
- Integrity

Reviewing this list or other similar lists from the Internet can be an illuminating exercise for leadership students and practitioners alike.

Sample Personal Values Statement

This real-life example of a personal values statement is provided courtesy of a healthcare executive who wishes to remain anonymous. She shared this with me as we discussed values-based leadership.

I really do have a personal values statement, and I have actually written it out. I compare my leadership to an actual journey, and I see my values as the guiding essentials on that journey. Each element has a name and includes various thoughts about that value.

Wind behind my back. I always want to journey to see new things and to make improvements.

Compass that points true north. I want to let the deeper forces within me that developed through my early years continue to guide me. Therefore, I do a lot of reflection while I am on the trail.

People on the trail with me. I have teams. Even though they may report to me, I view them as peers on this journey. The fact is that others help make me look good.

Sunshine ahead of me. I walk toward the light. I don't mean this in a religious sense, but this speaks to my interest in transparency and doing the right things.

Share lunch during the trip. I am grateful to live in a wealthy nation and work in a well-paid career. I try to give back as much as I can—not only to charities but to the workers around me.

My head is often down. This speaks to both my humility as well as to my keen focus on detail. Do it right, and do it right the first time.

Always carry a book. I have always been a lifelong learner. Books are gifts that broaden your view of the trail.

A song to sing. This is the cheesy part. I grew up listening to the rock band Journey. Their song "Don't Stop Believin'" is the song I sing on the trail. To me it means being positive about change and the work we all do.

An excellent example of a corporate leadership values statement is provided in exhibit 4.4. This text from Bayer could easily be used as an exemplary model for an individual leadership values statement as well.

Values Espoused in This Book

While the following values, which underlie the content of this book, may not precisely fit under a traditional definition of values, I contend that they are critical for effective leadership:

- Respect
- Ethical behavior
- Integrity
- Interpersonal connection
- Servant leadership
- Desire to make a change

Exhibit 4.4 Bayer Leadership and Integrity Values

Leadership
- Be passionate for people and performance
- Show personal drive, inspire and motivate others
- Be accountable for actions and results, successes and failures
- Treat others fairly and with respect
- Give clear, candid and timely feedback
- Manage conflicts constructively
- Create value for all our stakeholders

Integrity
- Be a role model
- Comply with laws, regulations and good business practices
- Trust others and build trustful relationships
- Be honest and reliable
- Listen attentively and communicate appropriately
- Ensure sustainability: balance short-term results with long-term requirements
- Care about people, safety, and the environment

Source: Reprinted with permission from Bayer (2016).

- Commitment
- Emotional intelligence
- Cooperation and sharing
- Cohesiveness and collaboration
- Trust
- Conflict management

The first three values must be strong in the complex world of healthcare. Respecting everyone, practicing ethical behavior, and possessing high integrity provide a firm foundation for those who lead in a field that cares for people in times of great need.

Interpersonal connection and servant leadership are logically tied to what is done in a service business such as healthcare. I am struck by how many leaders in healthcare list these as two of the more important considerations for effective leadership. Exhibit 4.5 explores some of the wisdom of Richard L. Hughes, Robert C. Ginnett, and Gordon J. Curphy, well-known authors in the leadership field, on the basic necessity of a good ethical foundation for those who exercise power.

Exhibit 4.5 Hughes, Ginnett, and Curphy on Values-Based Leadership

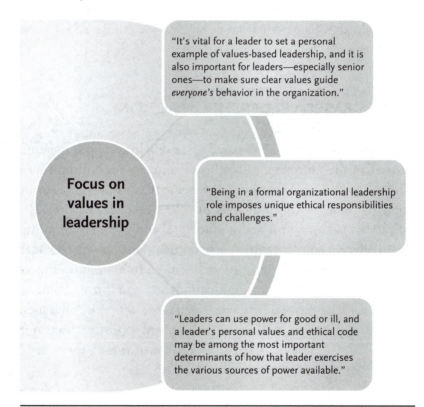

Focus on values in leadership

"It's vital for a leader to set a personal example of values-based leadership, and it is also important for leaders—especially senior ones—to make sure clear values guide *everyone's* behavior in the organization."

"Being in a formal organizational leadership role imposes unique ethical responsibilities and challenges."

"Leaders can use power for good or ill, and a leader's personal values and ethical code may be among the most important determinants of how that leader exercises the various sources of power available."

Source: Hughes, Ginnett, and Curphy (2015).

The desire to make a change is a value that has always fueled healthcare. The improvement of quality and patient safety, the development of new technology, discoveries in pharmacology, new approaches to the care model, and the eradication of diseases such as cancer all emanate from this value. If clinicians are drawn to the field in part because they want to make a change, certainly their leaders should share this same value.

Healthcare is a demanding career—for leaders as well as for all who serve. Thus, commitment is a required value for leaders.

Emotional intelligence, cooperation and sharing, and cohesiveness and collaboration are values that matter in a team setting, which is where most leadership takes place.

Trust surfaces on practically all lists of leader values.

Finally, the ability to manage conflict in a stressful field is a value that all effective leaders must have.

VALUES-BASED LEADERSHIP IN ACTION

Putting the concept of values-based leadership into context is useful. Harry Kraemer, former CEO of Baxter and current Northwestern University Kellogg School of Management Clinical Professor of Strategy, presents four principles of values-based leadership: self-reflection, balance, true self-confidence, and genuine humility. Essentially, Kraemer Jr (2011, 2) believes that the values-based leader is able to understand the self, can see situations from various perspectives, has a proper balance of self-confidence, and is truly humble. He states, "The way we treat customers, interact with colleagues, report to supervisors, deal with vendors, and so forth reflects our values. If we are not aware of those values, these interactions will not be effective."

> Successful leaders share values with those they lead.
>
> —Bernard M. Bass (2008)

Another way to better understand how values-based leadership works is to view it through three As: awareness, action, and achievement. A strong personal awareness of one's values and the values that drive highly effective leadership is a given for values-based leaders. One of the principles of this book is that internal values drive external behavior. If the values are the right ones, the resulting external behavior can serve to influence the actions needed to ultimately attain achievements that serve others. Exhibit 4.6 graphically portrays the three As.

Many executives who have read the earlier editions of this book have mentioned the uniqueness of viewing leadership from the lens of values. Yes, many aspects of leadership are soft; many do not easily lend themselves to quantitative proof. Yet this softer side often makes the difference. Using a values-based approach to studying leadership is an excellent way to maximize understanding.

FOUR STAGES OF LEARNING AND MASTERY

Highly effective leaders are always interested in learning and enhancing their leadership competencies. Values enable them to go through

---

Exhibit 4.6 Three As of Values-Based Leadership

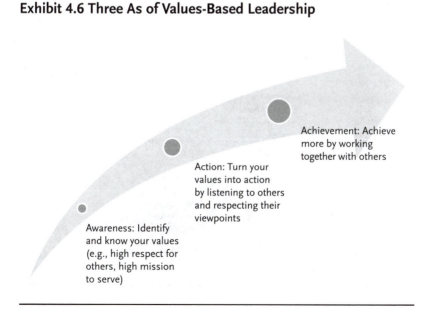

Achievement: Achieve more by working together with others

Action: Turn your values into action by listening to others and respecting their viewpoints

Awareness: Identify and know your values (e.g., high respect for others, high mission to serve)

---

the stages of leadership growth. Following is a description of each stage (also see exhibit 4.7).

Stage 1: Unconscious Incompetence

You don't know that you don't know. This stage is the most difficult for many leaders because they are unaware of their own mistakes and flaws. Often, they work in successful organizations and do not even consider whether problems with their leadership skills might exist. Leaders most likely to be at this level are those who have not started to develop appropriate leadership values or may be highly resistant to the input and feedback of others. As a result, they need training and awareness to enhance their self-understanding.

Exhibit 4.7 Learning and Mastery Process

Stage 2: Conscious Incompetence

You know that you don't know. Although this stage is the most important step toward learning, it can be the most challenging because sometimes you have to lose your job before you realize that your performance needs work. For others, this realization is a gradual process and may come as the result of the influence of a strong mentor or coach and a sincere desire to grow and improve.

> Moral leadership requires professional leaders to understand that it does matter that they like what they see in the mirror. It requires leaders to do, not just think of, what is right.
>
> —Elizabeth J. Forrestal and Leigh W. Cellucci (2016)

Stage 3: Conscious Competence

You know that you know. Some leaders are neither born nor strong, but at this stage, they start developing and honing their potential. Such leaders work hard to put into practice appropriate skills, but they sometimes fail because the skills are not part of their natural thinking habits yet.

Stage 4: Unconscious Competence

You don't know that you know. This stage is the ultimate level of leadership development because the activities here flow smoothly with neither great force nor hesitation. Leaders at this level seem to be naturals at their trade. Unconscious competence is truly descriptive of a born leader.

VALUES-BASED LEADERSHIP THEORY

One solid theory of leadership is that it is values-based. Copeland (2014, 130), in her excellent literature review of values-based leadership theory, states that "history has demonstrated repeatedly that leaders [who] lack ethical and value-based dimensions can have serious adverse consequences on their followers, their organizations, our nation and the world." James and colleagues (2021) also write that "nurse managers should recognize the potential benefits of a values-based leadership approach for staff well-being, enhanced professional collaboration and the nurse's voice, improved insight into clinical leadership attributes, and improvements in quality patient care."

Effective leadership is based on three factors: heredity, values, and competencies. As explained earlier, heredity in this context is the view that all persons are born with inherent characteristics (some have more than others) that enable them to practice leadership at some level of proficiency. Thus, the precept that leaders are born does carry logical support. The *values-based theory* of leadership posits that individuals develop certain (positive) values and behavioral skills or competencies that facilitate their practice of leadership—that is, leaders can also learn leadership.

But an individual must *desire* to be in a leadership position. Not everyone wants to be a leader. Many professionals in healthcare—particularly clinicians (e.g., physicians, nurses, pharmacists, therapists)—prefer to remain in clinical roles. As a result, they may not seek formal leadership positions. Certainly, they may act or serve as leaders within their clinical positions, but not consistently as full-time leaders do. Thus, motivation must be present for humans to engage in a particular behavior.

No matter the person's hereditary tendencies, values, and competencies, if the need or want (in other words, motivation) is absent, the person will not be a leader. Exhibit 4.8 presents this conceptually.

CONCLUSION

In summary, the concept of values is difficult to define. They are intensely personal, affecting individuals in profound ways. Despite

Exhibit 4.8 Components of Effective Leadership

some contributions to the literature over the past 20 years, values are not an area that many academics study. Perhaps it is because of the inspirational nature of values, which runs counter to the drily factual nature of academic inquiry. Perhaps it is because they are too deeply related to gestalt psychology, which is often considered a "soft" science. The origin of values is deeply personal, and each person's development of values is achieved though different experience and heredity. As much as we would like to define the concept absolutely, it will always remain abstract. Yet it is a critical component of effective leadership. Therefore, it is incumbent upon leaders to reflect on values and include them as part of our leadership studies.

Allowing positive values to be a primary influencer may be the most fundamental way that leaders can judge their own styles. Parts II and III of this book identify the values that guide leaders and team members. See appendix A for a professional and personal values assessment tool.

Self-Evaluation Questions

❏ What do I value? Do these values assist or hinder my leadership activities?

❏ Are my behaviors guided by personal values?

❏ What personal values of mine may conflict with my role and responsibilities as a leader?

❏ If I have written a narrative describing my leadership style, does it make reference to my personal values? Did I write this narrative to impress a search consultant or a potential employer, or did I do it to evaluate my strengths and weaknesses?

❏ Does my definition of leadership include some reference to values?

❏ What is my definition of leadership?

❏ List several successful healthcare leaders. What traits do they have in common? What values do they share?

❏ One Self-Evaluation Question in chapter 1 asks, "Do I view leadership as an act, a process, or a skill?" After reading chapter 4, how does my answer to this question differ?

Case and Exercises

Case 4.1

Three health system vice presidents (VPs) are discussing leadership over lunch. The first VP says, "Leadership is completely about relationships. It's about how you work with people and how you get to know them as individuals." The second VP replies, "I agree that people are important, but you can have a lot of happy people and not achieve any goals. That's not leadership in my book." The third VP comments, "You both have good points, but you're really missing the key of leadership—vision. A lot of what you're talking about is management. Leadership is developing a vision and getting the organization moving toward that vision."

You join these three VPs at the table, and they ask for your thoughts on this issue.

Case 4.1 Questions

1. Describe in detail how each VP's argument is right and wrong.

2. How might their differing viewpoints be melded together to provide a comprehensive and accurate definition of leadership?

Exercise 4.1

Find a list of values on the Internet. List the positive leadership actions that typically would emanate from these values.

Exercise 4.2

Review the following article on values-based leadership and discuss the portion of the article that states, "The study identifies literature that supports that when these VBL behaviors are found in leaders, the leaders are evaluated as more effective by subordinates" (p. 105).

Copeland, M. K. 2014. "The Emerging Significance of Values Based Leadership: A Literature Review." *International Journal of Leadership Studies* 8 (2): 105–35. www.regent.edu/acad/global/publications/ijls/new/vol8iss2/6-Copeland.pdf.

REFERENCES

Bass, B. M. 2008. *The Bass Handbook of Leadership: Theory, Research, and Managerial Applications*, 4th ed. New York: Free Press.

Bayer. 2016. "Our Mission; Bayer; Science for a Better Life." Accessed June 8. www.bayer.com/en/mission---values.aspx.

Copeland, M. K. 2014. "The Emerging Significance of Values Based Leadership: A Literature Review." *International Journal of Leadership Studies* 8 (2): 105–35.

Dye, C. F., and B. D. Lee. 2016. *The Healthcare Leader's Guide to Actions, Awareness, and Perception*, 3rd ed. Chicago: Health Administration Press.

Forrestal, E. J., and L. W. Cellucci. 2016. *Ethics and Professionalism for Healthcare Managers*. Chicago: Health Administration Press.

Frost, R. 2016. "The Road Not Taken." Poetry Foundation. Accessed June 17. www.poetryfoundation.org/resources /learning/core-poems/detail/44272.

Hughes, R. L., R. C. Ginnett, and G. J. Curphy. 2015. *Leadership: Enhancing the Lessons of Experience*, 8th ed. Burr Ridge, IL: McGraw-Hill Education.

James, A. H., C. L. Bennett, D. Blanchard, and D. Stanley. 2021. "Nursing and Values-Based Leadership: A Literature Review." *Journal of Nursing Management* 29: 916–30.

Kraemer, H. M. J. Jr. 2011. *From Values to Action: The Four Principles of Values-Based Leadership*. San Francisco: Jossey-Bass.

Kreitner, R., and A. Kinicki. 2012. *Organizational Behavior*, 10th ed. Burr Ridge, IL: McGraw-Hill Education.

Northouse, P. G. 2016. *Leadership: Theory and Practice*, 7th ed. Los Angeles: SAGE Publications.

Roberts, W. 1989. *Leadership Secrets of Attila the Hun*. New York: Warner Books.

Sarros, J. C., and J. C. Santora. 2001. "Leadership and Values: A Cross-Cultural Study." *Leadership and Organization Development Journal* 22 (5): 243–48.

Wooll, M. 2021. "The 13 Essential Leadership Values for Anyone Leading a Team." BetterUp Blog. Accessed November 15, 2021. https://www.betterup.com/blog/10-core-values-of -a-great-leader.

Zydziunaite, V. 2018. "Leadership Values and Values Based Leadership: What Is the Main Focus?" *Applied Research in Health and Social Sciences: Interface and Interaction* 15 (1): 43–58.

SUGGESTED READINGS

Alexander, C., D. Campbell, J. Leiferman, G. Mabey, S. Marken, C. Myers, A. Pengra, T. Reyburn-Orne, T. S. Sundem, and C. Zwingman-Bagley. 2003. "Quality Improvement Processes in Growing a Service Line." *Nursing Administration Quarterly* 27 (4): 297–306.

Boerma, M., E. A. Coyle, M. A. Dietrich, M. R. Dintzner, S. J. Drayton, J. L. Early II, A. N. Edginton, C. K. Horlen, C. K. Kirkwood, A. Lin, M. L. Rager, B. Shah-Manek, A. C. Welch, and N. T. Williams. 2017. "Point/Counterpoint: Are Outstanding Leaders Born or Made?" *American Journal of Pharmaceutical Education* 81 (3): 58.

Brown, M. E., and L. K. Treviño. 2006. "Socialized Charismatic Leadership, Values Congruence, and Deviance in Work Groups." *Journal of Applied Psychology* 91 (4): 954–62.

Carmeli, A., and M. Y. Halevi. 2009. "How Top Management Team Behavioral Integration and Behavioral Complexity Enable Organizational Ambidexterity: The Moderating Role of Contextual Ambidexterity." *Leadership Quarterly* 20 (2): 207–18.

Clark, L. 2008. "Clinical Leadership: Values, Beliefs and Vision." *Nursing Management* 15 (7): 30–35.

Dye, C. F., and A. N. Garman. 2015. *Exceptional Leadership: 16 Critical Competencies for Healthcare Leaders*, 2nd ed. Chicago: Health Administration Press.

Garman, A. N., and M. Johnson. 2006. "Leadership Competencies: An Introduction." *Journal of Healthcare Management* 51 (1): 13–17.

Hughes, R. L., R. C. Ginnett, and G. J. Curphy. 2015. *Leadership: Enhancing the Lessons of Experience*, 8th ed. Burr Ridge, IL: McGraw-Hill Education.

Karp, T., and T. I. Tveteraas Helgø. 2009. "Reality Revisited: Leading People in Chaotic Change." *Journal of Management Development* 28 (2): 81–93.

Miles, R. E. 2007. "Innovation and Leadership Values." *California Management Review* 50 (1): 192–201.

Reave, L. 2005. "Spiritual Values and Practices Related to Leadership Effectiveness." *Leadership Quarterly* 16 (5): 655–87.

Souba, W. W., and D. V. Day. 2006. "Leadership Values in Academic Medicine." *Academic Medicine: Journal of the Association of American Medical Colleges* 81 (1): 20–26.

Souba, W. W., D. Mauger, and D. V. Day. 2007. "Does Agreement on Institutional Values and Leadership Issues Between Deans and Surgery Chairs Predict Their Institutions' Performance?" *Academic Medicine: Journal of the Association of American Medical Colleges* 82 (3): 272–80.

Stanley, D. 2008. "Congruent Leadership: Values in Action." *Journal of Nursing Management* 16 (5): 519–24.

Yukl, G. 2010. *Leadership in Organizations*, 7th ed. Upper Saddle River, NJ: Prentice Hall.

CHAPTER 5

The Senior Leader Challenge

*Health care delivery is arguably the most
complex industry in existence.*

—John Glaser (2013)

THE CHALLENGES IN healthcare have been about the same for many years, usually centering on finance and quality. However, some of these issues have become more critical and new ones have surfaced, as mentioned in chapter 1. Certainly COVID-19 has created many ongoing trials and hardships. Following are specific challenges that senior leadership teams have encountered in the past few years:

- COVID-19 pandemic—at the top of the list for almost everyone, has touched every corner of healthcare
- Legislative changes—the continuing impact of the Affordable Care Act, perhaps the most substantive law since Medicare and Medicaid
- New risk/payment models—move toward pay for value, clinical integration, population health management, accountable care organizations

- Physicians—shortages, recruitment, retention, engagement, burnout, generational changes, and the need for more physician leaders
- Care outside the acute care facility—the need to control, or at least partially manage, non-post-acute care plus the growth of telehealth
- Improving outcomes, readmission prevention, increased emphasis on patient quality and safety
- Bigger entities—health systems getting larger, insurance company mergers
- Patients and families—their involvement within a consumer-driven market and retail healthcare
- Artificial intelligence and information technology (IT)—massive systems

Exhibit 5.1 describes the four-pronged challenges facing the field. This chapter gives voice to leaders' main concerns—be they internal or external to their organizations and the field. The intent here is to raise awareness of the fact that values-driven leaders have an advantage over these seemingly insurmountable challenges.

ORGANIZATIONAL FACTORS

Now more than ever, senior leaders need to depend on their strong values to effectively lead their hospitals and health systems. Chaos sometimes arises in part because leaders fail to anticipate, work through, and rise above the inevitable changes in the field. Some observers would suggest that the COVID-19 pandemic caught healthcare unprepared. To be fair, however, organizational factors do exist that can impede leaders' performance and can exacerbate the effects of current challenges. These factors are described in this section.

Exhibit 5.1 The Four-Pronged Challenge

- Making patient safety and quality a top priority
- Shifting from volume to value

- Facing continuing pressure to reduce costs
- Supporting growth in new areas such as population health

Quality

Costs

Engagement

Service and education

- Engaging physicians and staff
- Engaging patients in their own care

- Providing service to the *entire* community
- Educating future healthcare providers

Complex and Larger Organizational Structures

Mergers, acquisitions, alliances, affiliations, coalitions, federations, and other types of partnerships reinvented how healthcare services are delivered, paid for, and measured. This redesign created the need for more managers to oversee the quality and flow of even more services. Ultimately, a vast structural maze of managers with various titles emerged. Moreover, as organizations become larger and larger, authority becomes more ambiguous and communications lines more complex and confusing.

Many hospitals have become health systems, and to flourish or at least survive in a competitive market, they have created multiple business lines and adopted new approaches. Often, this expansion has created a schism between leaders who are involved in only external transactions (e.g., physician practice acquisitions, alliances, new business lines) and those who oversee day-to-day operations. It has also meant that decision-making is often shifted to "corporate" headquarters, often hundreds of miles away.

Rapid growth has also diversified the composition and enlarged the size of the typical senior leadership team. As a result, the personal and professional camaraderie that used to bind leaders is almost extinct, and the meetings have become too large for intimate and goal-driven interaction. Some teams convene as many as 20 to 30 people. Both research and common sense prove that a team this large cannot be effective. De Rond (2012) writes that "people tend to prefer teams of four or, at most, five members. Anything lower than four was felt to be too small to be effective, whereas teams larger than five became ineffective." Schmutz and colleagues (2019) state that "since larger teams exhibit more linkages among members than smaller teams, they also face greater coordination challenges. Also, with increasing size teams have greater difficulty developing and maintaining role structures and responsibilities." And Hackman (Coutu 2009) notes that "as a team gets bigger, the number of links that need to be managed among members goes up at an accelerating, almost exponential rate. It's managing the links between members that gets teams into trouble. My rule of thumb is no double digits."

A senior leadership team with more than 20 individuals is not at all unusual today. One executive laments that "our leadership team meets for longer periods of time and wastes more time than ever before." Some teams have become orchestrated show-and-tell sessions where the primary goal seems to be for each leader to showcase her great accomplishments. Rarely can teams of a large size engage in any true problem solving. Readers may want to ponder the *Bezos rule* (named after Amazon.com founder Jeff Bezos): Teams must be small enough to feed with only two pizzas (Cutolo 2021).

Haphazard Executive Search Process

Little preparation or forethought is given to the executive hiring process; organizations usually just jump in to start recruitment.

Although employers are clear on their intentions to search extensively and select the best candidate, they are vague on the actual execution of this plan. This type of hiring may also be classified as *start and stop*, whereby the organization moves quickly to advertise the vacancy or contracts with a search firm, then pauses the process for an indefinite period, and then slowly reenters it before getting back on track. Here, the message seems to be that the employer has bigger priorities, forcing it to delay the recruitment process.

Poor preparation causes executive hiring decisions to be made too subjectively or on gut feeling, not based on the organization's true needs or the position's expectations and qualifications. With gut-feeling hiring, many executive search processes become an endurance test for those involved, focusing almost exclusively on interpersonal style and fit. Sometimes the unfortunate result is the selection of a leader who has inadequate leadership competencies (see chapter 2) and knowledge of healthcare.

Moreover, with increasing leadership shortages, many organizations have realized that searching for candidates from outside the organization is no longer a viable option. More healthcare systems are devoting substantial resources to in-house leadership development programs. This trend is even more true of physician leadership, where the external supply is greatly limited and the risks involved in a hiring mistake are astronomical.

Litigious Environment

Some challenges faced by leaders today are new. Because these leaders have had no prior knowledge of or experience with the matters at hand, their decisions are often based on best guesses—a risky and potentially fatal move.

> A number of foundational shifts are arising from and being exacerbated by COVID-19's spread. Examples include consumers' increasing involvement in health care decision-making; the rapid adoption of virtual health and other digital innovations; the push for interoperable data and data analytics use; and unprecedented public–private collaborations in vaccine and therapeutics development. Amid these dynamics, governments, health care providers, payers, and other stakeholders around the globe are being challenged to quickly pivot, adapt, and innovate.
>
> —**Deloitte (2021)**

The legal ramifications of some of these issues further complicate decision-making processes. Recent challenges such as developing telehealth, protecting or securing the voluminous personal data compiled in IT systems, and instituting better corporate governance policies have compounded the complexity of legal issues in healthcare. With the continued growth of systems and consolidations, antitrust considerations become important. One CEO remarks that the "mission too often takes the back seat to legal maneuvering."

Fast Pace of Change

The traditional mindset in healthcare is to follow predictable, tried processes; therefore, many of its leaders are reluctant to adopt innovative or even alternative strategies or methods of operation. The proliferation of information on the Internet and the fast speed at which this information can be accessed encourage leaders to change with the times and make fast decisions. In fact, leaders who are reluctant to take part in a modern, technological world are seen as a liability because they fail to anticipate and thus capitalize on innovation and other advances. On the other hand, leaders who are advocates and first adopters of new technology are said to be informed, headed in the right direction, and even ahead of the competition.

Those characterizations may be right. However, there is a casualty in this fast-moving trend: The quality of the decisions suffers because leaders do not have enough time to consult with each other or to reflect on the implications of their decisions. A CEO from the Midwest admits that her board is often frustrated with the number and speed of significant decisions that her team has to make without thoughtful deliberation.

> The pandemic has been a tragedy that has tested us all. But COVID-19 has shone a bright light on systemic issues that have stymied progress in health care. With an expansion of value-based care, improvements in both our manufacturing and data collection infrastructure, expansion of access and enhanced maternal outcomes, we can usher in a series of important changes and overcome the entrenched status quo.
>
> —Susan Devore (2021)

Decision-making without proper analysis is prevalent in any industry; it is a product of the rapidly transforming world, with or without the Internet, mobile devices, and other technology-based media. A leader's strong values can help when both time and information are limited but demands are endless.

Lack of Time

Lack of time (specifically, the constant pressure to produce or decide in a limited time) has resulted in burnout and stress.

In addition, lack of time has led to the following:

- *Communication problems.* Because the meeting agenda is filled with so many pressing issues, not all members of the leadership team can convey their thoughts. Even those who have the opportunity to do so cannot properly elaborate on their ideas. On the other hand, some leaders may counter that so much time is spent on meeting minutiae that less time is appropriated for actual strategy evaluation.
- *Less interaction among leaders.* Frontline managers spend more time working together than do senior leaders. Many executive team members come together only occasionally and thus are less familiar and friendly with each other. At this level, personal and professional conflicts tend to be more common and can be more volatile. Competitive members use insider knowledge to intimidate and subdue opposing members. Knowledge is frequently withheld.
- *Reliance on e-mail and texting.* Time-strapped leaders share information and consult about decisions through e-mail and texts. While these methods are more efficient than a phone call, it prevents the proper airing out of issues and causes the input of stakeholders who are not privy to the e-mail or text sequence to be overlooked.

Lack of Shared Vision

Goals are achievable only when everyone on the team is deeply committed to them. Unfortunately, some executive team members move in the opposite direction from the rest of the team, have self-serving agendas, and possess little personal or professional compatibility with colleagues. While some leaders focus on external business development activities, others commit to managing acute care outcomes. Senior-level goals such as improving health system performance or enhancing quality and patient safety are broader and more abstract than the goals set by middle management teams. The threat of losing their jobs, which is always a possibility, especially in a financially difficult time, can turn some leaders into fierce competitors and create a negative political landscape.

The Pandemic Impact

COVID-19 certainly affected healthcare enormously, and its wake continues to touch all aspects of what leaders do. Huber and Sneader (2021) write, "There will be a health revolution. It's already under way. In-person visits to the doctor's office have given way to telehealth and that will continue. But science is not standing still. While the recent spending on healthcare may get dialed back, it has nevertheless been a massive step change." The challenges that confront healthcare include caregiver burnout, labor shortages, and supply chain complications. While some long for a "return to normal," the reality is that instead of rebuilding the healthcare ecosystem, effective leaders will have to look toward what Berlin and colleagues (2021) describe as a "new build." They suggest that what is necessary is "a vision for the workforce that incorporates learnings and aspirations for the future of work (for example, technology-enabled care models) and creates a realistic plan to make it happen."

CONCLUSION

One of the most important characteristics of strong leaders is the ability to objectively analyze their performance and their impact on the organization. This must be done with a full realization of the challenge factors described in this chapter. Highly effective leaders must keep a keen eye on the external factors affecting their organizations while at the same time assessing and measuring their own personal leadership performance. Part IV of this book provides various assessment tools. Consider the concepts in this chapter and apply them to your organization.

Self-Evaluation Questions

❑ How influential is the senior leadership team in my organization?

❑ Does the frequent turnover among senior leaders create a serious, negative effect on the team's effectiveness? Why?

❑ What is my organization doing to increase the number of and quality of physician leaders?

Exercises

Exercise 5.1

Question: Which group has the greater ability to change an organization—senior leaders or middle managers?

Viewpoint: Senior leaders have far more impact and ability to change an organization for several reasons. First, they create and interpret organizational policies. Second, they assess the environment and develop strategy. Third, they control the budget and make the ultimate decisions regarding executive hires. Fourth, they have better insight into environmental trends than do middle managers. Last, their span of control is greater, and they work closely with the board.

Exercise 5.1 Question

1. Do you agree with this viewpoint? Why? Why not? What points do you think are untrue of today's senior leaders?

Exercise 5.2

The layers of hierarchy between a senior leader and a middle manager continue to peel off in many industries, including healthcare. Using information gleaned from the Internet, contrast the role and activities of a senior leader with those of a middle manager. If possible, interview a senior leader and a middle manager.

Exercise 5.2 Questions

1. What are the typical responsibilities of a senior leader?

2. What are the typical responsibilities of a middle manager?

3. How is a senior leader rewarded and recognized? How do these acknowledgments differ from those received by a middle manager?

Suggested Readings for Exercise 5.2

- Henri Fayol's span of control theory may be found in any organizational behavior textbook. An excellent summary can be found at www.stybelpeabody.com/newsite/pdf/ceotime.pdf.

- Amy McCutcheon and Ruth Anne Campbell's "Leadership, Span of Control, Turnover, Staff and Patient Satisfaction." This article discusses the relationships among span of control, employee turnover, and patient satisfaction. See http://stti.confex.com/stti/inrc16/techprogram/paper_23430.htm.

REFERENCES

Berlin, G., M. Lapointe, M. Murphy, and M. Viscardi. 2021. "Nursing in 2021: Retaining the Healthcare Workforce When We Need It Most." McKinsey Healthcare System and Services. Published May 11, 2021. https://www.mckinsey.com/industries/healthcare-systems-and-services/our-insights/nursing-in-2021-retaining-the-healthcare-workforce-when-we-need-it-most.

Coutu, D. 2009. "Why Teams Don't Work." Interview of J. Richard Hackman, the Edgar Pierce Professor of Social and Organizational Psychology at Harvard University. *Harvard Business Review.* Published May. https://hbr.org/2009/05/why-teams-dont-work.

Cutolo, M. 2021. "Why Jeff Bezos's Two Pizza Rule Is One of the Secrets to Amazon's Success." Reader's Digest Blog. Accessed November 14, 2021. https://www.rd.com/article/two-pizza-rule-work-hack/.

Deloitte. 2021. *2021 Global Health Care Outlook: Accelerating Industry Change.* Accessed November 14. https://www2 .deloitte.com/global/en/pages/life-sciences-and-healthcare /articles/global-health-care-sector-outlook.html.

de Rond, M. 2012. "Why Less Is More in Teams." *Harvard Business Review.* Published August 6. https://hbr.org/2012/08 /why-less-is-more-in-teams/.

Devore, S. 2021. "Health Care in 2021: Five Trends to Watch." Health Affairs Blog. Accessed November 14, 2021. https:// www.healthaffairs.org/do/10.1377/hblog20210119.724670 /full/.

Glaser, J. 2013. "Managing Complexity with Health Care Information Technology." *H&HN Daily.* Published October 8. www.hhnmag.com/articles/6094-managing-complexity-with -health-care-information-technology.

Huber, C., and K. Sneader. 2021. "The Eight Trends That Will Define 2021—And Beyond." McKinsey and Company Podcast. June 21, 2021. https://www.mckinsey.com/business -functions/strategy-and-corporate-finance/our-insights /the-eight-trends-that-will-define-2021-and-beyond.

Schmutz, J. B., L. L. Meier, and T. Manser. 2019. "How Effective Is Teamwork Really? The Relationship Between Teamwork and Performance in Healthcare Teams: A Systematic Review and Meta-analysis." *BMJ Open* 9 (9): e028280.

SUGGESTED READINGS

Geerts, J. M., D. Kinnair, P. Taheri, A. Abraham, J. Ahn, R. Atun, L. Barberia, N. J. Best, R. Dandona, A. A. Dhahri, L. Emilsson, J. R. Free, M. Gardam, W. H. Geerts, C. Ihekweazu, S. Johnson,

A. Kooijman, A. T. Lafontaine, E. Leshem, C. Lidstone-Jones, E. Loh, O. Lyons, K. A. Fouda Neel, P. S. Nyasulu, O. Razum, H. Sabourin, J. S. Taylor, H. Sharifi, V. Stergiopoulos, B. Sutton, Z. Wu, and M. Bilodeau. 2021. "Guidance for Health Care Leaders During the Recovery Stage of the COVID-19 Pandemic: A Consensus Statement." *JAMA Network Open* 4 (7): e2120295.

Singer, S., and M. Kerrissey. 2021. "Leading Health Care Teams Beyond Covid-19: Marking the Moment and Shifting from Recuperation to Regeneration." New England Journal of Medicine Catlayst Commentary. July 27, 2021. https://catalyst.nejm.org/doi/full/10.1056/CAT.21.0169.

PART II

PERSONAL VALUES

CHAPTER 6

Respect as the Foundation of Leadership

When people respect you only because of your authority,
they will give you the minimum effort.

—Jim Whitehurst (2015)

JOHN GEORGE, A system CEO, and Julia Garrison, a senior vice president, were overheard discussing the beginning of the era of clinical integration and pay for value:

JULIA. John, healthcare seems to have greatly changed since you first entered it 25 years ago. The field and its workers are not as respected today. Would you agree?

JOHN. When I entered healthcare, many of us saw healthcare management as a calling. We wanted to serve people, to make a difference. I think now too many people go into it as just another career.

JULIA. I'm not sure I agree. Most of us new administrators are still service oriented. The problem is that healthcare leaders have been viewed as villains, even though we do a lot, directly and indirectly, to improve the health and lives of our patients and our workers. Don't you think the old days of the command-and-control healthcare CEOs may have something to do with this negative public perception? I think we could make some changes in our leadership's attitudes that would have a profound impact on our patients, physicians, and employees.

JOHN. Perhaps you're right, although I wouldn't say autocratic leaders are now a relic of the past. Unfortunately, they still exist, and they certainly harm the reputation of all healthcare administrators. I think, though, that the real requirement today is to have a deep and profound respect for workers and the care and services they provide.

Here is my challenge to you: Talk with your colleagues, do some research, and make a recommendation about how to effect a sea change in management. We'll discuss your findings, and we'll see how we can implement changes in our own backyard, so to speak.

RESPECT IS THE value that multiplies the desire of both the leader and follower to work harder and deliver consistently excellent performance.

> Leaders who respect others also allow them to be themselves, with creative wants and desires. They approach other people with a sense of their unconditional worth and valuable individual differences.
>
> —Peter G. Northouse (2021)

Leadership has traditionally been perceived as a prestigious position filled by influential people whose main role is to give orders and impose inflexible rules. This misconception may not be as prevalent now because more leaders have become aware that autocratic management begets only few and uneasy followers. Society frequently rejects selfish leadership. This type of behavior repeatedly leads to entitlement, greed, and other feelings of privilege, as has been frequently reported in the media in the past decade. As a result, many Americans distrust and are cynical about the C-suite—not just in healthcare but in all industries.

Respect for self and others is the nucleus of all activities, especially in management. It is a value that enables leaders to restrain ego, admit mistakes, pay attention, care about and honor others, keep an open mind, give credit or compliments, and ask for help or insight. Leaders must return to this basic value to regain trust and amplify their effectiveness. Although the task is daunting, the undertaking is worthwhile.

For many years now, I have spoken and written about the protocols of leadership. These protocols are the often-unwritten behavioral rules society and organizations expect from their leaders. These generally accepted standards of behavior cannot possibly cover all situations faced by leaders, but they share a common element: respect.

This chapter makes a distinction between self-esteem and self-centeredness, two opposing forces in management style. While self-esteem boosts the persuasiveness of a leader, self-centeredness undermines it altogether. In addition, the chapter also suggests several approaches for showing and gaining respect (see exhibit 6.1).

SELF-ESTEEM VERSUS SELF-CENTEREDNESS

Self-esteem is an individual's respect for her own convictions, actions, imperfections, and abilities. Without self-esteem, a person is not

---

Exhibit 6.1 How to Show Respect for Others

1. Give compliments, be courteous, and demonstrate good manners and pleasant deportment to show that you appreciate and honor the efforts that others bring to the organization.

2. Learn the strength of collective action through the cooperative work of teams.

3. Ask and listen to what others value, need, and expect.

4. Participate in others' activities to show you care about their interests.

---

mentally healthy; does not function well under pressure; cannot accept or give compliments and criticism; and tends to be egotistical, controlling, and in constant need of affirmation.

Self-centeredness, on the other hand, is an individual's overly favorable sense of his own abilities, views, decisions, and needs. A self-centered person is arrogant, insecure (yet feels superior), and a nuisance (if not harmful) in any social or professional setting.

Leaders who have low self-esteem but are highly self-centered

- do not respect or trust others;
- alienate others with a domineering attitude;
- are exasperating because they seek and demand so much approval;
- cause unnecessary work and waste time; and
- engender disloyalty, stress, and fear.

Exhibit 6.2 contrasts self-esteem with self-centeredness.

Exhibit 6.2 Self-Esteem Versus Self-Centeredness

Self-Esteem		Self-Centeredness
Respects self	vs.	Has overly favorable concept of self
Accepts and gives compliments and criticism gracefully	vs.	Demands constant approval while being unduly critical
Collaborates and cooperates with others	vs.	Alienates others with an arrogant approach
Stays efficient by relying on colleagues for aid	vs.	Doubts others, creating unnecessary work
Cultivates an inclusive, team-oriented atmosphere	vs.	Fosters disloyalty and suspicion in the workplace

---

THE CONCEPT IN PRACTICE

Following are some ways a leader can show respect in various facets of her position.

Become a Collaborator

Collaboration is a partnership among people who have shared goals but distinct strategies or priorities. The reasons for collaboration are varied and include the desire to expedite achievement of results; combine expertise, experience, and resources; minimize or prevent mistakes and waste in effort, time, and money; and produce a better product.

Leaders who become good collaborators learn to

- hold judgment until all the variables and others' opinions have been presented;
- listen actively;
- reflect before responding; and
- ask questions to understand, not to cast doubt.

Exhibit 6.3 is a basic guide to effective collaboration.

Senior leaders must push other executives to seek collaborations with those in lower-level positions. Why is this necessary? Because collaboration is about the equal exchange of ideas, not a privileged activity of those at the top of the organizational hierarchy. An inter-office collaboration that includes multilevel partners is a sign that leaders respect the insights and contributions of all employees.

Be Aware of Others' Definition of Respect

Respect means different things to different people. For example, Person A may perceive respect when he is asked for his opinion,

Exhibit 6.3 Key Requirements of Effective Collaboration

Common desired outcome. The collaboration must offer a reciprocal benefit to all partners or participants. The stakeholders must believe that they are getting something good in return for their efforts and that the end product improves the current situation.

Shared responsibility. The driving force of a true collaboration is shared responsibility—from decision making to implementation to monitoring and assessment. All members of the partnership, not just its leaders, must be able to voice their concerns, opinions, and questions. Consensus must be reached at all times. Responsibility for failure or negative consequences must also be shared by all involved.

Support. In a collaborative situation, parties to the process support each other's right to express ideas and suggestions. When a decision is made to move forward, all stakeholders support the conclusion.

Clear objective. The group must have a clear understanding of the collaboration's purpose or goal.

Trust. Trust is built when all partners commit to being transparent and sharing information. A willingness to admit mistakes also helps in this regard.

Open communication. Suspending judgment, not assigning blame, actively listening, being interested and inquisitive, and checking in or following up promote open communication among collaborators.

Celebration. Gains and accomplishments must be celebrated. Doing so encourages participants.

---

while Person B may feel respected if she is empowered to make an important decision.

For many people, the level of respect they give, get, or demand depends on superficial attributes such as job title. Unfortunately, respect for those who clean the facilities, for example, seems non-existent in many industries. Likewise, professors and students alike may not show as much respect for their university's security personnel or cafeteria staff. In clinical practice, physicians are traditionally more respected than are nurses or allied health professionals. In management, executives garner more respect than do receptionists and other frontline employees.

A good leader understands these dynamics and recognizes everyone's human dignity and basic need for respect. When asked how he shows respect, a successful CEO says, "I hire the very best people I can find, and then I show them the respect they are due by staying out of their way and letting them do their jobs." Another high-performing CEO reveals, "All of my executive team members think and act like each is my COO [chief operations officer]—and most important, they make most of their decisions without my involvement." These two quotes exemplify how leaders can show respect by empowering their staff.

> Being in a position to exercise power over other people . . . may be satisfying for a little while, but never in the long run. Ultimately it leaves you lonely. You command, and you receive fear and obedience in return, and what emotionally healthy person can live on a diet of fear and obedience?
>
> **—Harold S. Kushner (1986)**

Establish a Feedback System

The best feedback systems are those that provide constant, unfiltered, direct feedback and, when necessary, criticism. Feedback should be given on an ongoing basis and should be informal. The recipient of the feedback should be given an opportunity to respond, ask questions, or simply confirm his understanding.

In the book *Giving and Receiving Performance Feedback*, author Peter Garber (2004) indicates that in most organizations, it has become increasingly rare that true open dialogue occurs in traditional performance evaluation sessions. Executives' interactions are more often than not held in the C-suite,

> It is difficult to imagine how work group or team performance could improve without feedback.
>
> **—Richard L. Hughes, Robert C. Ginnett, and Gordon J. Curphy (2015)**

a setting that can intimidate most people. The fact that the leaders giving the evaluation have the power to hire and fire adds to the tension. As a result of these trappings, leaders may be less skilled at evaluating their direct reports and vice versa (Garman and Dye 2009).

Seeking and accepting feedback is a sign of respect, communicating that others' opinions are valued. When leaders interact with staff regularly, they appear accessible and are better informed.

Be Genuine

Genuineness is referred to as *authentic presence*. It can be conveyed by being visibly involved in organizational activities and showing a vested interest in others' work without being intrusive and pretentious. The unspoken message here is that "we are in this together." Forman (2010, 4) states, "We need to listen with what has been called the 'third ear.' This requires an open mind that embraces discovery and welcomes possibilities. To do this, we must temporarily set aside what we think or know and listen carefully."

Many CEOs practice management by walking around (MBWA), a popular strategy among leaders. MBWA's primary purpose is to witness the effectiveness or ineffectiveness of various services and, by extension, those who perform the work. Although MBWA provides great insight and breeds familiarity, it should be carefully managed to ensure that employees believe the approach is sincere.

This dialogue from the classic tale *The Velveteen Rabbit* (Williams 1922, 3–4) serves as a reminder of how everyone can develop an authentic presence.

"What is REAL?" asked the Rabbit one day. . . . "Does it mean having things that buzz inside you and a stick-out handle?"

"Real isn't how you are made," said the Skin Horse. "It's a thing that happens to you. . . ."

"Does it hurt?" asked the Rabbit.

"Sometimes," said the Skin Horse, for he was always truthful. "When you are Real you don't mind being hurt."

"Does it happen all at once, like being wound up," he asked, "or bit by bit?"

"It doesn't happen all at once," said the Skin Horse. "You become. It takes a long time. That's why it doesn't often happen to people who break easily, or have sharp edges, or who have to be carefully kept. . . . Once you are Real you can't be ugly, except to people who don't understand."

In Catholic hospitals, nuns (many of them top administrators) traditionally were known to be extraordinary influencers because they were frequently visible and consistently approachable. Physicians tend to gravitate toward physician leaders who are frequently seen in clinical areas and believe such leaders can better represent their needs, understand their concerns, and defend their demands. This tendency is even more true for the physician leaders who maintain some amount of clinical practice.

Give Credit and Acknowledge Accomplishments

The mark of a great leader is his ability to step back from the spotlight and publicly recognize someone else's excellent performance. This simple acknowledgment is one of the most powerful motivators, much quieter than a standing ovation but more valuable than money.

Offer Help or Coaching

Many leaders study coaching to enhance their abilities to evaluate, constructively criticize, and assist their staff's performance. By helping staff develop, the leader is saying, "I admire and respect your work so much that I want to invest in your growth and accomplishments."

Be Self-Aware

Leaders must be able to look inward to discover their strengths, weaknesses, goals, and impetus. Creativity often springs from being self-aware. In *Exceptional Leadership*, well-cultivated self-awareness is one of the four key cornerstones of superb leadership (Dye and Garman 2015). This approach requires strong feedback mechanisms as well as a willingness to consider with an open mind the input received.

Take Responsibility for Mistakes and Apologize

This approach is often the most overlooked way of showing respect. Many leaders fail to realize that by simply owning up to their mistakes and apologizing, they are loudly proclaiming that they are penetrable, they are vincible, and they are human—hence, on the same level as others. What others hear when leaders say "I made a mistake and I'm sorry" is "I respect you, so I will not pretend or make you believe that what happened was your responsibility."

Learn the Principle of Affirmation

The word *affirm* comes from an ancient legal principle: The higher court must approve the decision of the lower court. In hospitals and health systems, leaders function as the higher court that affirms the work and contributions of their employees (the lower court). This principle serves as a powerful, positive message and a great motivator for better performance.

Positive affirmations are statements and behaviors that build others up and boost their confidence and sense of well-being. They serve to minimize the many negative distractions that occur in the workplace. The advice that leaders give in the workplace and the atmosphere created by leaders in an organization help to shape the attitude that others in that organization have.

Show Appreciation

A note of congratulations, appreciation, or gratitude has always been a staple of good camaraderie. Many leaders still make time to handwrite notes, but this practice has declined as e-mails, phone calls, video conferences or chats, and even texts have become more common for their convenience and speed. Whatever the means of delivery, the idea is the same: A small token makes a big impression.

Show Enthusiasm

Some leaders may think that showing enthusiasm about an endeavor is inappropriate, unprofessional, or even silly. However, it has a positive effect on followers. Enthusiasm can energize people and boost loyalty to the undertaking.

Showing enthusiasm and support for the mission of the organization is also important because the rank and file models the behavior of its leaders. Employees can become cynical if they only hear but do not see their leaders' support of the mission.

Enthusiasm may also be expressed through attending or participating in employee events. Failure to make an appearance or embrace these events can drive a wedge between the C-suite and the front line, perpetuating the perception that senior leaders are only interested in activities that revolve around the power structure. As one executive's flippant remark expresses, "I really see no sense in serving hot dogs at the employee picnic. Let others handle that, and I'll handle my job."

CONCLUSION

Respect may be commonsense knowledge to some leaders. However, the concept is surprisingly novel to many others. Admittedly, showing respect is hard to master, and convincing people to try it is even harder, especially in today's healthcare workplace already overwhelmed with too many "must dos." But giving respect is not a temporary fix or trend; it is a fundamental value in all aspects of life.

Cases and Exercise

Case 6.1

Roberto Santiago has been CEO of St. James for the past three years, hired for his strategic visioning acumen. He spends his time in meetings with board members, community leaders, and physicians. Recently, he led a successful strategic planning retreat, garnering him strong support from the board and medical staff.

Roberto has put Jane Robbins, the chief operations officer, in charge of running St. James's daily operations. Jane oversees the vice presidents and attends all staff meetings. During a monthly housekeeping meeting, Jane fielded questions from the housekeeping staff. One asked, "We never see Mr. Santiago. Does he not care what happens to us?"

How would you answer this question if you were Jane?

Case 6.2

Courtney Sample is the new hard-charging, tough-as-nails CEO of a system hospital. She is well known for delivering great results, but sometimes at the expense of many. Previously, she executed a multiyear, multimillion-dollar turnaround of a bankrupt hospital, replacing the entire senior leadership team in the process.

Six months into her position, Courtney is frustrated.

She has not been able to finish a single project, and morale among her senior leadership team is at an all-time low. Many of the employees and physicians are unfamiliar with her, and those who know her avoid eye contact. She schedules an appointment with her longtime personal coach, Will Cheng, to seek his guidance. Will spends a day talking with Courtney's staff and then meets her over dinner.

WILL. You intimidate your staff. They didn't even want to talk to me. They think you view them like tools, just there to get the job done.

COURTNEY. Isn't that what we all are anyway? Tools to get the job done?

Case 6.2 Questions

1. How can showing respect help Courtney out of this scenario? What can Will do and say to correct Courtney's misguided attitude?

2. How is the concept of respect a constant in *all* leadership settings? Consider the leader who states, "Sometimes, I want my followers to fear me." Is this dynamic ever appropriate?

Exercise 6.1

Review one of the following academic articles and describe its findings on the role of respect in leadership.

Clarke, N. 2011. "An Integrated Conceptual Model of Respect in Leadership." *Leadership Quarterly* 22 (2): 316–27.

Ulrich, B. T., P. I. Buerhaus, K. Donelan, L. Norman, and R. Dittus. 2005. "How RNs View the Work Environment: Results of a National Survey of Registered Nurses." *Journal of Nursing Administration* 35 (9): 389–96.

REFERENCES

Dye, C. F., and A. N. Garman. 2015. *Exceptional Leadership: 16 Critical Competencies for Healthcare Leaders*, 2nd ed. Chicago: Health Administration Press.

Forman, H. 2010. *Nursing Leadership for Patient-Centered Care: Authenticity, Presence, Intuition, Expertise*. New York: Springer Publishing Company.

Garber, P. R. 2004. *Giving and Receiving Performance Feedback*. Amherst, MA: HRD Press.

Garman, A. N., and C. F. Dye. 2009. *The Healthcare C-Suite: Leadership Development at the Top*. Chicago: Health Administration Press.

George, B. 2016. "What's Your Life Goal? Success or Significance?" Published April 27. www.billgeorge.org/page /fortune-whats-your-life-goal-success-or-significance.

Hughes, R. L., R. C. Ginnett, and G. J. Curphy. 2015. *Leadership: Enhancing the Lessons of Experience*, 8th ed. Burr Ridge, IL: McGraw-Hill Education.

Kushner, H. S. 1986. *When All You've Ever Wanted Isn't Enough: The Search for a Life That Matters*. New York: Simon and Schuster.

Northouse, P. G. 2021. *Leadership: Theory and Practice*, 9th ed. Los Angeles: SAGE Publications.

Whitehurst, J. 2015. *The Open Organization: Igniting Passion and Performance*. Boston: Harvard Business Review Press.

Williams, M. 1922. *The Velveteen Rabbit, or How Toys Become Real*. London: Heinemann.

SUGGESTED READINGS

Denier, Y., L. Dhaene, and C. Gastmans. 2019. "'You Can Give Them Wings to Fly': A Qualitative Study on Values-Based Leadership in Health Care." *BMC Medical Ethics* 20 (35).

Ghutke, S., R. Jaiswal, and A. Thakur. 2014. "Case Analysis of 360 Degree Feedback." *International Journal of Advanced Research in Education, Technology and Management* 2 (3): 202–206.

CHAPTER 7

Ethics and Integrity

*Leaders with integrity inspire confidence in others because they
can be trusted to do what they say they are going to do.*

—Peter G. Northouse (2021)

IN A POPULAR graduate health administration course, the
professor turns to the topic of ethics: "How important is
ethics in healthcare leadership? And how do we determine
that someone is truly ethical?"

STUDENT A. First, you have to define what a leader is supposed to do. Then, you can determine the ethics from there.

STUDENT B. It's all about the end result. Outcomes are important in healthcare; that's what we are here to do—help make
positive changes for people.

STUDENT C. I have a problem with the idea that something
is ethical just because it benefits a great number of people.
That shortchanges the role that values need to play in leadership. What about the minority number who are inevitably
disadvantaged by the change? Don't they count? What about

the leader who ignored her moral compass just so she could provide for the many?

STUDENT D. But I think we're missing the core of the matter—frankly, if leaders don't have high integrity and ethics, they're not effective.

PROFESSOR. Excellent responses! There are no easy answers in ethics, which is why it's important to have discussions about these issues.

As ARE OTHER leadership values, ethics and integrity are interrelated. Ethics is a person's moral scope, and integrity is the person's capacity for staying within that moral scope. The general concept of both values is comprehensible, but their true meaning is elusive.

This chapter explores the tandem nature of ethics and integrity. It provides a guide for leaders on how to practice ethical behavior within the constructs of daily operation. While the vignette presents both a macro view and a micro view of ethics, this chapter focuses on leaders' daily activities.

DEFINING INTEGRITY

Practically all leaders believe they possess high integrity. However, when asked to name other leaders who have integrity, many demur by saying, "Integrity is hard to define." Why the contradiction? Three reasons are plausible.

> Leaders who do not behave ethically do not demonstrate true leadership.
>
> —J. M. Burns (1978)

First, many definitions for integrity exist, but none is universal. According to the *Merriam-Webster's Collegiate Dictionary, Eleventh Edition*, integrity is "the quality or state of being complete or undivided." To some people, the word could mean absolute honesty, while to others, it is a high degree of genuineness. My definition is that it is the quality that allows a person to differentiate right from wrong. Northouse (2021, 32), meanwhile, defines it this way: "Basically, integrity makes a leader believable and worthy of our trust." Each definition almost always reflects a person's sensibility (e.g., moral compass, bias, expectation). Thus, applying it to others can be a difficult proposition.

Second, our perception of integrity varies from one situation to the next. Everyone has his own concept of right and wrong, but we all stray occasionally from our own standards. For example, if Leader A, who is regularly lauded for her good ethical judgment, occasionally uses the organization's copy machine to copy personal paperwork or uses the company's computer to surf the Internet on her lunch hour, is she being unethical? Although Leader A's sensibility informs her that these actions are inappropriate, she continues because she does not deem them harmful to the organization. This scenario is an example of *ethical relativism* or contingency leadership. It provokes leaders into considering their own ethical anchors before facing complex situations.

Third, although difficult to define, integrity still ranks at or near the top of all lists of required leadership traits. Palanski and Yammarino (2007, 171) state that the "study of integrity, however, suffers from three significant problems: too many definitions, too little theory, and too few rigorous empirical studies." (This is the same argument I made in chapter 3 about popular leadership literature.) Nevertheless, many leadership books provide ample space for discussing integrity.

When you clarify the principles that will govern your life and the ends that you will seek, you give purpose to your daily decisions. A personal creed gives you a point of reference for navigating the sometimes-stormy seas of organizational life. Without such a set of beliefs, your life has no rudder, and you are easily blown about by the winds of fashion. A credo that resolves competing beliefs also leads to personal integrity.

—James M. Kouzes and Barry Z. Posner (2012)

THE CONCEPT IN PRACTICE

The ethical decisions of leaders, especially senior executives, are observed more closely—and are likely more scrutinized—than any other decisions they make. An ethical dilemma bears significant personal and professional risk because its resolution often compels a leader to reveal her private opinions. How can leaders lessen this risk but still handle these ethical challenges? The following approaches serve as a guide.

Adopt an Organizational Code of Ethics

An organizational code of ethics defines appropriate and inappropriate conduct in the workplace and identifies conduct that falls between those poles. It protects the organization from legal entanglement and employees from harassment and unfair treatment. Leaders should be enlisted to support the code and should educate themselves and others about its applications and benefits. Mechanisms to monitor employee adherence to the code must be developed as well.

The *Code of Ethics* and Ethical Policy Statement of the American College of Healthcare Executives, the leading professional association of healthcare leaders, are excellent guides for practicing leaders, managers, students, consultants, and others interested in the management field (see the *Code*'s Preamble in exhibit 7.1). Many healthcare organizations also have a corporate code of ethics or statement of values or a corporate responsibility program.

Several excellent examples can be found online. Premier Health posts a description of its commitment to integrity and ethics on its website at www.premierhealth.com/about-premier/about-us /integrity-and-ethics. Similarly, Ascension Health's comprehensive Corporate Responsibility Program can be found at https://ascension .org/about/corporate-responsibility.

Some organizations create ethics statements because of regulatory requirements and corporate compliance programs. However, an increasing number of healthcare organizations have put in place robust codes of ethics because doing so is the right thing and is beneficial to the enterprise as a whole.

Exhibit 7.1 Preamble to ACHE's *Code of Ethics*

The purpose of the *Code of Ethics* of the American College of Healthcare Executives is to serve as a standard of conduct for members. It contains standards of ethical behavior for healthcare executives in their professional relationships. These relationships include colleagues, patients or others served; members of the healthcare executive's organization and other organizations; the community; and society as a whole.

The *Code of Ethics* also incorporates standards of ethical behavior governing individual behavior, particularly when that conduct directly relates to the role and identity of the healthcare executive.

The fundamental objectives of the healthcare management profession are to maintain or enhance the overall quality of life, dignity and well-being of every individual needing healthcare service and to create a more equitable, accessible, effective and efficient healthcare system.

Healthcare executives have an obligation to act in ways that will merit the trust, confidence and respect of healthcare professionals and the general public. Therefore, healthcare executives should lead lives that embody an exemplary system of values and ethics.

In fulfilling their commitments and obligations to patients or others served, healthcare executives function as moral advocates and models. Since every management decision affects the health and well-being of both individuals and communities, healthcare executives must carefully evaluate the possible outcomes of their decisions. In organizations that deliver healthcare services, they must work to safeguard and foster the rights, interests and prerogatives of patients or others served.

The role of moral advocate requires that healthcare executives take actions necessary to promote such rights, interests and prerogatives.

Being a model means that decisions and actions will reflect personal integrity and ethical leadership that others will seek to emulate.

Source: Reprinted from American College of Healthcare Executives (2021).

Write a Personal Code of Ethics

Writing a personal code of ethics, or credo, serves two purposes: (1) to declare the values important to the person, and (2) to guide decision-making and prioritizing when difficult issues come up. In adopting a credo, a leader should consider how other people perceive her behaviors and actions. As one CEO simply puts it, "What do others think of you?"

Here are questions to ponder when developing a personal code of ethics:

- What does integrity mean to me?
- What do I value?
- What do I stand for?
- What am I willing to compromise or not compromise?

Committing to abide by this code of ethics is the next step. This commitment entails weighing the cost of not being ethical. The cost is significant, as illustrated by leaders in the field who have been caught peddling dubious schemes, misappropriating funds, or generally behaving badly. Here are questions to consider in this regard:

- What damage will this situation cause to my loved ones? To my career and livelihood? To my reputation in the community?
- Is the payoff worth everything I have worked hard to build?

Tell the Truth, and Do Not Exaggerate

In the strict ethical sense, telling the truth and not exaggerating are the same. Many people, however, differentiate between the two.

The argument for the difference is that telling the truth means telling no lies. On the other hand, exaggerating means stretching the truth to achieve a certain outcome or reaction.

For many, including healthcare executives, the latter has become accepted, commonplace practice. Many executives overestimate, engage in hyperbole, embellish the facts, provide misquotes, twist the truth, and overstate (or understate) their contribution or responsibility to fit their needs. Whether discussing budget or organizational performance, many communications are filled with subjective stretches of reality. Consider the following simple, but powerful, comments that are often rhetorical overstatements:

> Claiming more credit than you're due is yet another way we may fool ourselves about the moral virtue of our own decision making.
>
> —Richard L. Hughes, Robert C. Ginnett, and Gordon J. Curphy (2015)

- "We have cut all the fat out of our budgets. All that remains is absolutely necessary."
- "I have told the team that many, many times. They must not be hearing me."
- "I don't think I can cut any deeper—it will hurt patient care."
- "Everyone is very upset about this."

How many times have you heard these or similar statements, and how many times have you fully believed them?

Do as You Say

Become known as a leader who follows through. Often, integrity is measured less by failures in significant areas and more by the lack of follow-up on minor items. If a promise is made, it should be honored. One leader describes it as having a high "say–do" ratio.

Use Power Appropriately

Effective leaders are acutely aware that power can be used for good or bad. They understand the sources of their power, and they use it judiciously. Unfortunately, ineffective leaders and some new executives wield their power to attempt to gain respect, prestige, and favors.

Admit Mistakes

Admitting mistakes is a noble, impressive act. However, too many leaders believe that such an admission weakens their authority. The opposite is true. Power is not incrementally earned by being perfect all the time. Instead, power is bestowed on leaders by their followers. Followers can agree that an admission of fault serves to increase their leader's power.

March to the Beat of Your Own Drum

A clear understanding of and commitment to personal values is a leader's greatest defense against the temptation of following a negative example. An executive who is guided first and foremost by her own ethical standards, not by popular opinion or practice, behaves and performs with integrity. This type of leader does not need to beat her drum loudly to gain followers; people will follow naturally.

> Leaders face dilemmas that require choices between competing sets of values and priorities, and the best leaders recognize and face them with a commitment to doing what is right, not just what is expedient.
>
> —Richard L. Hughes, Robert C. Ginnett, and Gordon J. Curphy (2015)

Be Trustworthy

In their book *Judgment*, Tichy and Bennis (2007, 84) state, "Leading with character gives the wise leader clear-cut advantages. They are easier to trust and follow; they honor commitments and promises; their word and behavior match; they are always engaged in and by the world; they are open to reflective 'backtalk'; they can admit errors and learn from their mistakes."

> Neither shall you allege the example of the many as an excuse for doing wrong.
>
> —Exodus 23:2

Author Stephen M. R. Covey (2013) describes trust as the key way to avoid being viewed with suspicion; as such, trust reflects the essence of ethics and integrity. A leader is only as effective as the support that his followers grant him. Gaining that support is not possible if the leader does not earn others' trust and loyalty.

Manage Expense Accounts Judiciously

Leaders must require approvals for all reimbursements, especially for petty cash funds. This simple system of fund management does not create more bureaucracy, prevents temptation, and ensures that no one can question whether fund violation occurred.

Seasoned leaders agree that mismanagement of expenses is a common occurrence because it is so easy to overlook.

CONCLUSION

One of the greatest compliments to a leader is when others recognize her integrity and ethical uprightness. Ethics and integrity are always necessary ingredients in leadership. Leaders become great leaders when they follow their own moral instincts. Doing so focuses them in times of uncertainty, strengthening their resolve to do right no matter what.

Self-Evaluation Questions

❑ What would others say about my integrity? About my ethics?

❑ Does integrity really mean that much to me? How many times have I not followed through? Not done what I said I would do? Not gotten back to someone when I promised I would?

❑ As the old saying goes, "Actions speak louder than words." How do I stack up against this saying?

❑ Do I appropriately use the power granted to me?

❑ Have I ever cut corners and behaved in an ethically questionable manner?

Cases

Case 7.1

Jennifer Park, the chief financial officer of a hospital, is preparing for the year-end financial audit. She knows that several items in the books will draw the attention of the auditors. She meets with the CEO, Rob Cortez, to explain the situation. Rob responds, "Make certain that there are no comments in the audit. The audit has to be clean because the chair is new, and he won't tolerate an audit adjustment. Do whatever it takes."

Case 7.1 Questions

1. What is the implication of Rob's instruction to Jennifer?

2. What could happen behind the scenes if Jennifer follows Rob's order? If she does not follow his order?

Case 7.2

After checking references, Jerrod D'Amato, the human resources manager at a hospital, finds out that Cheryl Johnson, the number one candidate for a critical care nursing position, was fired for absenteeism at her last job. Because the position has to be filled immediately and this discovery will only slow down the process, Jerrod chooses to withhold the information from the hiring nurse manager. He does discuss the issue with Cheryl, who tells him she was going through a tough time but is now ready for a new start. Jerrod thinks that Cheryl deserves a fair chance and that her qualifications far outweigh the problems she had.

Case 7.2 Questions

1. Is Jerrod right or wrong? Explain your reasoning.

2. Is there a difference between "need to know" information and "nice to know" information?

REFERENCES

American College of Healthcare Executives. 2021. *ACHE Code of Ethics.* Amended December 6. https://www.ache.org/about-ache/our-story/our-commitments/ethics/ache-code-of-ethics.

Burns, J. M. 1978. *Leadership.* New York: Harper & Row.

Covey, S. R. 2013. *The 7 Habits of Highly Successful People: Powerful Lessons in Personal Change*, 25th anniversary ed. New York: Simon and Schuster.

Hughes, R. L., R. C. Ginnett, and G. J. Curphy. 2015. *Leadership: Enhancing the Lessons of Experience*, 8th ed. Burr Ridge, IL: McGraw-Hill Education.

Kouzes, J. M., and B. Z. Posner. 2012. *The Leadership Challenge: How to Make Extraordinary Things Happen in Organizations*, 5th ed. San Francisco: Jossey-Bass.

Merriam-Webster's Collegiate Dictionary, Eleventh Edition. (Springfield, Massachusetts: Merriam-Webster, Inc, 2014), "Integrity."

Northouse, P. G. 2021. *Leadership: Theory and Practice*, 9th ed. Los Angeles: SAGE Publications.

Palanski, M. E., and F. J. Yammarino. 2007. "Integrity and Leadership: Clearing the Conceptual Confusion." *European Management Journal* 25 (3): 171–84.

Tichy, N. M., and W. G. Bennis. 2007. *Judgment: How Winning Leaders Make Great Calls*. New York: Portfolio.

SUGGESTED READINGS

Bass, B., and P. Steidlmeier. 1999. "Ethics, Character, and Authentic Transformational Leadership Behavior." *Leadership Quarterly* 10 (2): 181–217.

Gardner, W. L., C. C. Cogliser, K. M. Davis, and M. P. Dickens. 2011. "Authentic Leadership: A Review of the Literature and Research Agenda." *Leadership Quarterly* 22 (6): 1120–45.

Greenbaum, R. L., M. J. Quade, and J. Bonner. 2015. "Why Do Leaders Practice Amoral Management? A Conceptual Investigation of the Impediments to Ethical Leadership." *Organizational Psychology Review* 5 (1): 26–49.

Manz, C. C., V. Anand, M. Joshi, and K. P. Manz. 2008. "Emerging Paradoxes in Executive Leadership: A Theoretical Interpretation of the Tensions Between Corruption and Virtuous Values." *Leadership Quarterly* 19 (3): 385–92.

Storr, L. 2004. "Leading with Integrity: A Qualitative Research Study." *Journal of Health Organization and Management* 18 (6): 415–34.

Interpersonal Connection

*Bad leaders perpetrate terrible misery on
those subject to their domain.*

—Robert Hogan and Robert B. Kaiser (2005)

ARTHUR ONLY HAD a reputation for being a great IT (information technology) manager at his health system. He
was on many task forces and assigned the lead on the critical
electronic health record (EHR) conversion. Arthur, who has
an MBA and a PhD in information technology, applied for the
chief information officer (CIO) position when its incumbent
retired. He got the job, beating other equally qualified but
more experienced candidates. This promotion to CIO pleased
many people at the organization, but it was surprising given
that Arthur was a middle manager—not necessarily next in
line for the job. Among employees, the situation has become
a favorite topic of discussion.

EMPLOYEE A. How did Arthur do it, landing a big CIO job so
fast? He never managed budgets or led a department. He
never worked directly with senior management. Granted, he

was heavily involved in the EHR conversion, but I can say the same for a lot of managers here, and they're not moving up the ladder.

EMPLOYEE B. My cousin runs a large IT outsourcing firm. The turnover in those companies is very high. People frequently leave for more money, and worker loyalty is nonexistent. Somehow, though, at my cousin's firm the turnover is low, although the employees could get so much more money if they worked somewhere else.

EMPLOYEE A. Those people must be crazy!

EMPLOYEE B. Maybe so, but my cousin is an ideal boss. He sets aside time during the day to visit his employees to listen to their concerns and input. He asks about their families, and he encourages them to take classes or go back to school to advance their careers. He respects their work, and he personally thanks them for their contributions. His employees feel welcomed in his office, and they know he puts people before numbers, so they are not afraid to approach him. He is humble, supportive, and helpful. Doesn't my cousin sound like Arthur? Don't you think people would prefer to work for someone like him over someone whose main focus is always money and business?

THE HEALTHCARE SYSTEM is the true industry of the people. No other field witnesses human afflictions, from diseases of the body to ailments of the spirit; hosts the most basic human need (interaction at the most inopportune moments); and serves as the most common human thread (everyone needs healthcare). Because of these truths, people—patients, employees, physicians, volunteers, contractors, communities—are the critical factor in organizational success.

The irony is that, though leading healthcare organizations find that improving relationships with their employees and patients is the key to excellence, most still focus on financial factors to measure success. Every organization has an annual financial audit, but only a few conduct annual human resources audits or even define what these human resources audits might be. Almost every board of trustees has a finance committee, but not all have human resources committees. Most organizations have balanced scorecards, but the financial portion of these scorecards receives the most time and attention.

> Leadership is a reciprocal relationship between those who choose to lead and those who decide to follow. Any discussion of leadership must attend to the dynamics of this relationship.
>
> —James M. Kouzes and Barry Z. Posner (1993)

In his well-known book *Good to Great*, Jim Collins (2001, 36) writes about the Level 5 leader. This person "builds enduring greatness through a paradoxical blend of personal humility and professional will." This type of leader puts people first (i.e., "gets the right people on the bus") and vision and strategy second. Financial success then follows this principle.

This chapter reiterates the significance of having people skills—a value so subtle that it can be easily undermined but so powerful that it can make or break an organization.

PEOPLE SKILLS

Leaders who have people skills are marked by a profound respect for the character of others and a deep faith in their potential, which is why they enjoy being with people and interact well with them. Often, the primary deciding factor in an executive search is the candidate's "chemistry" or ability to "blend" well with others, as illustrated in the vignette. Although almost all organizations place good people skills at the top of their recruitment requirement lists, they do not emphasize the importance of this attribute to their existing employees and do not provide appropriate tools for measuring it. Exhibit 8.1 lists definitions of "good people skills," as noted by healthcare leaders.

The backbone of people skills is reciprocity, because without it no interaction or relationship occurs. Every healthy

Chapter 8: Interpersonal Connection 127

relationship—personal or professional—is marked by a mutual exchange, a quid pro quo of sorts. This exchange strengthens the bond and encourages its duration. Nonresponsive, uninvolved rank-and-file employees can discourage even the most interactive leader.

THE CONCEPT IN PRACTICE

The following are ways to enhance interpersonal connections.

Listen

Many leaders are leaders because they are the ones in the know. For example, subject matter experts are designated to lead an initiative because of their knowledge and experience, not because of their ability to guide a group. Unfortunately, most of these leaders do too much talking, especially with subordinates, but not enough listening.

Exhibit 8.1 Definitions of "Good People Skills"

- "Practices active listening, and internalizes what others say so that she can reflect on it"

- "Is comfortable with his own humanity and readily admits mistakes and apologizes when necessary"

- "Is clear about her stance on an issue but respects others' perspectives"

- "Exhibits warmth, caring, and concern"

- "Has an air of genuineness and trustworthiness"

- "Gets along well with others"

- "Is open, is approachable, and cares about developing and sustaining strong relationships"

Hearing is easy because it is merely mechanical. Barring physical problems, we can all hear without exerting much effort. Listening, on the other hand, is a process that demands not only patience, time, energy, and respect but also an emotional and intellectual response. That is, listening is not (or should not be) a passive activity. In healthcare, many concerns are not articulated, if verbalized at all. Leaders must then listen more carefully to discover the root of a problem, and they must never assume the incorrect cliché "no news is good news."

Although listening is one of the most difficult tasks to master, especially in a high-stress, fast-paced environment, it is a critical skill. Exhibit 8.2 presents some techniques for improving listening.

Exhibit 8.2 How to Enhance Listening Skills

Ask a lot of questions. Be aware that the tone of your voice and the content of your questions can reveal your personal bias or opinion.

Ask clarifying questions. Do not assume the answers.

Restate the answers. Prevent misunderstanding by repeating or rephrasing in front of the person what he said.

Be open-minded. People will tell you less if they feel you are judgmental.

Be receptive to bad news. Leaders who cannot take negative news are intimidating for the wrong reasons. "Don't kill the messenger" may sound trite, but it is wise advice for every executive.

Minimize interruptions. Talking over people, acting distracted, taking phone calls, answering e-mails, and checking or posting on social media or websites are antithetical to good listening. Schedule a time for the discussion, and focus while it is happening.

Seek suggestions. Doing so sends a signal of respect and often encourages others to provide you more information.

Involve others in the conversation. Ask those who are quiet for their thoughts; their perspectives often get lost in the discussion.

Show Respect

In *Lions Don't Need to Roar*, author D. A. Benton (1992, 12) suggests that "sincerity and positive regard are two things that just can't be faked, and you need both to deal with people effectively." When asked what bothers them most about senior management, many employees state that leaders do not appreciate what they do "in the trenches." Often, this sort of observation means that executives do not make an effort to visit the units in which services are delivered; hence, they do not understand the stresses and challenges that front-line staff face on a regular basis. When leaders are absent, they cannot even thank, let alone become familiar with, those who do the work.

Strong leaders have great respect for others. They solicit ideas, share pertinent information, encourage participation in organizational initiatives and activities, show regard for others' well-being, and recognize their hard work, among many other actions. As discussed in chapter 6, "Respect is the value that multiplies the desire of both the leader and follower to work harder and deliver consistently excellent performance."

Save Time for Staff

The workday of an average healthcare executive is hectic, leaving him little time for unscheduled interactions with his direct supervisees and other staff. As a result, he can be viewed as unapproachable—someone who is too important to mingle with the rank and file.

Scheduled employee events (e.g., staff meetings, picnics, organizational socials, award luncheons, retreats, holiday parties) are ideal for a busy executive to attend. They give the leader an opportunity to connect with many people, including staff, physicians, community members, and even patients and their families.

Manage Perceptions

Perception is more important than reality because people will believe what they imagine to be true, even if it is not the actual truth. Otara (2011, 21) writes, "What people often observe or assess as your ability to be a leader and your effectiveness becomes their perception, which in turn becomes reality." Lee and I feel that managing perception is so important that we dedicate an entire chapter to it in our book *The Healthcare Leader's Guide to Actions, Awareness, and Perception* (Dye and Lee 2016).

For example, the firing of a popular manager can set off a thousand impressions, most of which would be incorrect. Specifically, it could create irrational fears or breed gossip, which could harm the culture. In this scenario, ignoring the reaction is not an option. Giving the pat "it's a confidential issue" statement is not an option either.

What leaders could do, instead, is offer the most plausible explanation to minimize the perception that someone is hiding something. In this age of more transparent leadership, employees do not tolerate secrecy and lies. The more they perceive a cover-up or wrongdoing (true or not), the more they develop a distrust for their leaders.

Leaders also have to manage perceptions about their jobs. Expensive lunches, dedicated parking spots, and other privileges send the message that leaders are more valued by the organization. Although such perks do get offered in healthcare and other industries, they are not common. When leaders receive (and accept) these perks, they must

> No matter how ambitious, capable, clear-thinking, competent . . . and witty you are, if you don't relate well to other people, you won't make it. No matter how professionally competent, financially adept, and physically solid you are, without an understanding of human nature, a genuine interest in the people around you, and the ability to establish personal bonds with them, you are severely limited in what you can achieve.
>
> —D. A. Benton (1992)

avoid the perception of any conflict of interest, which is something they expect employees to do as well.

Recognize Others

Some leaders try to promote their own accomplishments by suggesting that they, rather than the people who report to them, have done the good work. People-oriented leaders behave in the opposite manner—they highlight the skills and achievements of others, particularly their own staff members. They understand that leaders are measured by the successes of their teams or followers. Therefore, the more recognition the team members receive, the higher the leader is elevated and the greater the rewards to the team as a whole.

Manage and Channel Emotions Appropriately

Many leaders create problems for themselves by losing their temper and showing the negative side of their personality. Although everyone needs to vent, leaders must be careful not to lose control because uncontrolled emotions render them unprofessional, ineffective, helpless, and feared—qualities that impede genuine, equal interactions.

Moods—whether positive or negative—must be managed. Moodiness is usually seen as a symptom of poor mental health. If given a choice, I suspect most people would choose a constantly angry leader over a moody one because no guesswork is involved with the former.

Leaders who are in control of their emotions have good people skills. They remain calm in tense situations and focused in chaotic times. As a result, they are approachable to everyone. Exhibit 8.3 presents tips on managing emotions.

Smile and Be Courteous

Many leaders may deem this suggestion silly; however, stories abound in executive search circles about executives who seem unapproachable because they are curt or do not smile. Zig Ziglar, a very successful sales trainer and author, is well known for teaching and coaching executives about the power of a smile.

Visual, nonverbal cues communicate a leader's comfort with other people. For example, steady eye contact (without glaring or leering), smiling, and a relaxed posture send the message that a person is warm, caring, and friendly. These leaders create an atmosphere

---

Exhibit 8.3 How to Manage Emotions

Listen first, react second. By listening attentively to what is being said (e.g., suggestion, feedback, criticism, praise), you are delaying your natural impulse to react. True listening demands concentration, so it deflects attention and slows reaction time.

Change your mind-set and attitude. The workplace is not a battleground, regardless of the many "bullets" you must dodge in the course of the day. Therefore, do not prepare for any kind of battle, as doing so encourages negative and survivalist thinking.

Count to ten. If listening and having a positive attitude do not work, simply count to ten. This passing of time may dull the edges of your emotional response.

Cut off your anger as quickly as possible. Anger can be the biggest obstruction to reducing the charged nature of tense interpersonal situations.

Separate feelings from facts. Base discussions (or even arguments) on facts, not emotions or biases.

Be aware of your feelings' influence on your behavior. Realize that they can harm your judgment and abilities.

---

of trust and respect, where staff can state their opinions and not fear the repercussions.

Focus on the Needs of Followers

"Take care of them and they will take of you" is a phrase that echoes the most basic way a leader can develop and maintain strong interpersonal connections with followers. Good executives do not take their staff's loyalty for granted, so they strive to get to know these individuals. They understand the significance of being fair, providing worthwhile or meaningful work in a safe environment, and learning what matters most to people's professional and personal lives.

The enormous changes in healthcare—from the shift to pay for value to the increased complexities of managing larger and more intricate organizations—have taken a toll on workers and caused the public to be concerned about the cost, coverage, and quality of healthcare. On top of these challenges, workers have endured large-scale downsizing and displacement, service cuts, and reorganization. At times such as these, employees must feel and know that their leaders are representing their best interests, and doing so well.

Show Compassion

A basic understanding of life's challenges and empathy for people's experiences underlies compassionate leadership. Northouse (2021, 225) indicates that compassion "refers to being sensitive to the plight of others, opening one's self to others, and being willing to help them."

For example, many Catholic hospitals have maintained high employee morale and commitment. While the number of nuns serving in hospitals has greatly contracted, those who have worked in these organizations will attest to the influence of the nuns in instilling compassion and concern for people.

Eliminate Childish, Unprofessional Behavior

Yelling, slamming doors, constantly complaining, gossiping, ignoring and then insulting others, bragging, and showing off are just some of the inappropriate behaviors that dishearten even the most patient peer or subordinate. Leaders who are secure with themselves and their position, status, and influence do not commit acts that disparage, belittle, or discredit others. Such behaviors breed intolerance, fear, low morale, poor productivity, secrecy, high turnover, and a dysfunctional culture.

Be Optimistic

Optimism or hope, while difficult to define, can be a powerful motivator of good behavior. Leaders who have great interpersonal skills are eternal optimists. They inspire and encourage people to do their best. They rally projects that are languishing or behind schedule. They reinvigorate interest in smart but forgotten suggestions or decisions. They support innovation, action, and teamwork. Northouse (2021, 265) describes optimism as the "cognitive process of viewing situations from a positive light and having favorable expectations about the future." In many leadership situations, optimism is what gets staff focused and energized. Garman and I write that leaders "have more of an effect on staff motivation than they may realize; it is therefore an area that separates high-performing leaders from average performers" (Dye and Garman 2015, 114).

Dr. Lily J. Henson (2021), CEO of Piedmont Hospital in Atlanta, opines,

> Desmond Tutu said, "Hope is being able to see the light despite all the darkness." Ex Great leaders instill hope in those they lead. When faced with tight staffing, scarce resources and an overwhelming influx of patients during COVID-19, the most effective leaders helped their staff maintain the belief that they were providing the best care possible to their patients despite

the constraints they faced. These individuals prevailed, as Ben Franklin taught: "While we may not be able to control all that happens to us, we can control what happens inside us."

Being optimistic or hopeful can be learned, and it can become an imperative for leaders during a difficult time, such as a financial downturn; reorganization because of a merger, an acquisition, or budget cuts; mass layoff; unionization; and staff shortage. Of course, optimism and hope are not enough to stem the tide of workplace change or to fix the problem itself. However, it can do a lot to improve attitudes and mindset.

Practice the Golden Rule

In the wildly popular book *All I Really Need to Know I Learned in Kindergarten*, author Robert Fulghum (1988) repeated simple lessons from childhood that resonated with people from all walks of life: Share everything. Play fair. Don't hit people. Put things back where you found them. Clean up your own mess. Don't take things that aren't yours. Say you're sorry when you hurt somebody. And so on.

The genesis of this book was Fulghum's experience with writing a personal credo (see chapter 7 for a discussion on creating a personal code of ethics). In an increasingly cynical world, these "golden rules" may be deemed corny or unimaginative, but consider this: Healthcare fraud, including highly reported white-collar crime by health system chiefs, is almost always committed by those who have never understood the meaning of "don't take things that aren't yours." The same can be said of hospital leaders who opted not to apologize to victims when a medical error caused harm or death. Studies indicate that simple apologies could prevent a costly malpractice suit. On the other hand, no leader who has "played fair" (i.e., was accountable, transparent) can be accused of wrongdoing.

For the past ten years, I have used an adaptation of Fulghum's lessons, which I share in exhibit 8.4.

Exhibit 8.4 My Take on Fulghum's Kindergarten Lessons

1. Keep your organization simple—its mission, its rules, its bureaucracy, its structure. Be sure that everyone knows why the organization is in existence—and what their roles and goals are.

2. Ensure that authority is clearly understood in the organization.

3. Make sure that everyone knows her job and gets it done.

4. Take time occasionally to recognize the fact that the job did get done (celebrate, celebrate).

5. Treat everyone with respect, dignity, and fairness.

6. Have a reason for what you do.

7. Do not be afraid to say "no," but give a reason behind the "no."

8. Communicate effectively—and then communicate some more. Share information.

9. Hire right. Make hiring a top priority.

10. Be honest; be ethical.

11. Practice servant leadership.

12. Set clear expectations, give feedback more than once per year, and listen when you give feedback.

13. Listen some more.

14. Work together in teams—people really prefer it that way.

15. Be kind to your teammates.

16. Admit mistakes.

17. Understand and appreciate the fact that when you are in a leadership position, you have a lot of benefits and perks that the rank and file do not.

Foster Employee and Physician Engagement

Since the third edition of this book, the concept of employee engagement—and physician engagement—has garnered a large following. At the time of this revision, a Google search for "employee engagement" returned more than 517 million results. Harter (2021) writes that in 2021, Gallup indicated that only "36% of U.S. employees are engaged in their work and workplace." Certainly the COVID-19 pandemic has had a significant impact on healthcare. In the same article, Harter (2021) further states that "in the aftermath of 2020, employee quit rates are reaching record highs, according to the U.S. Bureau of Labor Statistics. Historically, Gallup research has found substantial differences in intentions to change employers as a function of the quality of the work environment." Some observers may believe that employee engagement in healthcare is higher than in other industries because of the service-oriented nature of healthcare work. Nonetheless, even if the percentage of disengaged people was half that of general industry, there is concern for healthcare leaders.

In a recent book on physician engagement (Dye 2021, 3), I contend that "making physician engagement a top strategic and tactical priority is simply mandatory if organizations expect to have success now and in the future. With such complex challenges as the redesign of much of the healthcare industry because of the pandemic, physician shortages, the needs of a large and rapidly aging population, population health management, new and different kinds of payment programs, value-based purchasing, cost containment, quality and safety concerns, care management, and Medicare penalties, physician engagement must be a top-level focus for all organizations."

Moreover, Hogan and Kaiser (2005, 175) report that "estimates of the base rate for managerial incompetence in corporate life range from 30% to 75%; a recent review reported the average estimate to be 50%." This finding led to their now-famous proclamation: "Bad leaders perpetrate terrible misery on those subject to their domain" (169). Could it be more evident that much of this misery is caused by poor interpersonal skills? Gruman and Saks (2011, 125) comment that "managers can encourage employee engagement by improving manager–employee communication and creating an environment where employees feel valued." Clearly, this outcome requires strong interpersonal skills.

CONCLUSION

Leadership is about building and maintaining relationships. The effectiveness of managing personal interactions is tied to how much leaders care about being and working with others. Many years ago, the chair of a health administration graduate program warned me: "If you want to thrive in this business, you really have to love working with and around people. If you don't have a passion for that, go into another field." I cannot say it better.

Self-Evaluation Questions

❑ What does "people are our greatest asset" mean to me?

❑ Have I ever put other people down?

❑ Has anyone ever described me as a people person?

❑ Was this a source of pride for me?

❑ Has anyone ever described me as a good listener?

❑ Was I able to enhance my interpersonal skills during the COVID-19 pandemic?

Cases

Case 8.1

Tiana White has just finished a meeting with Tina Garr, her vice president, when she runs into Mary Briones, a peer departmental manager, in the hallway.

MARY. You're frowning. What's wrong?

TIANA. Nothing. I'm fine.

MARY. You look stressed. You don't seem like the regular enthusiastic Tiana I know. Do you want to come into my office to talk about it?

TIANA. Keep this between us, but Tina is impossible to read. Sometimes she's warm and approachable. Other times, she acts as if I'm a stranger. I just tried to discuss with her my desire to take on more responsibility, because I just earned a master's degree and I've worked here for four years. I wanted her advice on what I could do to get promoted.

MARY. Those are valid questions. What did she say?

TIANA. She said, "You have too many projects right now. You shouldn't even be thinking of moving up." No explanation, no sugar coating. Then she said she had to go to another meeting. That's when I left.

MARY. No wonder you look dejected. Is there anything I can do to help?

Case 8.1 Questions

1. How could Tina have better handled the situation?

2. Is Mary displaying the interpersonal skills of a strong leader? How will these skills help Tiana?

Case 8.2

Rosemary Brezinski, a veteran chief nursing officer, is the new president of a rapidly growing system hospital. Most of her impressive career has been spent in large tertiary organizations known for research and medical innovations. Her new position is a significant promotion. She is now responsible for leading the hospital's response to its recent 10 percent growth in patient volume; improving morale and collaboration among managers, staff, and physicians; and planning and implementing the move of the system's teaching program to the hospital campus, something that only the senior management knows thus far.

In the first three weeks on the job, Rosemary has held several meetings with her senior management team and leadership groups in the hospital. She has distributed to these leaders a detailed, 80-item list of priorities that will serve as the team's agenda for the next 18 months. She has informed them that she will assign each priority to an individual or a group. Her message to everyone has been consistent since the beginning of her tenure at the hospital: "I have never failed in the past. I expect that we will make these changes happen on time and on budget." She has not spoken to the medical staff or the frontline employees.

Case 8.2 Questions

1. What interpersonal connection mistakes has Rosemary made so far?

2. How do you think the staff (including the physicians and managers) feel about her style?

3. Will her mandates for change work?

REFERENCES

Benton, D. A. 1992. *Lions Don't Need to Roar: Using the Leadership Power of Professional Presence to Stand Out, Fit In, and Move Ahead.* New York: Warner Books.

Collins, J. 2001. *Good to Great: Why Some Companies Make the Leap . . . and Others Don't.* New York: HarperCollins.

Covey, S. R. 1992. *Principle-Centered Leadership.* New York: Free Press.

Dye, C. F. 2021. *Enhanced Physician Engagement, Volume 1: What It Is, Why You Need It, and Where to Begin.* Chicago: Health Administration Press.

Dye, C. F., and A. N. Garman. 2015. *Exceptional Leadership: 16 Critical Competencies for Healthcare Leaders*, 2nd ed. Chicago: Health Administration Press.

Dye, C. F., and B. D. Lee. 2016. *The Healthcare Leader's Guide to Actions, Awareness, and Perception*, 3rd ed. Chicago: Health Administration Press.

Fulghum, R. 1988. *All I Really Need to Know I Learned in Kindergarten: Uncommon Thoughts on Common Things.* New York: Villard Books.

Gruman, J. A., and A. M. Saks. 2011. "Performance Management and Employee Engagement." *Human Resource Management Review* 21 (2): 123–36.

Harter, J. 2021. "U.S. Employee Engagement Holds Steady in First Half of 2021." Gallup Employee Engagement Report, July 29, 2021. Accessed Nov 17, 2021. https://www.gallup.com/workplace/352949/employee-engagement-holds-steady-first-half-2021.aspx.

Henson, L. J. 2021. Personal communication with author. December 15.

Hogan, R., and R. B. Kaiser. 2005. "What We Know About Leadership." *Review of General Psychology* 9 (2): 169–80.

Kouzes, J. M., and B. Z. Posner. 1993. *Credibility: How Leaders Gain It and Lose It, Why People Demand It.* San Francisco: Jossey-Bass.

Northouse, P. G. 2021. *Leadership: Theory and Practice*, 9th ed. Los Angeles: SAGE Publications.

Otara, A. 2011. "Perception: A Guide for Managers and Leaders." *Journal of Management and Strategy* 2 (3): 21–22.

SUGGESTED READINGS

Buch, R., G. Thompson, and B. Kuvaas. 2016. "Transactional Leader-Member Exchange Relationships and Followers' Work Performance: The Moderating Role of Leaders' Political Skill." *Journal of Leadership and Organizational Studies.* Published February 15. http://jlo.sagepub.com/content/early/2016/02/12/1548051816630227.abstract.

Chen, J. K. C., and T. Sriphon. 2021. "Perspective on COVID-19 Pandemic Factors Impacting Organizational Leadership." *Sustainability* 13 (6): 3230.

Collins, J. 2001. "Level 5 Leadership: The Triumph of Humility and Fierce Resolve." *Harvard Business Review* 79 (1): 66–79.

Jian, G., and F. Dalisay. 2015. "Conversation at Work: The Effects of Leader–Member Conversational Quality." *Communication Research.* Published January 8. http://crx.sagepub.com/content/early/2015/01/07/0093650214565924.abstract.

Laschinger, H. K., L. Borgogni, C. Consiglio, and E. Read. 2014. "The Effects of Authentic Leadership, Six Areas of Worklife, and Occupational Coping Self-efficacy on New Graduate Nurses' Burnout and Mental Health: A Cross-Sectional Study." *International Journal of Nursing Studies* 52 (6): 1080–89.

Tan, C.-M. 2013. *Search Inside Yourself: The Secret to Unbreakable Concentration, Complete Relaxation, and Effortless Self-Control.* New York: HarperCollins.

Uhl-Bien, M. 2006. "Relational Leadership Theory: Exploring the Social Processes of Leadership and Organizing." *Leadership Quarterly* 17 (6): 654–76.

Yeager, K. L., and J. L. Callahan. 2016. "Learning to Lead: Foundations of Emerging Leader Identity Development." *Advances in Developing Human Resources.* Published April 27. http://jlo.sagepub.com/content/early/2016/02/12/1548051816630227.abstract.

CHAPTER 9

Servant Leadership

The servant leader is servant first. . . . *It begins with the natural feeling that one wants to serve, to serve first. Then conscious choice brings one to aspire to lead. That person is sharply different from one who is* leader first, *perhaps because of the need to assuage an unusual power drive or to acquire material possessions. . . . The leader first and the servant first are two extreme types. Between them there are shadings and blends that are part of the infinite variety of human nature.*

—Robert K. Greenleaf (1970)

WHAT IS YOUR primary role as a leader?" Sister Mary O'Hara, the president and CEO of a soon-to-open community hospital, asked her newly formed management team. The answers varied:

- Work toward our mission and vision.
- Get everyone to work cooperatively.
- Manage efficiently and effectively.
- Meet our goals and make sure our employees do their jobs.

Sister Mary responded, "All of these are good ideas. What I want you to keep in mind most of all is this: Each of you is a servant leader. By that I mean that your job is to serve those who report to you. Help them do their work, and let them help you do yours. Be humble. You do not know all the answers and you're not the experts, so seek input from others. Give credit and praise liberally, and be generous with your time regardless of how busy you become. Listen before you speak. Ask how you can lend a hand. Teach and encourage learning. I realize that some of you may have a different view of leadership than what I just laid out. But the mission of our community hospital is to serve, and that is exactly what we are going to do—we will serve each other, regardless of our titles."

The management team applauded loudly in agreement.

THE HEALTHCARE FIELD was established with a simple, altruistic purpose: to serve the public. This purpose has been magnified because of the COVID-19 pandemic. Thus, healthcare leaders must subscribe to the same mission by becoming "servants" to the needs of their organizations and constituents. Servant leadership is not merely a trendy practice arising from political correctness or a cliché intonation of "following to lead"; instead, it is a management style that delivers desired outcomes, boosts morale, strengthens the organizational structure, and generates support for the leader.

According to Northouse (2021, 267), "Servant leadership argues unabashedly that leaders should put followers first, share control with followers, and embrace their growth. It is the only leadership approach that frames the leadership process around the principle of caring for others." Since it was first theorized in the 1970s, servant leadership has gained a large following, including experts in management and organizational behavior such as Peter Senge, Stephen Covey, Margaret Wheatley, and Ken Blanchard. Exhibit 9.1 contrasts traditional leadership with servant leadership.

Be mindful of this, though: Servant leadership does not connote waiting for others to move to action. In fact, servant leaders are very focused on goals and improvement. Sousa and van Dierendonck (2015, 1) state, "Whereas it may be possible to speak about servant leadership as one specific way of leadership, at a deeper level . . . there seem to be two overarching encompassing dimensions: a humble service-oriented side and an action-driven side, both coexisting and complementing each other."

Also, servant leaders are role models and teachers. They set an example for others, as one CEO does: "I gave each executive in the organization a small rock and a small ceramic monkey to place on their desks. The purpose of the rock and the monkey is to help them to be always mindful of what they need to do—keep the rocks and barriers out of the way so their staff can do their jobs. And if the staff can do their jobs, they [the executives] won't put inappropriate monkeys on their back." Another CEO echoes this principle: "My job is to take away any obstacles that keep [the people who report to me] from succeeding. . . . If there's an obstacle between you and any of our targets, I need to know about it."

> **A servant leader demonstrates the following behaviors:**
>
> 1. Focuses on the needs of followers
> 2. Eschews selfish behavior, personal biases, and pursuit of personal ambition
> 3. Sincerely respects all people
> 4. Realizes that the contributions of followers are what enable the organization to fulfill its mission
> 5. Helps, encourages, and counsels followers to hone their skills and become better at their positions because doing so brings the organization closer to its goals

Exhibit 9.1 Traditional Leadership Versus Servant Leadership

Motivation	To Lead	To Serve
Approach	Top-down, command and control	Bottom-up, collaborative
Basis	Power and authority	Stewardship
Primary focus	Finance	People
Self-awareness	Not important	Critical
Followers	May or may not grow	Definitely will grow

In essence, the success of leaders who serve depends on how well they meet their followers' needs. Followers are more efficient, productive, and satisfied when given autonomy, support, resources, and positive examples. As a result, they perform better than expected and grow personally and professionally. More important, they are more likely to become servant leaders themselves.

Servant leadership may be likened to transformational leadership in that both philosophies "show concern for their followers, [but] the overriding focus of the servant leader is upon service to their followers. The transformational leader has a greater concern for getting followers to engage in and support organizational objectives" (Stone, Russell, and Patterson 2003, 4).

THE CONCEPT IN PRACTICE

The following guidelines can hone a leader's servant skills.

Share Information

Sharing information freely with peers and subordinates opens communication pathways through which ideas travel. A two-way exchange of ideas signifies the leader's respect for other perspectives and trust in others' ability to contribute. Although information is power, a servant leader is disinclined to abuse the knowledge he acquires to manipulate the situation for his own good.

> A new moral principle is emerging which holds that the only authority deserving one's allegiance is that which is freely and knowingly granted by the led to the leader in response to, and in proportion to, the clearly evident servant stature of the leader.
>
> —Robert K. Greenleaf (1983)

Delegate Authority

Delegation not only increases productivity but also promotes teamwork, especially during times of crisis (although many leaders tend to take the reins when serious problems arise). In a crisis situation, servant leaders are not apprehensive about delegating authority to members of their leadership team because they have regularly included and coached them in brainstorming, problem solving, decision-making, and implementation. Thus, these leaders are confident of their staff's ability to perform under great stress.

Delegating authority should be a frequent practice in healthcare organizations because the challenges and responsibilities are often too intricate for one person to handle alone. In addition, frontline staff directly face the everyday dilemmas of the workplace and therefore often have more practical and sustainable solutions than what supervisors, directors, and vice presidents can offer. Servant leaders are aware of this dynamic.

> Understanding the tools needed for effective leadership is important, and the servant leadership philosophy offers leaders the opportunity to not only understand the needs of the organization but also . . . to incorporate one of the most valuable tools necessary in making the organization effective: followers.
>
> —Amy R. Savage-Austin and Andrew Honeycutt (2011)

Live the Mission and Pursue the Vision

Most mission statements of healthcare organizations include the word *serve*. Servant leaders take their missions to heart. They ensure that the organizational vision, values, culture, strategies, and activities are consistent with the mission. They enlist others, including physicians, in establishing policies and practices that support and advance the mission.

Servant leaders are also visionaries. Being future oriented and innovative, they seek to understand past events and current realities—any factors that have an impact on the future operation of the organization. They encourage staff to participate in this visioning work, aware that such an engagement facilitates the achievement of the vision.

Support and Promote Continuing Education

All employees can pursue continuing education to enhance their professional or vocational skills, which consequently improves their job marketability. Servant leaders not only apportion organizational funds to finance staff's educational pursuits (e.g., degree programs, professional seminars, certification courses) but also provide coaching.

"Teaching moments"—occasions that give leaders the opportunity to explain an organizational decision, policy, process, practice, or stance—are an excellent way to inform and engage the staff. For example, an adverse medical event is a teaching moment wherein leaders can review safety standards, reiterate quality policies, delineate the role of staff, and exchange questions and ideas about improvement.

Most important, professional and personal development must go beyond lip service. Policies (and budget) that support continuing education must be in place. Specifically, performance expectations should include a requirement to complete a certain number of continuing education hours by the next performance review. The onus of checking up on this requirement must fall on the leader.

Provide Opportunities for Accomplishments

Servant leaders do not set up their followers to fail. Structured objectives and clear instructions help staff reach their goals and complete their assignments. Moreover, these leaders provide coaching and support when needed, but they allow employees freedom to work toward their own objectives. In doing so, staff gain mastery of their jobs, greater enjoyment from their work, confidence, new skills, and feelings of achievement. They are proud to say, "We did this ourselves." Liden and colleagues (2008) found an empirical correlation between servant leadership behaviors and employee organizational commitment.

Establish a Succession Plan

The sudden departure of a leader (voluntarily or involuntarily) can cause much chaos and uncertainty in the organization. The situation can become even worse when no succession plan is in place that details that leader's replacement. Baby boomers continue to retire, and yet many healthcare organizations have no succession plans.

Although healthcare executives are cognizant of the importance of succession planning, they do not engage in the practice readily. According to one study (Garman and Tyler 2007) that yielded 722 responses, the most frequently cited reason for not conducting succession planning was that it was not a high enough priority (46 percent). Other reasons cited were because the current CEO was too new (31 percent) and that there was no internal candidate to prepare (25 percent). In contrast, succession planning is a priority for servant leaders because their first priority is the needs of their employees, who deserve strong and dependable leadership.

Learn About the Work

When employees complain that their leaders are "out of touch," they are mostly right. Leaders cannot empathize with frontline staff if they do not understand what this work entails. Visiting the units and talking with staff are some strategies for learning the work. But leaders could go a step further by shadowing employees and interacting with patients and their families.

Servant leaders partake in these experiences, enabling them to encounter firsthand the difficulties they only hear about, to speak the language of caregivers and support staff, and to discover areas

> Being a servant may not be what many leaders had in mind when they chose to take responsibility for the vision and direction of their organization or team, but serving others is the most glorious and rewarding of all leadership tasks.
>
> —James M. Kouzes and Barry Z. Posner (1993)

for improvement. In the process, both leaders and employees get to know each other better, paving the way for mutual understanding of their distinct roles.

Mentor Others

Clearly, healthcare executives are pressed for time, and mentoring often becomes a casualty of the rush. Mentoring is a critical competency that sets apart good leaders from great ones (see Dye and Garman 2015). Servant leaders are advocates for personal and professional development. As such, they provide coaching and support continuing education.

Hold Simple Celebrations

Servant leaders are acutely aware of the morale-boosting capability of simple celebrations and praise. A round of applause during a staff meeting, an acknowledgment in an organization-wide publication or on the intranet, or a plate of cookies are small gestures that carry great weight. For example, one chief financial officer holds a pizza party for the credit and collection workers when they meet their monthly numbers. The employees are gratified and motivated to repeat their achievement.

Change the Focus of Performance Reviews

Annual or midyear performance reviews are often met with dread. The main reason for this mindset is these assessments are essentially criticism—what mistakes were committed, what goals were not accomplished, what skills were not improved, and so on. As a result, the feedback is taken as a personal offense, not as a constructive comment. No one wants to feel attacked, so no one enjoys this type of review.

Leaders who serve are aware of this reaction, so they structure the performance evaluation differently:

- The focus is future performance, not past missteps or lost opportunities.
- Achievement of objectives is celebrated. Goals are developed with input from the employee and with consideration of the person's ability, environmental obstacles, available resources, and realistic timelines. These goals are monitored during the year.
- No blame is placed, and the factors that contributed to poor performance are discussed so that they are corrected or eliminated.
- Ongoing development is encouraged, regardless of how high the rank of the employee.

If organizational constraints do not allow for this type of progressive discussion, highly effective leaders then set aside other times to have conversations about performance and progress.

Make a Connection with Staff

Servant leaders are not aloof or detached. They maintain relationships and stay abreast of issues that affect all of their associates—staff, physicians, board members, community leaders, and peers.

Making a connection could be as simple as visiting departments or attending organizational events or as involved as getting to know the staff. Perhaps one of the best ways a leader can make a connection is by showing employees that she is one of them, as this example from Denise Brooks-Williams, FACHE—senior vice president and CEO North Market of the Henry Ford Health System, and former president of the National Association of Health Services Executives—illustrates:

> Whereas takers tend to be self-focused, evaluating what other people can offer them, givers are other-focused, paying more attention to what other people need from them.
>
> —Adam Grant (2013)

I lead by removing barriers and allowing my team to achieve their best in all they aspire to do. I am willing to assist all team members in any way I can. My position has allowed me to support many and help them reach career advancement. I recall a dietary team member who I supported on her advancement journey and today she is a public service officer in the organization. Mentoring is one of my greatest gifts to give. I truly love seeing those around me succeed and reach their full potential. (D. Brooks-Williams, personal communication, December 12, 2021)

CONCLUSION

Picture an organization in which everybody performs every activity with the primary intention of serving someone else. This vision seems like utopia, but it is achievable, and it starts with leaders. If subordinates feel that their leaders serve them, they will likely model that behavior toward others. As a result, service to patients will be enhanced, improving the organization's competitive advantage. As Garman and I write, "A fundamental polarity in leadership involves the balance between self-interest (what you do to serve your own needs) and selfless interest (what you do to serve the needs of others or the needs of the organization)" (Dye and Garman 2015, 17).

❑ Why am I in a leadership position?

❑ What is my leadership style? Does it place a heavy emphasis on controlling others?

❑ Does the idea of serving others make me think that I am a weak leader?

Case and Exercises

Case 9.1

Two students in an executive seminar, Rachel Goh and Santiago Perez, explore the basis of servant leadership in class.

RACHEL. I don't buy it. The idea that servant leaders are more committed to their followers and organization sounds too religious for me. The fact is, people are, at the core, selfish. We act with self-interest, first and always.

SANTIAGO. Servant leaders are manipulative, but in a good way. Take me, for example. My staff can't get along well without me because I provide them with everything they need—from advice to tangible resources. This is a win-win situation. I support their work, and in exchange I get the results I want.

Case 9.1 Questions

Do you agree with this summation that servant leadership is (a) not possible given the selfish nature of people and (b) secretly or outwardly manipulative but harmless? Explain your answer.

Using Greenleaf's definition of this theory (see www.greenleaf.org), discuss how servant leadership can guide executives in today's healthcare environment.

(continued)

(continued from previous page)

Exercise 9.1

Servant leadership is likely to work best in an organizational culture that supports it. That is, some cultures have a high level of trust and team orientation, while others are hierarchical or rely on command-and-control principles. What types of culture can support the practice of servant leadership?

See the following websites for a discussion on organizational culture:

- http://managementhelp.org/org_thry/culture/culture.htm

- http://study.com/academy/lesson/what-is-organizational-culture-definition-characteristics.html

- www.tnellen.com/ted/tc/schein.html

- www.thercfgroup.com/files/resources/Defining-Culture-and-Organizationa-Culture_5.pdf

Exercise 9.2

Two excellent academic reviews of servant leadership are provided by Savage-Austin and Honeycutt and Sokoll. Review both and summarize their key conclusions.

Savage-Austin, A. R., and A. Honeycutt. 2011. "Servant Leadership: A Phenomenological Study of Practices, Experiences, Organizational Effectiveness, and Barriers." *Journal of Business and Economics Research* 9 (1): 49–54. www.cluteinstitute.com/ojs/index.php/JBER/article/viewFile/939/923.

Sokoll, S. 2014. "Servant Leadership and Employee Commitment to a Supervisor." *International Journal of Leadership Studies* 8 (2): 88–104. www.regent.edu/acad/global/publications/ijls/new/vol8iss2/5-Sokoll.pdf.

REFERENCES

Brooks-Williams, D. 2021. Interview with author, December 12.

Dye, C. F., and A. N. Garman. 2015. *Exceptional Leadership: 16 Critical Competencies for Healthcare Executives*, 2nd ed. Chicago: Health Administration Press.

Garman, A., and J. L. Tyler. 2007. *Succession Planning Practices and Outcomes in US Hospital Systems: Final Report*. Chicago: American College of Healthcare Executives.

Grant, A. 2013. *Give and Take: A Revolutionary Approach to Success*. New York: Viking.

Greenleaf, R. K. 1983. *Servant Leadership: A Journey into the Nature of Legitimate Power and Greatness*. Mahwah, NJ: Paulist Press.

———. 1970. *The Servant as Leader*. Westfield, IN: Greenleaf Center for Servant Leadership.

Kouzes, J. M., and B. Z. Posner. 1993. *Credibility: How Leaders Gain and Lose It, Why People Demand It*. San Francisco: Jossey-Bass.

Liden, R. C., S. J. Wayne, H. Zhao, and D. Henderson. 2008. "Servant Leadership: Development of a Multidimensional Measure and Multi-level Assessment." *Leadership Quarterly* 19 (2): 161–77.

Northouse, P. G. 2021. *Leadership: Theory and Practice*, 9th ed. Los Angeles: SAGE Publications.

Savage-Austin, A. R., and A. Honeycutt. 2011. "Servant Leadership: A Phenomenological Study of Practices, Experiences, Organizational Effectiveness, and Barriers." *Journal of Business and Economics Research* 9 (1): 49–54.

Sousa, M., and D. van Dierendonck. 2015. "Servant Leadership and the Effect of the Interaction Between Humility, Action, and Hierarchical Power on Follower Engagement." *Journal of Business Ethics*. Published June 13. http://link.springer.com/article/10.1007/s10551-015-2725-y.

Stone, A. G., R. F. Russell, and K. Patterson. 2003. "Transformational Versus Servant Leadership: A Difference in Leader Focus." Servant Leadership Research Roundtable, School of Leadership Studies, Regents University, Virginia Beach, VA, August.

SUGGESTED READINGS

Bobbio, A., and A. M. Manganelli. 2015. "Antecedents of Hospital Nurses' Intention to Leave the Organization: A Cross Sectional Survey." *International Journal of Nursing Studies* 52 (7): 1180–92.

Newman, A., G. Schwarz, B. Cooper, and S. Sendjaya. 2015. "How Servant Leadership Influences Organizational Citizenship Behavior: The Roles of LMX, Empowerment, and Proactive Personality." *Journal of Business Ethics*. Published September. DOI 10.1007/s10551-015-2827-6.

Panaccio, A., D. J. Henderson, R. C. Liden, S. J. Waynes, and X. Cao. 2015. "Toward an Understanding of When and Why Servant Leadership Accounts for Employee Extra-Role Behaviors." *Journal of Business and Psychology* 30 (4): 657–75.

Parris, D. L., and J. W. Peachey. 2013. "A Systematic Literature Review of Servant Leadership Theory in Organizational Contexts." *Journal of Business Ethics* 113 (3): 377–93.

Swenson, S., G. Gorringe, J. Caviness, and D. Peters. 2016. "Leadership by Design: Intentional Organization Development of Physician Leaders." *Journal of Management Development* 35 (4): 549–70.

van Dierendonck, D., and I. Nuijten. 2011. "The Servant Leadership Survey: Development and Validation of a Multidimensional Measure." *Journal of Business and Psychology* 26 (3): 249–67.

VanMeter, R., L. B. Chonko, D. B. Grisaffe, and E. A. Goad. 2016. "In Search of Clarity on Servant Leadership: Domain Specification and Reconceptualization." *AMS Review* 6 (1): 59–78.

CHAPTER 10

Desire to Make a Change

Altruism is the quality that makes professionals think and act in the interest of serving the community. Without it, healthcare could become a profession of people pursuing their own interests or selfish goals, instead of a public service that everyone can rely on.

—Elizabeth J. Forrestal and Leigh W. Cellucci (2016)

SEVERAL YEARS AGO, Elaine Rostovich asked her boss Barb Valdez why she gave up overtime pay and shift differentials to become a nurse manager.

Barb answered, "The loss in pay doesn't matter to me as much as gaining the ability to make improvements around here. As a staff nurse, I couldn't change anything that was no longer working. Sure, I do a lot more paperwork and face more stress now, but it's satisfying to see that our clinical outcomes are better and our staff and patients are happier because we're now more efficient."

Barb's reasoning finally makes sense to Elaine as she listens to her mentor emphasize the importance of leading change: "Like a lot of healthcare CEOs, I entered the field because I wanted to make a difference in people's lives. This topic hasn't been researched a lot, but that desire is the true beginning of improvement. Those who have this passion work hard to make positive changes happen, and they don't do it for money, praise, or prestige. They do it because they understand that nothing is beyond improvement. They use all their resources, skills, and knowledge to accomplish their goals. They are some of the most well-informed people around, these change leaders."

THE DESIRE TO make a change is one of the most distinctive values of a strong leader. *Change makers*, as these leaders are known, are high achievers. They actively seek out flaws in the system and implement improvements. While campers abide by the rule "leave a campsite in better condition than you found it," change makers initiate upgrades even before they get to the campsite. They are proactive and innovative, and they welcome challenges.

CHARACTERISTICS OF A CHANGE MAKER

In the 1960s, motivational theorist David McClelland posited that individuals who have achievement motivation, as is the case with change makers, are likely to be goal oriented and uphold high standards of performance. These individuals are most likely to move into leadership positions because they can operate well and even flourish despite the high levels of stress and unceasing demands for long hours, critical thinking, and quick turnarounds. Such leaders also have broad strategic views. Bolman and Deal (2013, 24) state that "managers are supposed to see the big picture and look out for their organization's overall health and productivity." Moreover, Rylatt (2013) writes, "To be exceptional in influencing large-scale change requires an excellent grasp of the complexities and tensions of organizational culture and the sources of power and authority. High-performing change agents stand apart from others by virtue of their ability to negotiate more expansive and powerful job profiles that increase their capacity to generate meaningful outcomes."

Change makers have *restless discontent*—the inability to live with the status quo. They cannot tolerate ineffective processes that force people to muddle through ill-conceived standards and processes. One CEO defines this discontent as an "ability to sense opportunities." This description is fitting, as change makers are constantly on the lookout for new ideas. The discontent peels away as areas for improvement garner attention and the need for change earns buy-in from others, especially senior management. According to Hughes, Ginnett, and Curphy (2018, 560), "Leading change is perhaps the most difficult challenge facing any leader, yet this skill may be the best differentiator of managers from leaders and of mediocre from exceptional leaders."

> Our current success is the best reason to change things.
>
> —Iwao Isomura (1998)

For many healthcare leaders, the desire to make a change has become a professional calling. This approach is evident in the rise of the quality improvement movement in healthcare, which calls for

- establishing measurable goals and standards,
- developing systems for monitoring progress toward and achieving desired outcomes,
- disseminating lessons learned,
- celebrating successes, and
- continuing improvement efforts.

THE CONCEPT IN PRACTICE

Pay Equal Attention to All Measures of Performance

In flight school, student pilots are taught how to maneuver their planes guided only by their instrument panels. This technique teaches pilots to fly safely despite hindrances that may surround them—thick fog, utter darkness, raging storms, and other conditions that impair visibility. However, some pilots tend to pay the most attention to the altimeter, which tells the position and location of the plane on the horizon. Although the altimeter is an important gauge, this instrument is not the only one a pilot should check. Trouble almost always ensues when the other critical measures are overlooked. This danger is also seen in healthcare management.

All healthcare leaders—new or seasoned—have, at one point or another, focused only on the financial report when determining the status of their organization. This tendency is understandable; after all, without funds the operation will cease to exist, an especially salient issue in an environment filled with bankruptcies and acquisitions. However, healthcare is hardly a one-dimensional enterprise. If too much priority is given to revenue, capital, debt, investment, and other elements of finance, then not enough attention is given to human resources, patient safety, clinical outcomes, quality improvement, physician relations, and the like.

Change makers understand that the organization is a system and thus needs a system-based approach. Simply put, a flaw in one component can cause damage to another, ushering in a cascading effect.

Turn Satisfied Employees into Engaged Employees

High-performing organizations tend to have highly satisfied workers. However, satisfaction does not lead to engagement. Many happy employees walk in and out of their jobs daily without a desire to participate in the activities that cause their happiness. They may ignore areas that could use improvement because they think bringing about change is not part of their job responsibilities.

Employee engagement has been defined many ways, but practically all definitions indicate emotional connection or attachment to the work and goals of an organization. Engagement is neither satisfaction nor happiness. The fact is that employees can be satisfied and happy and yet not engaged. Harter and Adkins (2015) put it simply, stating that engaged employees are "involved in, enthusiastic about, and committed to their work and workplace." Harter (2020) writes, "Employee engagement is determined by factors such as feeling clear about your role, having the opportunity to do what you do best, having opportunities at work to develop, enjoying strong coworker relationships and working with a common mission or purpose. Importantly, these are all factors that managers can directly influence and that vary considerably in how they are executed across teams within most organizations." Gallup (2021) finds that "when employees are engaged, they are passionate, creative, and entrepreneurial, and their enthusiasm fuels growth. These employees are emotionally connected to the mission and purpose of their work." Exhibit 10.1 describes the linkage between employees' level of engagement and desire to make changes.

Note that more and more human resources firms are conducting employee engagement (as opposed to employee satisfaction) surveys. This practice signals a shift in mindset: Good employees have much to contribute to the viability of the organization. Seeking participation from employees could also bring out the latent change makers among them. Jim Haudan, the CEO of Root, emphasizes that for change and improvement to be fully executed, employees at all levels must be given the opportunity to internalize the thinking and rationale behind the strategy. Haudan (2021) reiterates that the most effective leaders create environments where employees are highly engaged.

Exhibit 10.1 Linkage Between Employee Engagement and Desire to Make Changes

Real engagement is multidimensional and can be effortless, natural, and magnetic. Throughout the past 25 years of working with businesses, [I have found] four proven approaches that truly drive powerful employee engagement have emerged. These approaches frame employees as customers and see engagement through the eyes of the people we serve as leaders. They help people feel enthralled, drawn in, and connected in a compelling and sustained way to the work that they do. They quickly become the foundation, or roots, for engaging your people. [These approaches] include (1) helping them feel like they're part of something bigger than themselves, (2) giving people a sense of belonging, (3) feeling like they're on a meaningful journey, and (4) showing people their contributions are making a difference.

Part of that engagement process comes in helping people understand the big picture of what the company is trying to achieve—arriving at the same conclusion on their own—and then recognizing their own role in helping drive those results. Most leaders leverage data and a show-and-tell process to engage people in the company strategy. But look at the following image [see exhibit 1.2 in chapter 1], which combines visuals, data, and stories.

While both the data and the image convey similar information about an organization, which one are you most likely to remember after one hour? One month? One year? Now think back to any PowerPoint or memo that you've received from a leader about the strategy or a list of ten key bullet points. How much of an impression do the words make compared to a visual? Imagine that, instead of sending out a memo to introduce your people to a new initiative, your organization rolled out a new strategy by holding small group discussions built around an image like this one. This is the power of metaphor, visualization, and discussion to truly drive engagement.

> Developing vision means that you see the future clearly, anticipate large-scale and local changes that will affect the organization and its environment, are able to project the organization into the future and envision multiple potential scenarios or outcomes, have a broad way of looking at trends, and are able to design competitive strategies and plans based on future possibilities.
>
> —**Carson F. Dye and Andrew N. Garman (2015)**

Be Objective Driven and Progress Oriented

Change makers are passionate about setting objectives for both professional and organizational purposes. Doing so helps them measure the effectiveness of their performance, decisions, and activities. Many leaders fail to set clear goals, delaying or impeding progress and achievement and frustrating those involved.

In addition, change makers admit that even the best organizations (and employees) must evolve with the times. Thus, they push to move forward, tracking their steps along the way with available measurement tools. SMART—specific, measurable, attainable, realistic, and timely—is still the best strategy for setting goals, although it is now more than two decades old (see Kouzes and Posner 1993 for more information). SMART goals allow organizations to focus simultaneously on the present and the future.

Welcome Change

Change makers enjoy new challenges and are not afraid of taking risks. For them, change is a normal part of leadership and presents opportunities. As such, they prefer to err on the side of overstudying or overanalyzing trends than to be misinformed. Being prepared serves as a defense against the unknown or sudden change that seems unmanageable.

The fear of making the wrong decision is endemic in healthcare. On the clinical side, an error could result in injury or death and subsequently costly and drawn-out lawsuits. On the business side, an error could result in loss of customers and consequently revenue. Certainly, cautious decisions are in order.

However, this general rule does not mean risks should not be taken. Progress and innovation—two words that most leaders would like to be associated with—are not driven by fear. They are possible only with leaps of faith, albeit calculated.

Celebrate Accomplishments

As discussed in chapter 9, people enjoy celebrations, especially if they highlight the product of their hard work. A celebration of accomplishments not only embodies the joy, relief, and pride of the team, it also underscores the gratitude of the leaders. People who are able to see that their efforts have made a difference and are appreciated are likely to repeat their performance in the future and feel empowered. Empowerment is a strong motivation because it makes people feel in control and valued.

Celebrations may also be used to improve morale. For example, one executive organizes a monthly "Breakfast of Champions" for employees. Individuals and departments who make progress toward goals are recognized during the program and given a box of Wheaties cereal as a token of appreciation.

Establish a Problem-Solving Method

Change makers follow specific problem-solving approaches, such as the following:

1. Identify the problem and describe it explicitly, including the effects it has on staff, operations, the bottom line, current and future goals, and patients.
2. Perform a root cause analysis.
3. Generate (or brainstorm) solutions, and weigh the pros and cons of each option.
4. Select the best solution.
5. Develop clear objectives with measures, including timelines and standards.
6. Assign clear roles and responsibilities to those involved in the task.
7. Implement the solution.
8. Monitor progress, making corrections or adjustments along the way if necessary.
9. Communicate with all stakeholders throughout the process.
10. Evaluate the process afterward.
11. Continue to monitor the cause of the problem to ensure no recurrence takes place.

Learn Contemporary Quality-Improvement Concepts

Lean management and Six Sigma are just some of the many tools that leaders can use to improve processes and manage change. Some instruments, such as those developed by the Institute for Healthcare Improvement, are specific to healthcare, but many are adopted from other industries. Change makers stay current about modern improvement techniques and are aware of their advantages, disadvantages, and applications.

Be Willing to Do More

By nature, change makers are always looking for areas to refine, enhance, or study. For some leaders, this improvement could mean increasing the number of their accomplishments for the organization, participating in task forces or forming new ones, or volunteering for new assignments. For others, this could mean expanding their control or creating a new service line. Those who seek added responsibilities or aim for higher achievements may be accused of feeding the needs of their egos. However, the results of this willingness to do more are often beneficial to the organization, yielding enhancements not previously considered.

Network and Benchmark

Change makers are competitive, compelled to compare their results and practices with those of others. They are drawn to data and measurement tools, and they keep abreast of current approaches to forecast future standards. As such, they interact frequently with peers and insiders, visit other sites to scope out new technology and initiatives, and attend conferences and workshops. In sum, these leaders take advantage of any networking opportunity to stay informed, competitive, and innovative.

In contrast, leaders who seldom network and benchmark lose their creative spark and even their perspective. Their strategies and decision-making are informed by outdated assumptions.

Learn Change Management

Today, one of the most requested attributes of a leader is the ability to manage and bring about change. Done effectively, change management is a structured process that uses various leadership theories and management models. Although not new, the concept has garnered renewed interest in these times of constant change. Change expert John Kotter (1996; 2002; 2014, 47) enumerates the basic components of change management:

1. Create a sense of urgency.
2. Build a guiding coalition.
3. Form a strategic vision and initiatives.
4. Enlist a volunteer army.
5. Enable action by removing barriers.
6. Generate short-term wins.
7. Sustain acceleration.
8. Institute change.

Change Leadership

In this time of turmoil, healthcare leaders must prioritize change. Kotter International (2011) explains that "change management, which is the term most everyone uses, refers to a set of basic tools or structures intended to keep any change effort under control. The goal is often to minimize the distractions and impacts of the change. Change leadership, on the other hand, concerns the driving forces, visions and processes that fuel large-scale transformation."

Make a Change for Progress's Sake, Not Yours

Some leaders get involved in change efforts because of an inappropriate and selfish need to gain personal fame. They take credit for other people's work and bask in the glory of accomplishment, but they contribute little and pass on the blame if something goes wrong. This behavior does not characterize true change makers.

Change makers pursue change and improvement for the sake of progress, not to strengthen their power or build up admirers and followers who shower them with adulation and gifts. A health system CEO sums it up well: "In this field, we are entrusted with the lives of people; it is a serious business. And we have to be certain that we make our changes for the betterment of the whole, not just to build our own personal legacies."

CONCLUSION

The leader's value of wanting to make a change is admirable, as it benefits the individual, the organization, and everyone else in between. Change makers strengthen the organization's competitive advantage and reputation, and they help keep out mediocre and stagnant practices and strategies.

Case and Exercises

Case 10.1

Kristen Photakis, CEO of a rural hospital, is talking with her friend Jason Weiss, a longtime healthcare consultant, about ways to better engage senior and departmental managers.

KRISTEN. It's frustrating that they sit back and wait for me to create the agenda, give them assignments, or study new trends.

JASON. How does the hospital develop strategies?

KRISTEN. We hold an annual board retreat. During that time, the board and I come up with 25 to 30 goals. When I return to the office, I meet with the vice presidents to tell them what was discussed. Then, I draft subgoals for each of the major objectives identified at the board retreat. The VPs and I hammer out the details until we come up with specific strategies and work plans.

(continued)

(continued from previous page)

JASON. There are several things wrong with that process. First, everything is developed at the top of the organization with little or no input from the lower ranks. Second, you've gotten into the habit of creating everyone's work plans rather than giving people the chance to develop their own. Third, you and the board set too many goals. You have to consider current workload and priorities, previous commitments, unfinished strategies, et cetera. No one can possibly keep up with all the details. And I must say rather bluntly that you are one of the few organizations I've heard of that does not involve the senior leadership team in the strategic planning retreats with the board. I would make that my starting point.

KRISTEN. Sounds like I have work to do.

JASON. Keep in mind that change is a group effort, not a solo practice. If you want your staff to get involved, you have to get out of the way and let them in.

Case 10.1 Questions
1. Is the consultant correct? Explain your answer.
2. What can Kristen do to improve the situation she has created?

Exercise 10.1
The Institute for Healthcare Improvement (IHI; see www.ihi.org) has had a profound impact on change and quality improvement in healthcare. Among IHI's many innovations is rapid-cycle testing, an approach to trying out an idea on a small scale before it is widely implemented. During the testing, the idea is modified if needed and then tried again; the

cycle continues until the ideal result is achieved. In the end, the idea is made permanent and applied on a large scale. A key component of rapid-cycle testing is the collection of small sets of data that can be quickly analyzed. These data samples must be carefully picked to ensure that they are representative of the larger data set.

Exercise 10.1 Questions

1. How can rapid-cycle testing improve or harm a leader's ability to make a change?

2. Name other improvement strategies used in the healthcare field today.

Exercise 10.2

Choflet, Packard, and Stashower (2021) provide an excellent guide to managing organizational change in the following article. In it, they state, "The COVID-19 crisis has created unprecedented demands for immediate and far-reaching organizational change in every healthcare delivery institution. Employees from executive to frontline staff are grappling with the pace, breadth, and depth of these demands. The field and practices of organizational change are being heavily challenged in terms of needs for change and pressures to make it happen more quickly than ever."

Choflet, A., T. Packard, and K. Stashower. 2021. "Rethinking Organizational Change in the COVID-19 Era." *Journal of Hospital Management and Health Policy* 5 (16): 1–13. https://jhmhp.amegroups.com/article/view/6699/pdf.

(continued)

(continued from previous page)

Exercise 10.2 Questions

1. What specific behaviors should leaders practice to ensure that change is welcome in times of crisis?

2. Making change too quickly is often the reason for failure. What can leaders do to minimize the chance of failure in times of quick change?

REFERENCES

Bolman, L. G., and T. E. Deal. 2013. *Reframing Organizations: Artistry, Choice, and Leadership*, 5th ed. San Francisco: Jossey-Bass.

Dye, C. F., and A. N. Garman. 2015. *Exceptional Leadership: 16 Critical Competencies for Healthcare Leaders*, 2nd ed. Chicago: Health Administration Press.

Forrestal, E. J., and L. W. Cellucci. 2016. *Ethics and Professionalism for Healthcare Managers*. Chicago: Health Administration Press.

Gallup. 2021. "Your Business Strategy Hinges on Employee Engagement." Accessed December 14. www.gallup.com/services/169328/q12-employee-engagement.aspx.

Harter, J. 2020. "4 Factors Driving Record-High Employee Engagement in U.S." Gallup Workplace Blog. Published February 4. https://www.gallup.com/workplace/284180/factors-driving-record-high-employee-engagement.aspx.

Harter, J., and A. Adkins. 2015. "Employees Want a Lot More from Their Managers." *Gallup Business Journal*. Published April 8. www.gallup.com/businessjournal/182321/employees-lot-managers.aspx.

Haudan, J. 2021. Personal communication with author, November 12.

Hughes, R. L., R. C. Ginnett, and G. J. Curphy. 2018. *Leadership: Enhancing the Lessons of Experience*, 9th ed. Burr Ridge, IL: McGraw-Hill Education.

Isomura, I. 1998. "Transformational and Charismatic Leadership." In *Organizational Behavior*, 4th ed., edited by R. Kreiter and A. Kinicki. New York: Richard D. Irwin.

Kotter, J. P. 2014. *Accelerate: Building Strategic Agility for a Faster-Moving World*. Boston: Harvard Business School Press.

———. 2002. *The Heart of Change: Real-Life Stories of How People Change Their Organizations*. Boston: Harvard Business School Press.

———. 1996. *Leading Change*. Boston: Harvard Business School Press.

Kotter International. 2011. "Change Management vs. Change Leadership—What's the Difference?" *Forbes*. Published July 12. www.forbes.com/sites/johnkotter/2011/07/12/change-management-vs-change-leadership-whats-the-difference/#78e0432818ec.

Kouzes, J. M., and B. Z. Posner. 1993. *Credibility: How Leaders Gain and Lose It, Why People Demand It*. San Francisco: Jossey-Bass.

McClelland, D. C. 1961. *The Achieving Society*. New York: Free Press.

Rylatt, A. 2013. "Three Qualities of Highly Successful Change Agents." Association for Talent Development. Published July 8. www.td.org/Publications/Magazines/TD/TD-Archive/2013/07/Three-Qualities-of-Highly-Successful-Change-Agents.

SUGGESTED READINGS

Hall, J. N. 2021. "The COVID-19 Crisis: Aligning Kotter's Steps for Leading Change with Health Care Quality Improvement." *Canadian Medical Education Journal* 12 (1): e109–e110.

Haudan, J. 2008. *The Art of Engagement: Bridging the Gap Between People and Possibilities.* New York: McGraw-Hill.

CHAPTER 11

Commitment

*One key to more flow in life comes when we align what
we do with what we enjoy, as is the case with those
fortunate folks whose jobs give them great pleasure.*

—Daniel Goleman (2013)

JUDITH D'AMATO AND Bob Graham, both seasoned vice
presidents at a large medical center, are talking about Blake
Cullen, the newly appointed CEO.

JUDITH. I am amazed at how different she is from the last two
CEOs—Larry Orestes specifically.

BOB. Exactly! Larry practically lived here. He worked more
hours than anyone did and rarely took a vacation. To his
credit, he accomplished a lot. But I can't tell you about a
single project that wasn't contentious or that followed the
initial agreed-on plan. He hated delegating or having others
take the lead. He was exhausting. That's probably why he's
not here anymore.

JUDITH. Blake's energy and focus are admirable. She has a
thick file for every initiative we have rolled out. She asks

questions and pores over material. Despite her packed schedule, she seems to have the time to attend staff events and welcomes people in her office. She's pleasant to be around, and she doesn't intimidate anyone with her skills and high rank.

BOB. Plus, she's so secure with her role that she's not threatened when someone else has better ideas. In fact, she invites and expects us to be part of the process, to do our job. The one thing she strongly demands is that we always keep the mission and vision at the forefront of all our activities.

JUDITH. It's also clear that she has a life outside of the hospital. Did you know she runs marathons with her grown kids? And every summer, she and her family spend two weeks volunteering to rebuild homes and plant trees in a depressed urban area. One of my nurses told me that. I was inspired.

BOB. That may be one of the major differences between Blake and Larry. She's here because she loves the job and respects the work we do. He was here because he was padding his résumé for the next big move.

EFFECTIVE LEADERSHIP IS a demanding master. It yields not to time. It bends not to excuses. It accepts only commitment.

Commitment is a value that measures the leader's dedication to his profession. Because commitment binds the leader to his work, it generates a strong work ethic, loyalty, pride, productivity, ownership, and even joy.

In exhibit 11.1, several healthcare leaders offer their own definitions of commitment. Some of these definitions use a sports analogy,

Exhibit 11.1 Commitment as Defined by Healthcare Executives

- "Getting the job done. You face all the hurdles and finish the race."

- "An attitude of excitement about any problem. Being committed means that you have the chance to fix it."

- "Having a solemn covenant that you will do whatever it takes to fulfill the mission of your organization."

- "We saw who was truly committed during the COVID crisis. They were the ones who got us through."

- "The old story of the chicken and the pig. The chicken gave eggs but the pig gave his life. That is true commitment. In some ways, I feel as though I have done the same for the healthcare organizations I have worked for."

- "Giving your all because any race worth running is a race worth winning."

equating the leader to an athlete and her commitment to an athlete's drive and competitiveness. The primary reason such an analogy is often used is that many leaders view their roles and responsibilities as an athletic event for which they continually train physically, mentally, emotionally, and spiritually.

Great leaders simultaneously act as coaches and players, inspiring and guiding others to do well and performing the work themselves. These leaders are also cheerleaders, boosting morale and applauding efforts. Highly effective leaders do function frequently as coaches, providing guidance, support, and correction. This approach requires a high level of energy and commitment to others. Garman and I describe the competency as mentoring and give specific suggestions on how to mentor (Dye and Garman 2015; see exhibit 11.2).

THE CONCEPT IN PRACTICE

Commitment to the profession is not a given in healthcare, especially in the current environment of high demands but low returns. The following simple strategies help in maintaining commitment.

Stay Focused on the Vision

The organizational vision can serve as a lighthouse and a compass for stewards navigating the choppy waters of healthcare management. It illuminates and points to the path to take. The vision, assuming it was not established arbitrarily and was the result of a careful participative process, takes away the guesswork and indecision about the future state of the organization. Commitment to the cause, so to speak, is easier with this desired outcome in full view. Great leaders prefer to know where they are going before they even start the journey.

Exhibit 11.2 How to Mentor

- Understand the career aspirations of your direct reports.

- Work with direct reports to create engaging mentoring plans.

- Support employees in developing their skills.

- Support career development in a nonpossessive way (e.g., know that moving up and moving out are necessary for the career advancement of support staff).

- Find stretch assignments and other delegation opportunities that support skill development.

- Model professional development by advancing your own skills.

Source: Adapted from Dye and Garman (2015).

Weigh Work and Life Pursuits

Working at home has long been a challenge to many healthcare leaders. As long as reports and deadlines have been around and as smartphones, tablets, and laptops make remote work straightforward, leaders working before and after business hours and even during vacations is de rigueur. The COVID-19 pandemic only intensified this situation. Everyone (even those in nonmanagement positions) now seems to be overworked, running ragged to keep up with heavy workloads and short turnarounds.

Unfortunately, leaders who are constantly working lose perspective and burn out. They place excessive demands on their staff and have unreasonable expectations. As a result, workplace morale declines; many mistakes are made; distrust spreads; productivity suffers; and employees become stressed out, fearful, and difficult to retain and manage. Employees do not even get a respite when overworked bosses are away from the office, as these leaders check in by e-mail or phone.

Another, and most important, casualty of overworking is the executive's personal life. For every high achiever, there is a patient and supportive family member (e.g., spouse, partner, parent, child) who has been overlooked or a personal pursuit (e.g., hobby, advanced degree, creative aspiration, spiritual development) that has been pushed aside. Over the long run, this situation could result in resentment at best and family and social breakdown at worst.

A new school of thought argues that maintaining a work–life balance has become a fallacy in a deadline- and travel-intensive global market. What matters, according to this theory, is the flexibility to respond to both work and life demands and an awareness of the consequences when one is chosen over another. In this sense, work and life are integrated, not separate entities that do not meet. That said, leaders should learn ways to cope with the demands of both work and life with the goal of doing their best at these two components. Exhibit 11.3 offers strategies for maintaining career success without sacrificing personal interests.

Find an Enjoyable Outlet

Healthcare pushes many of its executives to the limit. Many leaders are fatigued and tapped out and want to change careers.

An undertaking that has nothing to do with the field can refresh a leader who is suffering from burnout. It presents opportunities for developing out-of-the-box solutions and stimulates thinking. It also hones teamwork and learning skills, as well as the leader's humility, as she is now a follower instead of the main person in charge.

Simply spending time with family and friends can be an enjoyable outlet.

Show Initiative

The greatest proof of a leader's commitment is her initiative. Initiative is the drive to chart a new direction with no outside encouragement or command. Some healthcare leaders define initiative as follows:

- "Doing more than is required—going the extra mile."
- "Actively seeking out issues and problems."
- "Being proactive, not reactive."
- "Engaging in positive thinking."
- "Not being a minimalist."
- "Avoiding the negativity of blaming others and acting like a victim of circumstances."

Exhibit 11.3 How to Maintain Both Work and Life Pursuits

Minimize meetings. Many meetings are often unnecessary. Before you attend or host one, ask the following questions:

- What is the goal of this meeting?
- Can this goal be achieved without my presence?
- Can this goal be accomplished through other means, including e-mail exchanges or memos?
- What other work could I do if I do not attend this meeting?
- Could I delegate attendance at this meeting to someone else?

Prioritize work and life to-dos. First, write two comprehensive lists—one for work responsibilities, one for personal priorities. Second, categorize items on both lists as urgent (U), important (I), or can wait (CW). Third, assign an order to the items in each category (1 for first to be done, 2 for next, etc.) according to level of importance. Such a priority list serves as a visual reminder and a stress reducer because the items are part of your daily functions, not just weighing on your mind.

Allow for regular downtime. Schedule a block of time every week, for at least two to three hours, to get away from job stressors. Even if you cannot physically leave the workplace and stop all tasks, take time out to tend to low-pressure activities. Some executives take one or two days away from the office every couple of months to regroup. Unplugging from wireless devices or smartphones for at least several hours a day is also a wise move.

Be flexible with time. A tight schedule does not allow for the surprises inherent in healthcare operations. The same is true for personal life. Being flexible does not mean ignoring the calendar altogether, but it does mean having a willingness to accommodate unplanned or unforeseen demands, whether they are work related or home related.

Get regular exercise. Regular physical activity boosts energy levels and helps clear the mind.

Volunteer. Giving back to the community not only improves your reputation but also gives you fresh perspectives. Join the board of a local service organization, participate in fund-raising activities, or perform outreach work for a cause you would like to advance. Volunteering is an ideal activity in which to involve your friends and family.

Only by taking the initiative can you follow your own course. As the Spanish poet Antonio Machado (2003, 239) writes, "Traveler, there is no road. . . . As you walk, you make your own road."

Be Prepared to Make Sacrifices

Leadership expert John C. Maxwell (2007, 198) says, "Sacrifice is a constant in leadership. It is an ongoing process, not a one-time payment." The advice "you must pay your dues" is often given in healthcare, which is primarily hierarchical in structure. As such, the expectation is that those interested in moving up the organizational ladder need to yield to the demands (and politics) of their positions, investing much energy and time in their projects and performing work that no one else opts to do. For example, new health administration program graduates are assigned tasks, such as copying and cold calling, that do not require an advanced degree. Similarly, middle managers are sent out to attend time-consuming, low-level meetings or to handle face-to-face patient complaints. The purpose of these seemingly menial assignments is not to punish the employees but to test their team orientation, "get-to-it-tiveness," and commitment to their careers.

Making sacrifices, however, is not confined to non–senior management staff. Executives are also expected to make concessions for the good of the enterprise or the team. Over time, such sacrifices build up, giving the executive a bank of goodwill that can be drawn on when needed.

> Subordinates often become committed to goals simply by seeing the sincere and enthusiastic commitment of top leadership to them.
>
> —Richard L. Hughes, Robert C. Ginnett, and Gordon J. Curphy (2018)

In a way, making sacrifices is an American value because it is based on the principle of "hard work merits rewards." The American public generally scoffs at people who rely on their good fortune, not years of honest effort and even failure, to become successful.

Think Positively

Positive thinking is a deliberate act, a choice that can be made in the face of negative scenarios. It transforms bad attitudes and victim mentalities, and it overtakes people's tendency to fear the worst. Committed leaders make a conscious decision to think positively and have a good attitude because they want their initiatives to succeed. Even when an effort is, by all indications, going to have less-than-optimal outcomes, committed leaders dwell on the bright side—that is, they look for lessons, instead of mistakes. Mistakes have a negative connotation that makes people wary and defensive. Lessons, on the other hand, focus on improvement and development.

Positive thinking has its share of detractors who contend that it shields us from reality and thus sets us up for disappointment. This pessimistic view, however, may breed bad attitudes that only perpetuate the difficulty of any situation and weaken commitment. Perhaps a more relevant possibility to consider is the one proposed by Collinson (2012, 87), who suggests that "leaders' excessive positivity is often characterized by a reluctance to consider alternative voices, which can leave organizations and societies ill-prepared to deal with unexpected events." He continues to argue that this type of leadership "encourages leaders to believe their own narratives that everything is going well and discourages followers from raising problems or admitting mistakes" (87). However, Mohanty (2014, 61) presents the counterargument: "The leader's attitude tends to spread and affect others drastically. A good leader truly cares about the morale of the team [and] motivates his team with respect [and] a relentlessly positive attitude. The success of any organization is very much dependent on the leadership attitude. The role of a leader is to inspire people so that they can contribute their best to the organization and also inspire them to become more confident in their work to achieve their personal and group goals, [which] reflects the attitude of a leader."

Exhibit 11.4 provides Gandhi's insight into the power of a positive spirit and its impact on literally all that you will do.

Be Mindful of Body Language

A leader's body language and facial cues communicate many messages. For example, a leader's frown as he paces the hallway could signal stress, while his warm smile and leisurely walk may represent his approachability. Commitment (or lack thereof) can be displayed through body language as well. Uncrossed arms, eye contact, leaning slightly into the other person, and standing or sitting to be equal in height with that person are just some examples.

Promote Employee Participation and Engagement

As discussed in chapter 10, ensuring staff satisfaction is no longer enough; leaders must also encourage employees to take part in organizational efforts. One way to support engagement is to delegate responsibility to staff.

Many healthcare workers, including managers, are highly reliable and intelligent. They await an opportunity from their superiors

---

Exhibit 11.4 Positive Attitudes: From Your Thoughts to Your Destiny

Keep your thoughts positive, because your thoughts become your words.

Keep your words positive, because your words become your behavior.

Keep your behavior positive, because your behavior becomes your habits.

Keep your habits positive, because your habits become your values.

Keep your values positive, because your values become your destiny.

—Mahatma Gandhi

Source: Reprinted from Gold (2002).

to use their skills and judgment on an important initiative. Such an assignment contributes to the employee's sense of commitment to her job and to the organization, not to mention to the processes and outcomes of the project or task.

> The more one's authority and breadth of responsibilities increase, the more control there should be over one's own time and commitments.
>
> —Ted W. Engstrom and Edward R. Dayton (1984)

This manager–worker connection could inspire other involvement, including that of physicians, patients, and families. Employee engagement could increase morale and help in the recruitment and retention of high performers. Exhibit 11.5 enumerates the contributors to employee engagement.

Exhibit 11.5 Organizational Factors That Contribute to Employee Engagement

Excellent organizational reputation. Highly engaged employees are found in organizations known for providing high-quality care and other public services to their community.

Clear job expectations. Highly engaged employees know exactly what their roles, responsibilities, and goals are.

Close relationships with supervisors. Highly engaged employees report to managers who leverage the staff's individual capabilities and meet their professional needs.

Regular feedback. Highly engaged employees receive frequent comments on their individual and team performance for the purpose of learning and improvement.

Recognition and celebration. Highly engaged employees appreciate rewards and celebrations for their efforts.

Career advancement and continuous education. Highly engaged employees are encouraged to pursue educational interests and in-house promotional opportunities.

Develop a Strong System of Personal Organization

Being organized is a symbol of being committed. It signals that the leader is always in control of her time, tasks, and priorities, among other things. Such a leader uses all available tools, such as filing systems, calendars or planners, and smartphones. A personal assistant helps the leader manage her schedule.

CONCLUSION

To committed leaders, work is not drudgery or toil; instead, it offers great satisfaction. In the classic book *The 7 Habits of Highly Effective People*, Stephen Covey (2013) lists being proactive as the first habit. According to Covey, being proactive is a function of commitment and work ethic. Now, imagine an organization teeming with proactive workers and leaders, then realize that your organization can become one, too. As the saying goes, "Practice makes perfect."

Self-Evaluation Questions

❑ What does commitment mean to me?

❑ Am I paying a price for the work I do? Is that price worth the rewards I am receiving? Do I enjoy my work?

❑ What does "paying dues" mean to me?

❑ If my staff were to describe my facial expressions at work, what would they say?

❑ To what degree am I organized? Do I regularly run behind schedule? Do I keep a daily or weekly to-do list and accomplish most, if not all, of it?

❑ Consider this quote from Katzenbach and Smith (1993, 105): "Team [members] work hard and enthusiastically. They also play hard and enthusiastically. No one has to ask them to put in extra time; they just do it. No one has to remind them not to delegate jobs to others; again, they just do the work themselves. To outsiders, the energy and enthusiasm levels inside teams are unmistakable and even seductive." To what extent does this description apply to my contributions to the team?

Case and Exercises

Case 11.1

Children's Hospital has a reputation for having the lowest turnover rate among the six hospitals located in the area, despite the fact that its average wages are approximately 10 percent lower than those offered by its competitors. In addition, Children's Hospital has the highest rate of employee engagement. In contrast, University Hospital, which provides the largest compensation and benefit packages in the area, has the highest rate of turnover and the lowest rate of employee engagement.

Dori Shimbuku, a human resources consultant hired by University Hospital to study its recruitment and retention patterns, comes to the conclusion that University employees, including its leaders and managers, lack commitment.

Case 11.1 Questions

1. What does Dori mean? What should she recommend University Hospital do to increase employee and leadership commitment?

(continued)

(continued from previous page)

2. How might commitment be measured?

Exercise 11.1
Several online articles discuss employee engagement. Choose two of them and develop a presentation that answers the following questions:

1. What are the primary causes of high employee engagement?
2. What is the relationship between an employee's level of engagement and his relationship with his boss?
3. What practices should senior leaders develop to build employee engagement in their organizations?

The online resources on Employee Engagement included at the end of this chapter may be useful for this exercise.

Exercise 11.2
Physician engagement has become a widely discussed topic. Conduct an online search for information about physician engagement, and determine the applicability of the concept of commitment to enhancing physician engagement.

REFERENCES

Collinson, D. 2012. "Prozac Leadership and the Limits of Positive Thinking." *Leadership* 8 (2): 87–107.

Covey, S. R. 2013. *The 7 Habits of Highly Successful People: Powerful Lessons in Personal Change*, 25th anniversary ed. New York: Simon and Schuster.

Dye, C. F., and A. N. Garman. 2015. *Exceptional Leadership: 16 Critical Competencies for Healthcare Leaders*, 2nd ed. Chicago: Health Administration Press.

Engstrom, T. W., and E. R. Dayton. 1984. *The Christian Leader's 60-Second Management Guide*. Waco, TX: Word Books.

Gold, T. 2002. *Open Your Mind, Open Your Life: A Little Book of Eastern Wisdom*. Kansas City, MO: Andrews McMeel Publishing.

Goleman, D. 2013. *Focus: The Hidden Driver of Excellence*. New York: HarperCollins.

Hughes, R. L., R. C. Ginnett, and G. J. Curphy. 2018. *Leadership: Enhancing the Lessons of Experience*, 9th ed. Burr Ridge, IL: McGraw-Hill Education.

Katzenbach, J. R., and D. K. Smith. 1993. *The Wisdom of Teams: Creating the High-Performance Organization*. Boston: Harvard Business Press.

Machado, A. 2003. *There Is No Road*. Translated by M. C. Berg and D. Maloney. Buffalo, NY: White Pine Press.

Maxwell, J. C. 2007. *Ultimate Leadership: Maximize Your Potential and Empower Your Team*. Nashville, TN: Thomas Nelson.

Mohanty, S. 2014. "A Leader with Positive Attitude and Thinking Can Bring Great Success." *International Journal of Emerging Research in Management and Technology* 3 (2): 61–63.

SUGGESTED READINGS

Collinson, D., and D. Tourish. 2015. "Teaching Leadership Critically: New Directions for Leadership Pedagogy." *Academy of Management Learning and Education* 14 (4): 576–94.

Cunha, M. P., A. Rego, S. Clegg, and P. Neves. 2013. "The Case for Transcendent Followership." *Leadership* 9 (1): 87–106.

Dye, C. F. 2021. *Enhanced Physician Engagement, Volume 1: What It Is, Why You Need It, and Where to Begin.* Chicago: Health Administration Press.

———. 2021. *Enhanced Physician Engagement, Volume 2: Tools and Tactics for Success.* Chicago: Health Administration Press.

Lewis, K. R. 2015. "Everything You Need to Know About Your Millennial Coworkers." *Fortune.* Published June 23. http://fortune.com/2015/06/23/know-your-millennial-co-workers/.

Turkel, M. C., G. Reidinger, K. Ferket, and K. Reno. 2005. "An Essential Component of the Magnet Journey: Fostering an Environment for Evidence-Based Practice and Nursing Research." *Nursing Administration Quarterly* 29 (3): 254–62.

Yahaya, R., and F. Ebrahim. 2016. "Leadership Styles and Organizational Commitment: Literature Review." *Journal of Management Development* 35 (2): 190–216.

Zhang, X., N. Li, J. Ullrich, and R. van Dick. 2015. "Getting Everyone on Board: The Effect of Differentiated Transformational Leadership by CEOs on Top Management Team Effectiveness and Leader-Rated Firm Performance." *Journal of Management* 41 (7): 1898–933.

ONLINE RESOURCES ON EMPLOYEE ENGAGEMENT

Banerjee, D., and M. Rai. 2020. "Social Isolation in Covid-19: The Impact of Loneliness." *International Journal of Social Psychiatry* 66 (6): 525–27.

Gallup. 2020. "Gallup Q12® Meta-Analysis" Accessed December 14. https://www.gallup.com/workplace/321725/gallup-q12-meta-analysis-report.aspx.

Harter, J., and A. Adkins. 2015. "What Great Managers Do to Engage Their Employees." *Harvard Business Review*. Published April 2. https://hbr.org/2015/04/what-great-managers-do-to-engage-employees.

Lanaj, K., A. S. Gabriel, and N. Chawla. 2021. "The Self-Sacrificial Nature of Leader Identity: Understanding the Costs and Benefits at Work and Home." *Journal of Applied Psychology* 106 (3): 345–63.

Reinwald, M., S. Zimmermann, and F. Kunze. 2021. "Working in the Eye of the Pandemic: Local COVID-19 Infections and Daily Employee Engagement." *Frontiers in Psychology* 12: 654126.

CHAPTER 12

Emotional Intelligence

*Even people with many apparent leadership strengths can
stand to better understand those areas of EI where we have
room to grow. Don't shortchange your development as a
leader by assuming that EI is all about being sweet and
chipper, or that your EI is perfect if you are—or, even worse,
assume that EI can't help you excel in your career.*

—Daniel Goleman and Richard Boyatzis (2017)

DURING LUNCH AT an off-site leadership seminar, a group of middle managers from the same health system participates in an open dialogue about the vice presidents in their various hospitals.

KYLA. The strongest of the group is Melissa Varga. Her departments meet budgets year in and year out. Their clinical outcomes are high, and their retention is great. I'd like to work for that vice president.

ANDREW. Well, I do work for her and I wish I didn't. Melissa is an emotional roller coaster. Some days she is calm, and some days she just seems crazed. Behind closed doors, she is not beyond using threats to get us to achieve our goals, but often all that outsiders see is this calm and controlled leader. She's far from that. We're expected to work many hours, and she's always frowning when we take vacation. My business units are all work and no play. We're really stuck with her because she has all the clinical departments reporting to her.

BJ. I heard she throws tantrums. I was going to apply for a job working for her, but someone warned me. I'm glad to work for Mike Randolph. This guy is one cool cucumber. He constantly gets things done and does not get overexcited when things go wrong. He expresses thanks to us and respects our work, so we respect him back. He has very good interpersonal skills and controls his emotions. Even under pressure, he doesn't lose his composure.

KYLA. He sounds like a robot, but better than Melissa, it seems. What's the difference then—they actually both achieve high results?

ANDREW. Both of them are pretty strong execs. I think the difference is emotional intelligence.

BJ. Well, that's just a catchall phrase without much meaning. What is it, really?

KYLA. It means the person has a good grasp of his or her emotions and feelings and those of others, and how those are displayed externally. Leadership is not exclusively about getting results. It's getting results without emotional outbursts or allowing anger to take over. Actually, I think there's some pretty good research that shows that emotional intelligence is a legitimate thing.

IN THE LATE 1990s, writer Daniel Goleman popularized the concept of emotional intelligence, setting off further inquiries into the relationship between feelings and intellect. Researchers Peter Salovey and Jack Mayer (1990, 189), two pioneers of emotional intelligence, define the term as follows: "Emotional intelligence [is] the subset of social intelligence that involves the ability to monitor one's own and others' feelings and emotions, to discriminate among them and to use this information to guide one's thinking and actions."

Emotional intelligence has two components: energy and maturity. Energy (or the spark or zeal for life) refers to the liveliness and stamina with which people approach their work. It keeps leaders fresh and motivated when others have had enough and are ready to give up. Maturity, meanwhile, refers to people's refinement, social graces, tact, capacity to grow and change, and ability to interpret signals from others. It makes leaders aware of signals from others. It reminds leaders to apologize, express gratitude, harbor no ill will, empathize, have a sense of humor, and respect others. Also, maturity keeps leaders poised during times of distress and wise during times of pressure. Although maturity is often associated with old age, it can be learned at a young age.

Emotionally intelligent leaders make every effort to develop their leadership skills, knowledge, and abilities. They also work hard to be aware of their inner emotional selves and the world around them. They are confident and enthusiastic and have self-esteem and a positive attitude. They discern nuances in (and thus are sensitive to) people's words and actions. They are aware of the effect that their (and others') needs, beliefs, motivations, and feelings have on their surroundings. They know how damaging passive-aggressive behaviors and one-upmanship can be in the workplace. They are watchful of situations in which they and others deal with conflict, criticisms, stress, pressure, and difficult people. They use a self-awareness lens, which enables them to see the communication and behavioral patterns that showcase the worst in people, including themselves.

The COVID-19 pandemic also showed the importance of emotional intelligence. Drigas and Papoutsi (2020, 22) state that

"Awareness, management, empathy, basic components of emotional intelligence, are especially important for people to control difficult situations as the one we are going through. Moreover, people with high emotional intelligence can better manage and mitigate stress and adopt strategies of resilience and control." And Kantor and colleagues (2020, 568) note, "Integrating emotional intelligence allows hospital medicine leaders to anticipate, identify, articulate, and manage the emotional responses to necessary changes and stresses that occur during a crisis such as the COVID-19 pandemic."

Simply put, emotionally intelligent leaders have a robust capability for reading people and receiving and giving critical feedback. This ability comes from their firm understanding of their own and others' feelings and the environment in which they operate. Northouse (2021, 40) suggests that "people who are more sensitive to their emotions and the impact of their emotions on others will be leaders who are more effective."

THE SELF-AWARENESS FACTOR

In the book *Emotional Intelligence at Work*, author Hendrie Weisinger (1998) sets out the following steps to improving emotional intelligence:

1. Develop high self-esteem.
2. Manage your emotions.
3. Motivate yourself.
4. Develop effective command skills.
5. Develop interpersonal expertise.
6. Help others help themselves.

According to Weisinger, self-awareness is the main driver of these steps. Self-awareness is a universal panacea for negativity and enables leaders to

- accept (even anticipate) constructive criticism;
- avoid feeling defensive;
- support those around them;
- be assertive but not aggressive;
- have confidence in their ability to initiate change;
- view scenarios as win-win;
- not be hostile, overbearing, or impatient; and
- take charge of situations.

Conversely, leaders who are not self-aware misinterpret events and others' comments, throw tantrums or act out, and are reactive rather than proactive.

Many executives, because of their high rank, have become so removed from daily operations and workers that they do not even realize how others in the organization perceive them. When in the office, they primarily deal with their direct reports, a group that mainly consists of other senior managers who are likely also isolated from staff. As a result, these executives' workplace reality becomes distorted and their emotional intelligence dulls.

Worse, their self-awareness is based on incomplete information or incorrect assumptions about themselves and others.

THE CONCEPT IN PRACTICE

The following principles can enhance emotional intelligence.

Develop Personal and Social Competence

Experts suggest that emotional intelligence may be managed through learning and improving both personal and social competencies. Personal competency includes self-awareness, self-control, and self-motivation. Social competency, meanwhile, includes social awareness, empathy, collaboration, and teamwork. According to Singh (2010, 41), "An attempt to develop the personal competencies of executives in [an] organization can go a long way to improve their emotional intelligence."

Characteristics of Emotionally Intelligent Leaders

Comfortable and self-aware. They are confident with their skills, goals, and visions but value continuous improvement. Thus, they welcome feedback.

Reflective listener. They show a genuine interest in other people and their ideas. They encourage others to lead discussions or give input. They rarely interrupt, preferring instead to wait their turn.

Nonthreatening and nonintimidating. They are open and approachable. They do not use power to manipulate their followers, and they are aware that the trappings of their high rank are easily misunderstood and could corrupt their reputation.

Available. They avoid appearing constantly busy, as it signals that they do not highly regard the everyday tasks and challenges of employees. They invite others to speak with them directly, and they attend events of great importance to staff.

Seek Feedback

Emotionally intelligent leaders do not feel threatened by feedback, whether from direct discussions or through 360-degree assessment tools. These executives relish the chance to receive ratings and comments from peers, subordinates, and other associates because they understand the role of feedback in their personal and professional development.

Appendix B presents the Emotional Intelligence Evaluation Form, a tool that leaders can use to obtain direct feedback. This instrument works best when there is participation from staff and associates at all levels of the organization so that a comprehensive result can be generated. To ensure the confidentiality of the feedback, participants are discouraged from sharing their comments. Ideally, a neutral third party should administer the tool, collate comments, and provide a full report to the leader being evaluated.

> I saw how the inability to manage emotions and communicate effectively often led to unresolved and repetitive conflicts among staff, low morale, and diminished productivity.
>
> —Hendrie Weisinger (1998)

Set a Personal Path and Follow It

Many individuals—leaders included—possess little sense of personal direction, especially when they get caught up in the busyness of daily operations. These leaders may be effective in establishing and monitoring organizational objectives, but they may fall short when managing their own careers.

Emotionally intelligent leaders, in contrast, frequently take stock of where they have been and what they have accomplished. They know their long-term and short-term personal goals and seek to work in organizations that provide opportunities for fulfilling those goals. In other words, they look for fit between their personal mission and the organization's mission so that both entities can benefit from the union. For example, an individual who intends to make a difference in the public health system is not served well by working in a large for-profit. Some emotionally intelligent leaders weigh their career options by occasionally interviewing for open positions even when they do not intend to leave their jobs. This exercise allows them to compare their skills and accomplishments with current standards and expectations.

Leaders who are not attuned to their personal intentions or path can more easily get derailed by the unceasing demands of healthcare management.

View Annual Retreats as a Time for Self-Reflection

Most members of religious orders and some laypersons often take religious retreats. These are planned getaways, lasting a few days to a week, that focus on intense introspection. Although these retreats are intended to reconnect participants with their original aspirations, some people go a step further: They reflect on their own strengths and weaknesses and incorporate their abilities into their leadership style. One nun admits to designing a succession plan while on a retreat.

Get a Coach

Executive or leadership coaching has become one of the fastest-growing areas of consulting, as leaders have realized the benefits of having a neutral adviser. These coaches can assess current behavior, management style, and performance; offer unbiased feedback; and teach practical skills for improvement and for managing perceptions. In addition, coaches are helpful in establishing a clear career vision or direction. Large numbers of physician leaders, in particular, use leadership coaches. Winters (2013) reports that they "feel under-qualified to lead," so they seek coaches to understand leadership and emotional intelligence issues more keenly.

Many emotionally intelligent leaders rely on their coaches, with whom they discuss private details of their jobs and from whom they seek counsel. The book *Exceptional Leadership* (Dye and Garman 2015, 195–203) presents an entire chapter on how to use executive coaches. Several coaching websites also offer information on this topic—see, for example, www.theexecutive coachingforum.com and http://executivecoachingroundtable.com /Practicaladvice.pdf.

Manage Your Emotions

Managing emotions is not the same as lacking emotions. In this era of social media—when sharing personal information, opinions, and reactions has become routine practice for anyone with an account—it is easy to assume that those who maintain composure have no feelings or are "robots." Emotionally intelligent people do, in fact, have a lot of emotions—only they tend to show more positive feelings (e.g., optimism, sympathy, confidence) rather than negative ones (e.g., defeat, anger, vengeance). Most important, they *manage* their emotions.

Emotionally intelligent leaders know that positive messages are influential, inspiring followers and keeping them enthused about initiatives, even the difficult ones. Negative emotions, on the other hand, are not motivational. They instill fear and anxiety, and they could erode trust and respect.

Executives do reach points at which their frustrations take over— a natural occurrence in management. Over time, these emotional outbursts could devolve into an angry personality that the person is not able to discern in himself. Cursing, shouting, name-calling, chronic complaining, and impatience are some signs of poor emotional control. Weisinger (1998) notes that physiological changes can be observed in people who "lose their cool," including heart palpitations, perspiration, and rapid respiration.

> Emotional competence is particularly central to leadership. . . . Interpersonal ineptitude in leaders lowers everyone's performance: It wastes time, creates acrimony, corrodes motivation and commitment, builds hostility and apathy.
>
> —Daniel Goleman (1998)

Although emotions are a natural response to everyday stimuli, they can become detrimental in the workplace if they are not appropriately displayed. Leaders should watch out for their personal emotional triggers (and the responses described by Weisinger) in an effort to slow down or transform their reactions.

Expect Setbacks

Leaders respond to setbacks differently. Because they are more optimistic, emotionally intelligent leaders cope well with challenges. Some of these leaders take a mental or physical break from the activity and return with renewed commitment, while others view setbacks as a personal test they must pass. To better deal with setbacks, one CEO carries around a laminated card with the following message:

> You will get knocked down at times.
> You will taste dirt occasionally.
> But it is through this process that
> You will better enjoy the return to the air above.

Maintain Physical and Mental Health

Healthcare delivery is physically and mentally exhausting work, even for those who do not provide direct care. As such, healthcare leaders must maintain their health, which enables them to be of service to their staff and patients. Appropriate amounts of rest, sleep, and exercise and a balanced diet go a long way toward wellness. A regular visit to the doctor, vacations or time off, and a stress-decreasing routine also help.

The point is that leaders who are too tired or too physically and mentally run-down are ineffective, negative, and short-tempered. They are not approachable, and they behave unpredictably, to the detriment of the employees and the organization. Emotional intelligence cannot be developed and sustained in an unhealthy mind and body. And while it may go without saying, pandemics in healthcare make this an even more important matter.

View Everything Holistically

Highly effective leaders know that life has ups and downs, and that, as leaders, they will likely have more ups and downs than other workers do. Maintaining perspective and seeing the whole picture, however, helps them manage emotions. Exhibit 12.1 shows how this flows.

CONCLUSION

Emotional intelligence is more critical today given that the command-and-control style of leadership is no longer the norm. More and more leaders understand that they have to earn—not expect—respect and trust. Being emotionally intelligent is one way to practice this understanding. Emotionally intelligent leaders do not use their power to gain an advantage over others; are aware of their intentions, accomplishments, and shortcomings; manage their emotions; and welcome feedback. This level of maturity requires a lot of work, something that an emotionally intelligent leader puts in every day.

Exhibit 12.1 Flow of Holistic Thinking

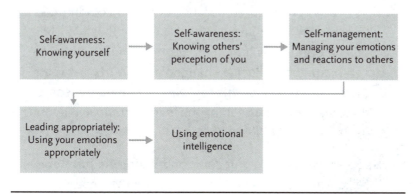

Case and Exercises

Case 12.1

Mike Sebastian has been the director of facilities for more than 30 years. Up until the past three years, the facilities department had low turnover. Today, however, the turnover rate is 30 percent, causing concern for Rena Shah, the chief human resources officer at the hospital.

To understand the problem, Rena pays a visit to several of Mike's former employees.

> FIRST WORKER. I retired because of him. I couldn't take the constant panic he gave me. He wasn't that bad when he first started—a little temperamental but nothing to complain about. But he changed a lot in my last years there. He would blow his top when he found out something was not done or someone made a complaint about us. It was hard to live with.

> SECOND WORKER. I quit six months after he hired me. Mike was a screamer. People outside the department didn't know because he seemed great with everyone

else. Behind closed doors, though, he could dress you down. No job was worth that. Even though I needed the money and was really looking forward to being eligible for the pension plan, I decided to leave for my own peace of mind.

THIRD WORKER. Forget about talking to him! He would never listen. He's old school. He thinks it's his way or the highway. I once tried to reason with him to calm down the situation, but he fired me. And I put in the best years of my life in that job. With all due respect, Ms. Shah, you should give him the boot and give him a taste of his own medicine.

Case 12.1 Questions

1. How should Rena address the problem with Mike?

2. What do you think triggered Mike's transformation in the past three years?

Exercise 12.1

As mentioned earlier, emotional intelligence may be managed through learning and improving both personal and social competencies. Personal competency includes self-awareness, self-control, and self-motivation. Social competency, meanwhile, includes social awareness, empathy, collaboration, and teamwork.

Go to the website of Consortium for Research on Emotional Intelligence in Organizations (www.eiconsortium.org) and develop a list of the specific leadership behaviors that characterize emotional intelligence. How do these behaviors match up with your own?

(continued)

(continued from previous page)

Exercise 12.2
Review the following article and consider various ways that healthcare leaders can apply the principles contained within.

Kantor, M. A., S. K. Apgar, A. M. Esmaili, A. Khan, and M. B. Sharpe. 2020. "The Importance of Emotional Intelligence When Leading in a Time of Crisis." *Journal of Hospital Medicine* 15 (9): 568–69.

REFERENCES

Drigas, A., and C. Papoutsi. 2020. "The Need for Emotional Intelligence Training Education in Critical and Stressful Situations: The Case of Covid-19." *International Journal of Recent Contributions from Engineering, Science & IT (iJES)*, 8 (3): 20–36.

Dye, C. F., and A. N. Garman. 2015. *Exceptional Leadership: 16 Critical Competencies for Healthcare Executives*, 2nd ed. Chicago: Health Administration Press.

Goleman, D. 1998. *Working with Emotional Intelligence*. New York: Bantam Books.

Goleman, D., and R. Boyatzis. 2017. "Emotional Intelligence Has 12 Elements. Which Do You Need to Work On?" *Harvard Business Review* 84 (2): 1–5.

Kantor, M. A., S. K. Apgar, A. M. Esmaili, A. Khan, and M. B. Sharpe. 2020. "The Importance of Emotional Intelligence When Leading in a Time of Crisis." *Journal of Hospital Medicine* 15 (9): 568–69.

Mycek, S. 1997. "Getting Beyond Industrial Logic: Renewing Our Faith in the Value of Health." *Healthcare Forum Journal* 40 (4): 16–20.

Northouse, P. G. 2021. *Leadership: Theory and Practice*, 9th ed. Los Angeles: SAGE Publications.

Salovey, P., and J. D. Mayer. 1990. "Emotional Intelligence." *Imagination, Cognition, and Personality* 9 (3): 185–211.

Singh, K. 2010. "Developing Human Capital by Linking Emotional Intelligence with Personal Competencies in Indian Business Organizations." *International Journal of Business Science and Applied Management* 5 (2): 29–42.

Weisinger, H. 1998. *Emotional Intelligence at Work: The Untapped Edge for Success.* San Francisco: Jossey-Bass.

Winters, R. 2013. "Coaching Physicians to Become Leaders." *Harvard Business Review*. Published October 7. https://hbr.org/2013/10/coaching-physicians-to-become-leaders/.

SUGGESTED READINGS

Boak, G. 2016. "Enabling Team Learning in Healthcare." *Action Learning: Research and Practice* 13 (2): 101–17.

Jafri, M. H., C. Dem, and S. Choden. 2016. "Emotional Intelligence and Employee Creativity: Moderating Role of Proactive Personality and Organizational Climate." *Business Perspectives and Research* 4 (1): 54–66.

Murray, L. K. 2020. "How to Lead with Emotional Intelligence in the Time of COVID-19." Johns Hopkins Academics Blog. Published April 21, 2020. https://publichealth.jhu.edu/2020/how-to-lead-with-emotional-intelligence-in-the-time-of-covid-19.

Persich, M. R., R. Smith, S. A. Cloonan, R. Woods-Lubbert, M. Strong, and W. D. S. Killgore. 2021. "Emotional Intelligence Training as a Protective Factor for Mental Health During the COVID-19 Pandemic." *Depression and Anxiety* 38 (10): 1018–25.

Sadovyy, M., M. Sánchez-Gómez, and E. Bresó. 2021. "COVID-19: How the Stress Generated by the Pandemic May Affect Work Performance Through the Moderating Role of Emotional Intelligence." *Personality and Individual Differences* 180: 110986.

Schlaerth, A., N. Ensari, and J. Christian. 2013. "A Meta-analytical Review of the Relationship Between Emotional Intelligence and Leaders' Constructive Conflict Management." *Group Processes and Intergroup Relations* 16 (1): 126–36.

Spano-Szekely, L., M. T. Quinn Griffin, J. Clavelle, and J. J. Fitzpatrick. 2016, Feb. "Emotional Intelligence and Transformational Leadership in Nurse Managers." *Journal of Nursing Administration* 46 (2): 101–18.

Thompson, J. A., and R. Fairchild. 2013. "Does Nurse Manager Education Really Matter?" *Nursing Management* 44 (9): 10–14.

Tyczkowski, B., C. Vandenhouten, J. Reilly, G. Bansal, S. M. Kubsch, and R. Jakkola. 2015. "Emotional Intelligence (EI) and Nursing Leadership Styles Among Nurse Managers." *Nursing Administration Quarterly* 39 (2): 172–80.

Ungaretti, T., K. R. Thompson, A. Miller, and T. O. Peterson. 2015. "Problem-Based Learning: Lessons from Medical Education and Challenges for Management Education." *Academy of Management Learning* 14 (2): 173–86.

PART III

TEAM VALUES

CHAPTER 13

Cooperation and Sharing

The reliance on teams is due partially to increasingly complex tasks, more globalization, and the flattening of organizational structure.

—Peter G. Northouse (2021)

THE PROFESSOR OPENS his class with a question: "As you know, I do a lot of executive team building and executive coaching with senior leaders across the country. What do you think is the greatest challenge in getting senior executives to work together in a collaborative and cooperative way?"

His students volunteer the following responses:

- Most of them don't have the time to be part of a good team.
- A lot of their work takes place outside the team with other teams and groups of people. They really aren't together that much.
- Executives do not fit well into teams. They are pretty arrogant, probably don't play well in the sandbox together, and have to follow what the CEO says. I just don't see them as team players.

- At that level, there's more interest in who gets the credit for the job.
- They're not really all equals. Probably the chief financial officer or the chief nursing officer or someone like that is really viewed at a higher level than the others. Without equality, you can't get a team to work.

The professor replies, "Those are all good thoughts! The real challenge, from what I have experienced, has been participation—that is, active participation. If all the team members participate, then I can help them build an atmosphere of sharing. That's when the team becomes focused on shared goals and mutual trust."

TOO MANY MEETINGS today have a hypnotizing show-and-tell style: One by one, meeting attendees tell the others about their project and show (with PowerPoints and handouts) how the project is progressing. Questions and answers are volleyed, but often very little attention is given to identifying the problems that could arise, or have arisen, from the undertaking. No one asks about the details of or the reasons for the project, and few volunteer their help. And there is always the "sneak peek" at e-mails or texts. At the end of these meetings, people file out no more involved with others' projects. Consequently, when successes or failures happen, they become an individual's accomplishment or failure, rather than a team's celebration or setback.

Although the healthcare field prides itself on emphasizing individual authority and accountability (especially in a physician clinical environment), it should also support and encourage team dynamics. Building teams means encouraging efficiencies.

Teams are predestined for failure when they lack the fundamental values of teamwork: cooperation and sharing. Both elements require team members' willingness and the team leader's encouragement and support. Simply put, cooperation and sharing demand that team members sacrifice some of their individuality for the benefit of the entire team.

THE CONCEPT IN PRACTICE

Strengthen your team with the following strategies.

Build the Right Team from the Start

Most CEOs who come into an organization rebuild all or at least part of their executive team. They do this for two reasons: (1) to establish their mark on the organization and (2) to assemble a team of people who espouse similar values. Most executives who are tapped to become part of the new team are excited about the opportunity. Often, this excitement translates to wanting to share and cooperate.

When recruiting, leaders must consider people who believe in the concept of teams. They should evaluate prospective members with the following guidelines:

1. Ask prospects to recount an actual situation in which they worked with a team and by doing so

Team effort enhances . . .

Coordination, reducing bureaucracy. Assigning specific functions to people helps eliminate overlapping responsibilities, duplication of duties, and red tape.

Involvement and support. Because everyone works together toward a common goal, the focus shifts from receiving personal glory and recognition to supporting the team's objectives and valuing the contributions of others. "That's not my job" is replaced by "It's everybody's job."

General oversight, reducing problems that fall through the cracks. Everyone is involved in making sure that nothing is overlooked or undermined.

The joy of celebrations. One of the reasons sports bind people together is that everyone enjoys watching the exhilaration of team victories. An accomplishment is always grander when more people share and enjoy it because it represents the combination of each person's hard work, sacrifice, and dedication.

Creativity. When more people are involved, various perspectives and new ideas are generated and better results are achieved.

developed a solution that was much better than their own. Listen carefully for the candidate's behavior and their inclination—or disinclination—toward teamwork.

2. Ask prospects to recount an actual situation in which they had problems working with teams. Ask them how they handled their frustration.

3. Ask prospects to describe a situation in which team efforts do not work very well.

4. Ask prospects to name the values that drive effective team interaction (see chapter 17).

5. Administer a validated personality assessment, such as the Hogan Personality Inventory, to assess the prospect's personality and leadership style and how she would support effective team interaction.

6. When speaking to references, ask specific questions about team behavior. Ask references to describe how the prospect gets along with fellow team members. Ask for examples of how the prospect argues or debates issues during team sessions. A good idea is to ask the extent to which the prospect plays politics among fellow team members.

Understand Team Processes

Tuckman's (1965) well-known concept of forming, storming, norming, and performing is an easy-to-remember phrase describing how teams form and function. A more current view suggests that teams actually process their activities through two major steps—transition and action. Exhibit 13.1 shows these two activities and how they drive a team toward its goals. The two steps are tied to team goals. Knowing how these major functions work and the challenges they bring can be the key to achieving team success. Morgeson, DeRue, and Karam (2010, 7) write, "As teams work across the transition and action phases they encounter numerous challenges that arise from the team, organization, and environmental contexts in which the team is operating. These challenges can threaten team viability and make it difficult for them to accomplish their goals, in part because the challenges make it difficult for teams to regulate their goal-directed behavior." The next several suggestions help prevent these problems.

Discuss Team's Value and Values

All team members should learn their individual roles and expectations, evaluate their personal worth to the team, and participate in establishing the values that drive team interactions and behaviors. Doing so improves relationships and cooperation. Because team members are often so busy with their own daily activities, they may

---

Exhibit 13.1 How Teams Accomplish Their Goals

Transition: Teams evaluate their strategies and tactics then plan their actions to achieve their goals.

Action: Team members execute work activities that support the achievement of their goals.

Team goals

---

fail to invest the necessary time to fully grow and develop as a unit. The team atmosphere should encourage spirited but respectful debate, because better decisions emerge through this exchange.

Under an autocratic CEO, open discussion is unlikely to occur. Teams under such a leader are formed merely to fulfill an organizational convention. Members cannot, nor do they know how to, partake in actual decision-making. As a result, members are not aware of their roles and importance. Of course, the underlying problem in this scenario is the leader; however, such a team can be salvaged by a new leader, who can ingrain the values of teamwork with constant dialogue and team exercises.

Demonstrate the Value of "Teaming"

Team leaders must involve all members in setting achievable short-term goals. Achievement of these goals demonstrates the team's value and contribution to improving the organization. An effective leader can demonstrate the value of teaming by bringing tough issues to the group and asking every member to suggest solutions and alternatives. Too often, leaders prefer to handle especially difficult problems themselves or to delegate them to a small subset of the senior management team. Exhibit 13.2 lists strategies for increasing team member participation.

Determine the Purpose of the Team

Unfortunately, many teams do not know why they exist. When asked, most teams respond with, "We share information" or "We discuss strategy," while some say (perhaps mistakenly), "We run the organization."

Ideally, the team, as a unit, should determine its purpose; however, the leader could establish it as well. This purpose provides a framework for what the team must accomplish, so it must be clear and must be understood by every team member. Clarity of purpose prevents the team from taking on activities and goals (or prospective members) that are vague or inappropriate.

Engage in Team-Building Exercises

Any exercise that confirms the collective strength of the team, assesses the dynamics of the team, and aids in the interaction among members is beneficial. Common team exercises range from simple personality assessment tools (e.g., Myers-Briggs Type Indicator, DiSc) to

---

Exhibit 13.2 How to Increase Team Member Participation

Establish a clear connection between the team's purpose and activities and the organization's mission and vision. Members need to know not only what they are doing but also how their individual tasks tie in with the bigger goals.

Forge personal relationships with members. Genuine camaraderie is built on members' familiarity with each other's personal interests and pursuits.

Allow and encourage informal discussions (e.g., dialogue about children, movies, personal interests) before or after team meetings. Occasionally, food may be brought in or the group could conduct the meeting over an off-site lunch.

Reward and recognize hard work and accomplishments. A portion of the organization's incentive program should be allotted for team bonuses. If this policy is not an option, the team leader should plan and provide some other form of celebration.

Make team decisions within the confines of team meetings. Members must be present during deliberations and when a final decision is made; merely announcing the decision to the team will harm team morale and discourage future involvement of its members.

Treat all members equally. No one member should be a favorite, regardless of how frequently that person volunteers and how much that person contributes to the team function.

---

more sophisticated assessments (e.g., Hogan Personality Inventory; Hogan Development Survey; Hogan Motives, Values, Preferences Inventory) to extensive physical activities (e.g., Outward Bound).

These exercises offer practical knowledge and skills in a fun and relaxed environment. A note of caution is in order: The person who plans these activities must be an expert on the group's methods, team-building techniques, and objectives. Having a neutral third party to lead the team through these exercises is usually preferable—otherwise, the program could become an expensive time waster for all involved, or worse, could cause irreparable harm in team dynamics.

Confront Relationship and Conduct Issues

Conflicts between team members should be expected. Sometimes such clashes require the leader to intervene, such as when they create disruptions in team functioning. Other times, however, the team itself will police behaviors, discuss ways to stem the conflict, and dole out appropriate punishment if necessary.

Developing a team code of conduct is a valuable team-building exercise. Not only is this activity cooperative, but it also delineates the rules that protect members and monitor their behavior and interactions. Many senior management teams work together on a team code

Several years ago, I led a senior management team retreat. Before the retreat, I met individually with team members to ask them the following questions:

- What are the primary reasons for the existence of this senior management team?

- What are the primary reasons for the meetings of this senior management team?

- Does the content of the meetings support the primary reason for the existence of the team?

The responses were varied, but most members indicated that their reason for being was to "collectively lead the organization."

During the retreat, it was revealed that team meetings were show-and-tell sessions, not the mutual interaction that members envisioned. This revelation led to an in-depth discussion about the need to (1) shape and follow a clear purpose and (2) restructure meeting patterns. The team **decided to meet every other week solely to discuss strategy and to meet weekly to discuss day-to-day operations.**

This team, save for a few members who left to pursue other opportunities, remains intact today. The members report being closer and managing conflicts more effectively.

of conduct during their retreats. Exhibit 13.3 is an example of team conduct expectations; this code has been adopted by many healthcare organizations and is currently used by a midwestern health system. Another example, albeit focused on physician practices and developed by the American Medical Association, can be found at www.stepsforward.org/modules/conducting-effective-team-meetings.

Match Words with Actions

A team leader's words and actions carry greater weight than those of members. As such, the leader has to ensure that her behaviors are consistent with her messages, and both must be consistent with the organization's mission, vision, and values. Any discrepancies team members observe could, at best, become fodder for gossip and, at worst, weaken the trust and respect the leader worked hard to

---

Exhibit 13.3 Example of a Senior Management Team Code of Conduct

- Each of us has a right to his own opinion and has the right to state it. Each of us expects that others will carefully and respectfully listen to our opinion and seriously consider it before rejecting it.

- Although our CEO has the authority to make unilateral decisions, she will engage all of us in giving input in as many issues as possible. We respect her right to "some days count the votes and some days weigh the votes."

- We recognize that some decisions are better made with subsets of our team. However, except in unusual situations, we agree that these decisions will not be finalized until the entire team is notified and has the chance to provide final input.

- Each of us has the right to campaign for our issues outside of team meetings and meet individually with other team members to petition for support. However, we agree to tell the team that this campaigning has been done.

- Mystery, intrigue, and politics are fatal diseases. We will strive for openness, honesty, and tact.

---

establish. It could decimate the participative way of the team, with members perceiving that the leader only preaches about cooperation and sharing but does not really practice these team concepts.

Even in informal interactions, the leader must be watchful of his body language and casual banter to ensure that he remains appropriate, professional, and a role model for others on his team.

A classic example of how *not* to be a leader is Nathan Jessup, the fictitious well-decorated lieutenant colonel played by actor Jack Nicholson in the 1992 movie *A Few Good Men*. Here is how Colonel Jessup defends his leadership: "I have neither the time nor the inclination to explain myself to a man who rises and sleeps under the blanket of the very freedom I provide, then questions the manner in which I provide it! I'd rather you just said thank you and went on your way." Although Colonel Jessup has achieved much, he is not someone a team will choose as, or be proud to call, its leader.

Challenge the Current Boundaries

The hierarchy in every organization creates boundaries, including the following (Band 1994):

- Boundaries of authority—who is in charge of what?
- Boundaries of task—who does what?
- Boundaries of politics—what is our payoff?
- Boundaries of identity—who are we as a group?

Although boundaries are necessary, they can impede decision-making and workflow. The leader must allow team members to challenge these boundaries when necessary by setting "must" (critical) and "should" (recommended) guidelines. For example, the team *must* first gain approval from department directors before implementing a process, but the team *should* include all levels of employees in decision-making. In this way, the team knows which boundaries are off-limits and which are flexible. To promote cooperation, one leader tells his team: "I expect all of you to work together as though you had authority over the entire organization. Leave your claims of functional turf at the door."

This balance is often difficult. Hughes, Ginnett, and Curphy (2018, 511) describe organizations with a hierarchical culture as ones that have "formalized rules and procedures; they tend to be highly structured places to work. Following standard operating procedures, or SOPs, is the rule of the day. The emphasis is on ensuring continuing efficiency, smooth functioning, and dependable operations."

CONCLUSION

Decision-making, problem-solving, brainstorming, planning, and implementation are activities that are most effective when executed by a team, not by one person alone. Cooperation and sharing are team traits that do not happen without an open dialogue among team members and without support from the team leader.

Self-Evaluation Questions

❑ Has my team ever discussed its purpose?

❑ Do my team members truly believe in the value of teams?

❑ Do they believe in the value of team deliberations?

❑ Does my team regularly participate in team-building activities?

Cases

Case 13.1

Lakshmi Patel is the new CEO at a medical center. The agenda for her first meeting with the senior management team includes the following questions:

- What has been the primary purpose of the senior management meetings in the past? What was discussed? What was accomplished?

- What do you want to be the primary purpose of these meetings moving forward? What should we discuss? What should we accomplish?

- What meeting format do you prefer? Do you think that format will enable us to better meet our goals?

- Do each of you have a clear understanding of your roles? Do each of you help one another? How much cooperation and sharing should we expect from this team?

Case 13.1 Questions

1. You are one of Lakshmi's vice presidents. How would you answer these questions?

2. Should Lakshmi discuss these questions privately with each senior management member before raising them in the full group meeting (and therefore getting more open feedback than in an open meeting)? If so, how should she proceed after these private meetings?

Case 13.2

Cynthia Sanchez is the CEO of a large suburban community hospital. Her senior leadership team is made up of 17 people,

5 of whom report directly to Cynthia; the rest report to the chief operations officer. Every Tuesday, the entire 17-member team meets for two hours, and often the meetings run longer by about another hour.

During the meeting, Cynthia gives a summary of all the meetings she attended in the previous week. Then, she turns to the chief medical officer (CMO) to discuss physician issues and to the chief financial officer (CFO) to discuss the budget. During these conversations, no one else but Cynthia poses questions and comments to the CMO and the CFO. The rest of the group stays silent or prepares their own reports.

By the time Cynthia ends her conversation with the CMO and CFO, only 15 to 30 minutes are left. The team members then go around the table to give their respective department or project updates. Most team members use this time to tout their accomplishments, but no one pauses for congratulations or recognitions, as time is running out. During these updates, Cynthia is on her laptop, checking e-mail or answering correspondence. Occasionally, she asks for clarification or offers advice.

Recently, Cynthia hired Luann Crosby, an executive coach. Luann sat through one of these meetings. Afterward, Luann pulled Cynthia aside.

Luann. You know there was a problem with that meeting, right?

Cynthia. What do you mean? They're a little long, but no one complains about them.

(continued)

(continued from previous page)

Case 13.2 Questions

1. You are Luann. Give Cynthia an extensive diagnosis of the meeting. Include as many details in your diagnosis as possible.

2. Give Cynthia specific recommendations on improving the meeting.

3. How will you get Cynthia to buy into your suggestion? How will you coach her to gain buy-in from her team?

REFERENCES

Band, W. A. 1994. "Touchstones: Ten New Ideas Revolutionizing Business." In *Organizational Behavior*, 4th ed., edited by R. Kreiter and A. Kinicki. New York: Richard D. Irwin.

Hughes, R. L., R. C. Ginnett, and G. J. Curphy. 2018. *Leadership: Enhancing the Lessons of Experience*, 9th ed. Burr Ridge, IL: McGraw-Hill Education.

Katzenbach, J. R., and D. K. Smith. 1993. *The Wisdom of Teams: Creating the High-Performance Organization*. Boston: Harvard Business School Press.

Morgeson, F. P., D. S. DeRue, and E. P. Karam. 2010. "Leadership in Teams: A Functional Approach to Understanding Leadership Structures and Processes." *Journal of Management* 36 (1): 5–39.

Northouse, P. G. 2021. *Leadership: Theory and Practice*, 9th ed. Los Angeles: SAGE Publications.

Tuckman, B. W. 1965. "Developmental Sequence in Small Groups." *Psychological Bulletin* 63 (6): 384–99.

SUGGESTED READINGS

Balters, S., N. Mayseless, G. Hawthorne, and A. L. Reiss. 2021. "The Neuroscience of Team Cooperation Versus Team Collaboration." In *Design Thinking Research: Interrogating the Doing*, edited by C. Meinel and L. Leifer. Cham, Switzerland: Springer.

De Cooman, R., T. Vantilborgh, M. Bal, and X. Lub. 2016. "Creating Inclusive Teams Through Perceptions of Supplementary and Complementary Person-Team Fit: Examining the Relationship Between Person-Team Fit and Team Effectiveness." *Group Organization Management* 41 (3): 310–42.

Kukenberger, M. R., and L. D'Innocenzo. 2020. "The Building Blocks of Shared Leadership: The Interactive Effects of Diversity Types, Team Climate, and Time." *Personnel Psychology* 73 (1): 125–50.

Lanaj, K., and J. R. Hollenbeck. 2015. "Leadership Over-emergence in Self-managing Teams: The Role of Gender and Countervailing Biases." *Academy of Management Journal* 58 (5): 1476–94.

Morrison-Smith, S., and J. Ruiz. 2020. "Challenges and Barriers in Virtual Teams: A Literature Review." *SN Applied Sciences* 2 (6): 1–33.

Owens, B. P., and D. R. Hekman. 2016. "How Does Leader Humility Influence Team Performance? Exploring the Mechanisms of Contagion and Collective Promotion Focus." *Academy of Management Journal* 59 (3): 1088–11.

Reiter-Palmon, R., V. L. Kennel, and J. A. Allen. 2021. "Teams in Small Organizations: Conceptual, Methodological, and Practical Considerations." *Frontiers in Psychology* 12: 889.

Tannenbaum, S. I., A. M. Traylor, E. J. Thomas, and E. Salas. 2021. "Managing Teamwork in the Face of Pandemic: Evidence-based Tips." *BMJ Quality & Safety* 30 (1): 59–63.

Wankmüller, C., and G. Reiner. 2020. "Coordination, Cooperation and Collaboration in Relief Supply Chain Management." *Journal of Business Economics* 90 (2): 239–76.

Weer, C. H., M. S. DiRenzo, and F. M. Shipper. 2016. "A Holistic View of Employee Coaching: Longitudinal Investigation of the Impact of Facilitative and Pressure-Based Coaching on Team Effectiveness." *Journal of Applied Behavioral Science* 52 (2): 187–214.

White, B. A., J. Johnson, A. C. Arroliga, and G. Couchman. 2020. "Ad Hoc Teams and Telemedicine During COVID-19." *Baylor University Medical Center Proceedings* 33 (4): 696–98.

Zeuge, A., F. Oschinsky, A. Weigel, M. Schlechtinger, and B. Niehaves. 2020. "Leading Virtual Teams—A Literature Review." https://www.researchgate.net/profile/Andreas-Weigel/publication/343473371_Leading_Virtual_Teams_-A_Literature_Review/links/5f2bcb6392851cd302dfc180/Leading-Virtual-Teams-A-Literature-Review.pdf.

CHAPTER 14

Cohesiveness and Collaboration

Team-based organizations have faster response capability because of their flatter organizational structures, which rely on teams and new technology to enable communication across time and space.

—Peter G. Northouse (2021)

AT A FOCUS group during a leadership conference, Rakesh Jaya, facilitator and organizational development researcher, asked participants from different organizations to explain the structure and results of their own senior management meetings.

JAMES SMITH, CHIEF OPERATIONS OFFICER. All of our meetings are preplanned and highly structured. We don't meet unless there's a clear reason for it. We follow the agenda strictly and honor the time allotment for each agenda item. A detailed follow-up list is prepared at the conclusion of every meeting. Everyone is required to come well prepared for his or her reports and to participate in all the discussions.

MELANIE RODRIGUEZ, CHIEF EXECUTIVE OFFICER. Our team meets every two weeks, and the meetings last for four to six hours. Long ago, the team collectively decided that we wouldn't use an agenda because it's too limiting. Our meetings are open-ended, so we have the freedom to explore and deliberate on an issue fully. We arrive at many of our decisions this way, and we think this is a creative approach to thinking about and resolving our problems. We realize that this structure is not for everyone, so only the senior-level members of our team are invited to the meetings. But we do provide a summary of our discussions to the rest of the team, and they are encouraged to speak to their vice presidents if they have any concerns or comments.

AMY BRODERICK, CHIEF FINANCIAL OFFICER. I work for a large system, and our team is composed of 25 members. Every week, the chief executives from our nine hospitals meet for two hours to discuss strategic issues. Each of these meetings is focused on one issue and is led by a sponsor. This way, all team members have an opportunity to run a meeting and be well informed about at least one strategy. Then, every month, the entire 25-person team meets to exchange reports about business unit outcomes, ongoing and upcoming strategic initiatives, and some operations-related issues. If needed, we invite staff outside of the team to provide input and share information.

STEVE MICHAEL, SENIOR VICE PRESIDENT OF COMMUNICATIONS AND MARKETING. We built subgroups into our team to increase our efficiency and effectiveness. The subgroups meet every week, and they report their discussions and decisions to the full team when we all meet twice each month. Our CEO trusts our judgment and skills, so she gives us much autonomy but expects us to be accountable for our outcomes. Before the start of our monthly meeting, we open with a breakfast and the CEO says with a huge smile on her face, "Tell me something I don't know," then people start talking about their children's wedding or a movie they just saw. There's always an opportunity for us to get to know each other in a more personal way. We all know and respect each other, and I think that because of that we offer help to those who are struggling with their operations or projects.

MANY LEADERSHIP TEAMS in healthcare strive to capture the entrepreneurial spirit of successful businesses. This spirit makes a team cohesive, as it cheers team members on through conception, development, rollout, and marketing of new products or services. Unfortunately, this spirit is temporary and can be undermined by old-fashioned jealousy and selfish tendencies.

When a business expands its operation, new members are added to the existing team. Although a logical move, this addition could be destructive to the cohesiveness of the team, as current and new members feel tension or quarrel over whose ideas are better, who has the power to make decisions, who is responsible for which tasks, or what improvements need to be pursued (or not pursued). As the rift grows, member support for the common goal diminishes. Although cohesiveness increases team productivity, morale, and camaraderie, it does not prevent schism brought on by territorial battles and other issues. Exhibit 14.1 lists the downsides to cohesiveness.

Collaboration, on the other hand, pulls together divided parties to work toward a mutually accepted goal. It transcends traditional compromise in that no exchange of services is necessary to achieve the preferred outcomes of both parties; it demands only equal input and dedication to the cause. Most important, collaboration often results in conflict resolution.

> Team members (in shared leadership) step forward when situations warrant, providing the leadership necessary, and then step back to allow others to lead. Such shared leadership has become more and more important in today's organizations to allow faster responses to more complex issues.
>
> —Peter G. Northouse (2021)

Exhibit 14.1 Disadvantages of Team Cohesiveness

Low performance norms and poor performers. Performance norms are the standards expected from all team members. They dictate the quality and quantity of work—how vigorous, effective, and productive the work is; what goals should be achieved; and what contributions should be tendered. In a cohesive environment, these norms (primarily unwritten) are low. Highly competent members pick up the slack (perhaps even gladly) for members who have subpar abilities. As a result, those who need skills improvement remain undeveloped and dependent on the high achievers. In a contentious environment, however, low performance norms become a source of conflict. The best performers resent the fact that they have to cover for the poor performers. Worse, many competent members are too polite to deliver constructive criticism.

Proliferation of groupthink. Groupthink is, simply, unanimous thinking. When the team is cohesive, its members tend to lose their individual perspectives. As a result, new and creative thoughts are blocked off, objections are stifled, and concurrence becomes the standard. Instead of pursuing the goals of the organization as a whole, keeping the solidarity of the team becomes the team's main purpose.

Low tolerance for change. Founding team members are loyal to the initial team purpose, composition, rules, norms, and goals they helped establish. They believe that these components strengthen team cohesiveness, which is given high value. As such, they are uncomfortable with change, even when they recognize that evolution could improve team functions. New members are often viewed as disruptive outsiders and detrimental to the cohesiveness of the team.

Team goals take precedence over organizational goals. A highly cohesive team is fanatical about the welfare of its members. Some leadership teams have reduced clinical and support staff but maintained administrators. Some have paid executive bonuses despite financially tight years, a practice that has gained significant public disapproval.

Conflicting parties typically respond in one of the following ways:

- Avoid the other party and thus the conflict
- Give in to the demands of the other party

- Compete, with the goal to win
- Compromise or strike a deal
- Collaborate, with a goal to achieve

Consider the last three approaches. Competition is never an appropriate response because it amplifies the damage and makes it irreversible. Historically, compromise was often recommended, but it leaves both parties only partially satisfied and distorts the quid pro quo practice of "saving" favors (see chapter 15) to be redeemed in a later conflict. If neither party anticipates future dealings with one another, then a compromise is usually a better approach than collaboration. Conversely, if the parties continue their relationship and expect further dispute, then collaboration is the only responsible solution. The latter situation is the case with senior leadership teams.

Cohesiveness begets collaboration, and collaboration begets cohesiveness. Although one can exist without the other, one cannot be as effective without the other.

THE CONCEPT IN PRACTICE

Despite its disadvantages, cohesiveness is an important component of collaboration. The following methods can help in forming a cohesive and collaborative team.

Minimize Selfish Behavior

In teams, selfishness is a contagious disease that can easily spread to all members. The team leader, as the role model, must demonstrate that she works on behalf of others' interests, not just her own. If not, team members will suspect the leader's motives and cohesiveness will decline. The leader is also responsible for confronting members who contribute only to advance their own pursuits, not the team's. Appropriate team behavior must be established and put in writing—possibly during a retreat (see discussion about team code of conduct in chapter 13).

Assess the Size of the Team

Mergers and acquisitions, new service lines, and corporate partnerships extend the reach of an organization's leadership team and expand its size. As new members and responsibilities are added, the team loses its camaraderie and cohesiveness. A team that has more than 11 or 12 members often experiences a split, whereby the members form their own factions because they cannot find a commonality among the entire group. In a large team, the members also do not receive enough individual attention.

The generally accepted principle is that the team should have between 6 and 11 members. However, there is no ideal size. Here are several important considerations for setting the team size:

- If the task is repetitive, the team may have many members.
- If the task is complex, a large team can slow down the decision-making process.
- If a lot of collaboration is required, teams larger than 11 or 12 members can create problems.

If reducing the team size is not an option, the leader could manage perception about the size through the following approaches:

- Divide operations executives and strategy executives into two teams.
- Hold less frequent meetings with the entire team, but convene subgroups more often.
- Do not replace a team member when turnover occurs.

Get to Know One Another

Team leaders should socialize with members at every opportunity presented, including before or after meetings, organizational events, and informal celebrations. These interactions not only create a personal bond between the leader and members but also communicate that the leader is interested in the person behind the executive.

Consider the following bonding practices used by several successful leaders:

- Every fourth Friday, one CEO takes her senior management team to an off-site location for a full-day retreat. The first half (from breakfast until lunch) of the retreat is dedicated to business and operations. The second half is reserved for non-work-related matters, such as getting-to-know-you exercises.
- After its monthly meeting with the board, one leadership team spends the day at an off-site location to enjoy each other's company and catch up. The different venue serves to refocus the team and inspire creativity.
- One CEO holds a weekly no-agenda lunch session with his team, allowing team members to interact with one another in an informal setting.

Minimize the Influence of Cliques

Unfortunately, cliques are not confined to junior high school; they are prevalent in the workplace as well. The larger the organization, the larger the teams; the larger the team, the greater the possibility of cliques forming. Cliques are detrimental to any team because they represent cohesiveness without collaboration. That is, such groups are powerful because of their solidarity and focus on a common goal, but members of cliques fail or even refuse to partner with others to achieve that objective. Thus, they alienate others and disrupt the normal function of a team.

The leader can address the challenges of cliques in the team in several ways:

1. *Occasionally acknowledge the clique's existence during team meetings.* For example, one CEO announces (only half-jokingly), "I already know that the operations people have come to a conclusion on this matter a long time ago. Now I want to know what they talked about before this meeting!" By publicly recognizing the clique, the leader is making it clear that side negotiations will not be tolerated.

2. *Confront the clique privately.* Generally, a clique engenders negativity among team members because it has its own agenda. Divide and conquer could be one of the approaches a clique can use to sway the opinion of team members who are undecided about a certain decision or plan. By confronting the clique, the leader is directly appealing to its sense of propriety while strongly emphasizing the need to work together, not sabotage, team efforts. This confrontation must be done calmly so as not to widen the rift between the team and the clique.

3. *Assign clique members to a task force related to their area of expertise.* The goal of this strategy is to capitalize on the clique's strengths to benefit the team. Many members of

a clique are experts in their fields, and they withhold this knowledge from the team to further their own agendas. If the leader delegates them to a task force specific to their areas—for example, a clinical quality-improvement task force—clique members are more likely to apply their skills and abilities and teach other team members.

4. *Have an open discussion with the entire team about the damage a clique, or any subgroup, can inflict on cohesiveness and collaboration.* Such a discussion (which is a good topic for a retreat) is sensitive and should be done with an expert facilitator.

Discuss and Evaluate the Team's Purpose

Over time, the team's composition changes. As old members leave and new members take their place, the team's reason for being evolves as well. The team must regularly (annually, perhaps) redefine its purpose, reassess its goals, and reestablish its expectations. This discussion must involve all team members, because nothing inspires commitment more than 100 percent participation from those who embody the principles and implement the changes.

Treat All Members Fairly and Equally

An imbalance of power produces divisiveness, which is counter to the ideas of cohesiveness and collaboration. The fact that some members fill higher positions or have more organizational and community clout than do the rest of the team should not affect the way the leader regards all team members.

For example, if two members (say, the chief operations officer and the chief nursing officer)

> Group cohesion is the glue that keeps a group together. It is the sum of the forces that attract members to a group, provide resistance to leaving it, and motivate them to be active in it.
>
> —Richard L. Hughes, Robert C. Ginnett, and Gordon J. Curphy (2021)

commit the same indecent behavior (say, sexual harassment), the leader cannot excuse one but censure the other. Not only will this action spark a protest among the team, but it will also run counter to the service mission of both the team and the organization. The same can be said for personal relationships. The leader cannot pick and choose which member he will befriend or get to know better. Doing so will send a message that the leader plays favorites and will cause team members to distance themselves.

Designate a Team Role for Each Member

A team role is a specific character or function that each member consciously or unconsciously inhabits at any team gathering (e.g., meeting, retreat). Roles include cheerleader, devil's advocate, team conscience, team historian, and meeting planner. A member's personality or professional background lends itself to role assignment. For example, a member who has worked for the organization for 30 years could be named the historian.

Although seemingly simple, the practice of role designation reinforces members' sense of belonging to the group and clarifies their contributions.

Reassess the Compensation Policy

The organization's compensation structure indirectly affects team cohesiveness. That is, if the pay policy is designed primarily to recognize and reward individual performance, the message is that team participation and outcomes are not as valued. As a result, team members may reserve their best work for their own individual projects (the accomplishment of which will yield a bonus or raise) or develop hidden agendas that could conflict with the team's. Although compensation is beyond the purview of this book, money is an important consideration for the leader.

Rally the Team

As detailed in chapter 1, today's executives are faced with multidimensional and interrelated challenges. The most difficult times are always the most opportune times for the leader to pull the team together, especially if the team has experienced infighting and division.

Rallying the team should go beyond vocal cheerleading to boost morale, however. It should be backed up by practices that ease conflict and promote unity. For example, at the end of every meeting, the leader exclaims, "We're a great team! Let's get those quality numbers up!" However, at the next meeting, the leader publicly berates one group for the poor outcomes it achieved while exalting another group for its remarkable performance. Worse, he does not offer guidance or advice to those who are struggling. This leader's mixed message facilitates unhealthy competition, retards collaboration, and discourages improvement. At the end of the day, team members will hear, "We're a great team!," but not believe it.

CONCLUSION

Without cohesiveness and collaboration, a team is merely a collection of people who sit around a conference table when they are told to do so. Such a team produces nothing without difficulty and waste, which in turn cascade to the rest of the organization. More important, this kind of team does not advance the mission and vision of the organization or meet the needs of the community it supposedly serves.

Self-Evaluation Questions

- Why does my team meet? What do we accomplish when we meet?

- Would outside observers describe my team as cohesive?

- Has my team studied collaboration? Have we had training in conflict resolution?

- Consider the symptoms of groupthink listed earlier in this chapter. What symptoms does my team exhibit?

Case and Exercise
Case 14.1

St. Nicholas Health System is an integrated health delivery organization comprising St. Nicholas Medical Center, Suburban Western Health Center, Suburban East Health Center, St. Nicholas Employed Physician Practice, St. Nicholas HMO, and St. Nicholas Home Care and Durable Medical Equipment Corporation. The health system operates in a highly competitive city of 2.5 million residents.

Headed by CEO Serena Parris, the leadership group has 25 members, including the executive vice president and chief operations officer (EVP/COO), several system senior vice presidents, assorted system vice presidents, and the site administrators from each business unit. The senior team meets weekly to discuss tactical and strategic operations as well as ongoing projects (if time allows, which is rare).

The site administrators do not feel they are part of the executive team, given that they report to the COO and not to the CEO, and that most of the discussions relate to the system rather than the individual business units. In fact, at

St. Nicholas, much of the work is accomplished through interactions between the vice presidents or executive directors and administrators or middle managers. Because Serena is a hands-off leader, she has given her EVP/COO freedom to make ongoing operations decisions. The EVP/COO gives the site administrators much autonomy to run their own facilities.

Serena depends heavily on only three executives on the team—the EVP/COO, the senior vice president of medical affairs, and the chief financial officer. The rest of the 25-member team is aware that Serena has frequent daily communications with these three executives.

Case 14.1 Questions

1. What are the strengths of this team? Its weaknesses?

2. Do the site administrators belong to this group? Explain your answer.

3. What message does Serena send to her team by relying so much on three team members over everyone else?

4. If you were a consultant, what advice would you offer Serena to strengthen the team?

Exercise 14.1

Some leadership experts argue that members of the senior management team independently work on their own issues and come together only occasionally to coordinate organizational activities and set organizational strategy.

Consider the following thoughts regarding the work of senior leaders and their teams:

1. The job of a typical healthcare vice president has an individual focus. That is, she spends most of her

(continued)

(continued from previous page)

time on activities that have nothing to do with the work of the senior management team of which she is a member.

2. Working challenges faced at the middle management and frontline supervisory levels are usually short-term in nature (there is an immediacy to the nature of the issue), and the problems that must be solved are usually clearer. Issues at the senior management level are much grayer, involving strategy and longer-term decisions.

3. Compared with the problems faced by middle management, the challenges encountered by the senior management team require strategic (not operational), long-term responses. Similarly, the purpose of a senior management team (e.g., achieve a 4 percent margin) is more abstract than the purpose of any other organizational team.

4. Senior-level leaders have two, often overlapping, performance goals—a corporate goal and an individual goal.

5. At the senior leadership level, complementary skills are less important than position. In true team situations, the extra performance capability that a real team provides comes mostly from its complementary skills—that is, executives with clinical backgrounds are knowledgeable about patient care operations, while leaders with financial backgrounds are adept at business concepts.

6. Establishing and maintaining team standards of behavior are difficult for a senior management team

because this group meets less frequently than do other teams.

7. Members of senior management teams are not "mutually accountable" to each other; rather, they are individually accountable to the CEO. Mutual accountability is hard to establish because one executive has too many responsibilities.

Exercise 14.1 Questions
1. If these points are correct, how should senior executives enhance their working effectiveness? Can executives create real teams?

2. If you were starting an organization from scratch, how would you assemble the leadership team?

REFERENCES

Hughes, R. L., R. C. Ginnett, and G. J. Curphy. 2021. *Leadership: Enhancing the Lessons of Experience*, 9th ed. Burr Ridge, IL: McGraw-Hill Education.

Northouse, P. G. 2021. *Leadership: Theory and Practice*, 9th ed. Los Angeles: SAGE Publications.

SUGGESTED READINGS

Andrews, R., S. Greasley, S. Knight, S. Sireau, A. Jordan, A. Bell, and P. White. 2020. "Collaboration for Clinical Innovation: A Nursing and Engineering Alliance for Better Patient Care." *Journal of Research in Nursing* 25 (3): 291–304.

Dolan, K., V. Hunt, S. Prince, and S. Sancier-Sultan. 2020. "Diversity Still Matters." *McKinsey & Company.* Published May. https://static1.squarespace.com/static/561d0274e4b0601b7c814ca9/t/5ede28f14191b966b7436ae0/1591617786565/Diversity-still-matters-McKinsey+2020_06.pdf.

Kim, S., H. Lee, and T. P. Connerton. 2020. "How Psychological Safety Affects Team Performance: Mediating Role of Efficacy and Learning Behavior." *Frontiers in Psychology* 11: 1581.

Marler, H., and A. Ditton. 2021. "'I'm Smiling Back at You': Exploring the Impact of Mask Wearing on Communication in Healthcare." *International Journal of Language & Communication Disorders* 56 (1): 205–14.

O'Donovan, R., and E. McAuliffe. 2020. "Exploring Psychological Safety in Healthcare Teams to Inform the Development of Interventions: Combining Observational, Survey and Interview Data." *BMC Health Services Research* 20 (1): 1–16.

Shaeffner, M., H. Huettermann, D. Gebert, S. Boerner, E. Kearney, and L. J. Song. 2015. "Swim or Sink Together: The Potential of Collective Team Identification and Team Member Alignment for Separating Task and Relationship Conflicts." *Group and Organization Management* 40 (4): 467–99.

Tang, C. M., and A. Bradshaw. 2020. "Instant Messaging or Face-to-Face? How Choice of Communication Medium Affects Team Collaboration Environments." *E-learning and Digital Media* 17 (2): 111–30.

Whitelaw, S., A. Kalra, and H. G. Van Spall. 2020. "Flattening the Hierarchies in Academic Medicine: The Importance of Diversity in Leadership, Contribution, and Thought: The Authors Present a Rationale for Team-based Leadership in Medicine, Shifting Away from Traditional Hierarchical Leadership Models of Today. *European Heart Journal* 41 (1): 9–10.

CHAPTER 15

Trust

When you are not present, people can tell.
When you are, people respond.

—Amy Cuddy (2015)

MAJOR **MICHELLE HARRIS,** an Army Medical Service Corps officer, has just returned to the United States from a third deployment overseas. As a healthcare executive, she is active in her professional society's local chapter. In one meeting, she and Chuck Hall, a fellow executive, discuss the concept of trust in leadership.

CHUCK. Michelle, in your position, it must be great to simply give orders that your team won't question or distrust. I'd love to do the same in my hospital. But I have to sell every idea, earn my colleagues' trust every step of the way.

MICHELLE. No, that's not how it works in the military.[1] There's a book called *Leadership Lessons from West Point.* It points out that in the military, trust is even more critical than in civilian situations.

CHUCK. How so?

MICHELLE. In the military, we ask—note that I say "ask," not "command"—people to put their lives on the line, so we work harder to earn their trust. We provide constant training to ensure high levels of competency and safety. We demonstrate that we care about our people, and a high degree of openness can be observed in our training. We have to be on the same page, especially in combat situations. Everyone has a deep understanding of our missions and the dangers and payoffs they present. Movies about the military don't accurately depict the high levels of trust that underlie everything we do.

CHUCK. That's quite impressive. I'd like to invite you to speak to my senior management team next month, if you have time to spare.

TRUST IS THE first value all team members must learn. Without trust, team members engage in fierce competition, backstabbing, and hypocrisy (see exhibit 15.1).

Merriam-Webster's Collegiate Dictionary, Eleventh Edition, defines trust as the "assured reliance on the character, ability, strength, or truth of someone or something." In leadership teams, trust is the members' confidence in each other's ability and resolve to uphold the team's principles and to work toward its goals. It is what allows one member to vote for another's untested, seemingly outlandish proposal. It is what makes members stand behind their leader in moments of failure or scrutiny. Exhibit 15.2 enumerates the essential bases of trust, and exhibit 15.3 is a behavior guideline for all team members to promote a culture of trust.

Cuddy, Kohut, and Neffinger (2013) state that "trust also facilitates the exchange and acceptance of ideas—it allows people to hear others' message—and boosts the quantity and quality of the ideas

Exhibit 15.1 Consequences of Lack of Trust

- Team members keep important and relevant information to themselves for fear that others will steal or sabotage their ideas.

- The team leader or high-ranking team members undermine the suggestions or plans submitted by lower-level members.

- Competition for resources among team members is excessive.

- Side deals or negotiations constantly occur.

- Many team members are deliberately left out of the planning and decision-making processes.

- Cliques have more influence on and power over team members than does the leader.

- Political maneuvering is rampant and viewed as a necessary practice.

Exhibit 15.2 The Five Components of Trust

1. *Integrity*—honesty and truthfulness

2. *Competence*—technical and interpersonal knowledge and skills

3. *Consistency*—reliability, predictability, and good judgment

4. *Loyalty*—willingness to support, protect, and save someone else

5. *Openness*—willingness to share ideas and information freely

Source: Adapted from Robbins and Judge (2013).

that are produced within an organization. Most important, trust provides the opportunity to change people's attitudes and beliefs, not just their outward behavior."

An exchange of tangible or intangible favors or goodwill is common practice among team members. This transaction is modeled after the economics of bartering or the *social exchange theory*. This theory posits that individuals decide the fairness of a relationship on the basis of a self-measured give–take ratio. If a person thinks he

---

Exhibit 15.3 How Team Members Can Engender Trust

Speak your mind. The truth could hurt, but it could also pave a path for improved and increased communication. Be calm while you express yourself, and be receptive to the responses.

Maintain confidentiality. A lot of leadership team matters are confidential, and for good reason. Such matters, including informal or casual conversations, must not be discussed or shared.

Actively support the team. Do not refer to or speak about the team negatively, inside or outside the team setting. People's poor perception of the team extends to their poor perception of you, if only because you belong to the group.

Embrace openness. Trust develops in an open and candid environment.

Practice due process. In the team setting, due process means that all team members have the right to be heard fairly.

---

is giving more than he is receiving, he will perceive the exchange as unfair, and thus he may withdraw from giving. Conversely, if the person believes the things he gives and receives are of comparable value, he will continue the exchange relationship. The same idea is true of trust: It is a commodity that team members can exchange.

Unlike other favors, however, trust is not easily earned. A team member must prove her trustworthiness to the rest of the group by showing and having faith and concern; being transparent and accountable; providing support, assistance, information, and resources; and aligning with the general consensus without sacrificing personal values. More important, the team member must display these behaviors consistently and over time.

Once earned, trust must be maintained.

When team members cease to trade trust, a "depression" occurs, prohibiting members from cooperating, sharing information, and collaborating. It harms the cohesiveness of the unit and ultimately leads to various dysfunctions.

THE CONCEPT IN PRACTICE

The following approaches can enhance trustworthiness and trust levels among team members.

Acknowledge the Quid Pro Quo Practice

Honesty engenders trust. By publicly recognizing and discussing the fact that favors are exchanged to help forward the team's initiatives, team members can use that fact to achieve the most optimal outcomes. The concept may be woven into trust-building exercises.

Earn, Do Not Expect, Trust

Trust does not develop overnight, especially in a field such as healthcare that is in a constant state of flux. A leader cannot order her team members to trust her, nor can she think that trust comes automatically with the position. She must first assess her true self and either improve or maintain her trustworthiness. Trust building is a multistep and multiyear journey that can be easily derailed by a small move in the wrong direction.

Display Consistent Behavior

In some respects, trust is about predictability and consistency. Team members will be hard-pressed to have confidence in a leader who does not do what he says or is fickle, temperamental, indecisive, impulsive, or too spontaneous. Moreover, followers are discouraged

> People want to feel understood by their leaders. Trust comes before strength and it becomes a conduit of influence. Your strength is a little bit threatening before people trust you. But when they trust you and you are their leader, it's a gift to them. Presence allows you to build that trust because you are saying, "I'm here, I care about you. I'm listening and what I am telling you to do is not just based on my own personal opinion but what I'm observing and hearing from you."
>
> —Amy Cuddy (quoted in Schawbel 2016)

when the leader's words and deeds are contradictory. For example, one CEO declares that he wants to create a culture of empowerment, but he insists on reviewing everyone's work all the time and giving the final approval on every single decision. An erratic or unpredictable leader is viewed as unreliable and hence not deserving of trust.

Drive Out Fear

In his well-known book *The Five Dysfunctions of a Team*, Patrick Lencioni (2002, 43) presents a pyramid that shows his theory of the five types of dysfunction. Notably, he puts lack of trust at the bottom of the pyramid, indicating that it is the most serious of the five. Most readers would agree that when trust is absent in the work culture (or any culture for that matter), uncertainty and ultimately fear can easily develop.

Clearly, fear has no place on any team. Following are some strategies for driving fear away:

- Establish and sustain a culture in which people can express opinions, concerns, suggestions, and even dissent without putting their jobs, reputation, undertaking, or team membership in jeopardy.

- Do not discuss or negotiate anything in secret. Confidentiality is markedly different from secrecy, and the latter breeds suspicions, gossip, and disloyalty. Secrets are always revealed, and when they are, team members feel left out and threatened. Everyone on the team must practice transparency.

- Persuade members to participate in team activities. One leader holds "Think Out Loud" meetings, where the team brainstorms ideas. The goal of this session is to stimulate creative thinking and generate novel approaches to old challenges.

- Be accessible. The executive suite should not be a hiding spot; it should be one of the places a leader can be found, in addition to the hallways, patient care units, conference rooms, cafeterias, other people's work spaces, and so on. Presence at organizational events and community functions as well as the availability of contact information are two ways a leader can become more accessible.

Avoid the Perception and Reality of Conflict of Interest

Many situations in healthcare present a conflict-of-interest challenge because healthcare delivery and management entail so many types of exchanges, some of which could work in the self-interest of those involved in the exchange.

Full disclosure is one way to combat the perception of a conflict of interest. For example, the Cleveland Clinic now publicizes the business dealings of its physicians and other clinicians with drug and medical device makers. In April 2009, the Institute of Medicine issued the report *Conflict of Interest in Medical Research, Education and Practice* (Office of News and Public Information 2009). The report discusses how "disclosure by physicians and researchers not only to their employers but also to other medical organizations of their financial links to pharmaceutical, biotechnology, and medical device firms is an essential first step in identifying and managing conflicts of interest and needs to be improved."

Many healthcare organizations, including professional associations and healthcare businesses, already have a conflict-of-interest policy in place. However, more needs to be done in this area to minimize (if not eliminate) the risk of conflict of interest and its subsequent consequences to the reputation of the organization, its leaders, and its staff.

Be Candid

Candor is the sincerity and frankness of speech and behavior. It runs counter to lying, condescending, or exaggerating. Speaking candidly means

- retaining eye contact and a steady voice,
- stating facts and withholding opinions that could hurt,
- focusing on the situation and not going off on a tangent,
- inviting questions or comments, and
- giving the other person a chance to respond.

Retreats are optimal moments for candid discussions, as John Kotter (1996, 132) proposes in his book *Leading Change*: "Most of the time must be spent encouraging honest discussion about how individuals think and feel with regard to the organization, its problems and opportunities. Communication channels between people are opened or strengthened. Mutual understanding is enlarged. Intellectual and social activities are designed to encourage the growth of trust."

> Trust in a relationship generally develops gradually over time through the course of personal interaction. Taking some kind of risk in relation to the other person and feeling you weren't injured (emotionally or physically) in the process is what moves trust to new levels.
>
> —James M. Kouzes and Barry Z. Posner (2003)

Unfortunately, many team members recoil from voicing their opinions and concerns in front of the whole team, as my experience with leading senior management retreats has shown. Although these members were willing to be candid with me in private, they preferred not to speak when faced by the other members. To combat this phenomenon, I started meeting individually with team members before the retreat. I emphasized the merits of being open and honest, and I recruited them to contribute to the group dialogue. Also, I occasionally brought a list of concerns, with permission from the team, to serve as a starting point for our candid discussion.

Use Finesse

Finesse does not cost anything, but it is worth a small fortune. However, like a battery, finesse is negatively and positively charged. Dealing with someone with decorum and courtesy is a plus, but it can also be a minus: It can prohibit the confrontation needed to reveal underlying conflicts. For example, a cohesive leadership team that has been together for many years and has rarely argued over issues does not take kindly to confrontation. As suggested in chapter 14, a cohesive team does not necessarily make a productive team because many of its members have grown complacent; thus, the team can use a little shake-up once in a while. Having tact, however, prevents boorish behavior.

> High-performance teams are characterized by high mutual trust among members. That is, members believe in the integrity, character, and ability of each other. But as you know from personal relationships, trust is fragile. It takes a long time to build, can be easily destroyed, and is hard to regain. Also, since trust begets trust and distrust begets distrust, maintaining trust requires careful attention by management.
>
> —Stephen P. Robbins and Timothy A. Judge (2013)

Expect and Welcome Resistance

The process of earning trust—essentially, being open—puts a person in a vulnerable position. The leader (or a team member) should be prepared for criticism, doubt, resistance, and reluctance but should not take these responses personally. One CEO puts this risk in perspective: "If you want trust within your management group, you have to expect to get shot down sometimes. Then you get back up, thank the person who shot you, and move on."

Do Not Take Advantage

A leadership position offers many opportunities for inappropriate conduct. Sadly, in the past decade alone, high-level executives in and out of the healthcare field have exploited this truth. Taking advantage for the purpose of personal gain is wrong in any situation, as this act almost always has a victim. A leader could keep herself from taking advantage by obeying the golden rule of bartering: The exchange must be of equal value.

Grant Authority Appropriately

The power to bestow decision-making capabilities on team members falls on the leader, so he must exercise extreme care and judgment. Personal friendships, resentment or anger over past insults, and even lack of information can cloud the leader's ability to grant this authority. A poor choice can lead to infighting, charges of favoritism, and resistance. It could also erode the leader's trustworthiness. The best defense against such a scenario is always awareness and wisdom, which can come from being fully present physically, mentally, and emotionally.

Understand the Links Between Trust and Mission and Action

As this chapter's opening vignette indicates, military operations exemplify how trust is the basis of mission fulfillment. Trust essentially powers the actions that support the mission. Without trust, the action either does not occur or is performed haphazardly, causing grave harm. As retired Major General David Rubenstein, FACHE (2021), states:

> The first thing that comes to mind when talking about trust is the chain of events that occur in the Army from words to actions to trust to mission accomplishment. A soldier will hear his or her leader's words but waits to see the leader's actions. When action matches words, the soldier starts to build a trust that says, "I'll go in harm's way to do my job because I trust you." When I hand my static line to the jumpmaster, 800 feet above the ground on a moonless night, I'm saying, "I'm ready

to jump out of this plane because I trust you've ensured that my equipment and I are ready." And always remember, people should be the number one priority.

CONCLUSION

Trust is the assurance of goodwill between two people. It builds over time and must not be taken for granted. Trust among team members is a commodity that can be traded, facilitating ongoing relationships and improving the likelihood of collaboration, cooperation, and sharing of information.

Lacking trust is like walking into a room full of complete strangers. You have a problem: You need to finish an important project, but you have no time to do so. Imagine asking these strangers in the room to help you. Imagine handing them the incomplete work. Imagine sharing with them valuable and confidential information about the project. Imagine encouraging them to collaborate and cooperate with each other. Imagine giving them a quick deadline. Imagine doing all of this without feeling paranoid, doubtful, desperate, exasperated, and doomed.

Self-Evaluation Questions

❑ How is trust displayed among my team members? Do we barter trust, and do we understand its function in the team?

❑ Is my leadership style marked by openness and honesty? Do others easily approach me?

❑ To what extent am I known as a good team player?

❑ Is my communication with the team candid and straightforward? To what extent do I encourage this communication style?

Team Evaluation Questions

To what extent do team members

- ❑ believe in each other's abilities and competence?
- ❑ believe in each other's inclinations and intentions?
- ❑ believe in each other's integrity?
- ❑ get along with each other?
- ❑ share the same goals?
- ❑ rely and depend on each other?
- ❑ have confidence in each other's motives and behaviors?

Cases

Case 15.1

New CEO Doug Wright has a problem. His leadership team displays dysfunctional behaviors. Infighting is rampant, and cooperation and sharing of information are nonexistent. At meetings, most team members do not participate in the discussion, resigned to sitting quietly after they give an update on their respective responsibilities. Recently, two chief executives suddenly quit, leaving the other team members gossiping about the reasons.

Doug has spoken to the team (both as a group and individually) at length about the problem. He has touted the values of openness, honesty, and trust. He has encouraged the team members to speak their minds and has informed them of the no-recrimination policy he has just instituted. But still, the team seems removed, content with doing as it is told.

Frustrated, Doug contacts Roxanne Samanski, an organizational development consultant. The first question he asks her is, "Shall I fire all of them and start fresh?"

Case 15.1 Questions

1. If you were Roxanne, how would you respond to Doug? What suggestions would you offer?

2. What role does lack of trust play in this situation?

3. Do you think it's important to find out the history of this team to understand its current dysfunctions?

Case 15.2

Ralph O'Riley is a dynamic CEO of a large for-profit system. He is well known in the community. He is a brilliant businessman, and he is highly rewarded for it, enjoying various perks such as a beautifully appointed office suite, a company car, and a parking spot right outside the hospital entrance.

He rarely attends employee-related functions, and he only occasionally visits the other facilities in the system, let alone the units on his own campus. He is a mythical figure among employees and intimidates his own leadership team. He shows up to meetings late, relies on his chief executives to "fill him in on the agenda," and does not know all of his staff members' names or positions. He does not participate in operational discussions, but he gives orders that affect operations, something that confounds his team and angers the rank and file.

Once during a retreat, Ralph was overheard by some of his team members boasting about his golf game and his power. "This is a waste of my time," he complained over his cell phone. "It's not PC to say it, but I own these people. They do what I tell them to do. I made a lot of money for this system. Now they should give me a break."

(continued)

(continued from previous page)

Case 15.2 Questions

Obviously, everything Ralph is seems to run counter to the practices that build and enhance trust.

1. What long-term effects does Ralph's behavior have on his team, the employees at large, and the organization as a whole? Are these effects irreversible?

2. Ralph is clearly a financial wizard and has great business instincts. How should he leverage these competencies to create a better culture? To make himself even more powerful by being approachable and trustworthy?

3. What role does power play in Ralph's success?

Case 15.3

Review the following article:

Ahern, S., and E. Loh. 2021. "Leadership During the COVID-19 Pandemic: Building and Sustaining Trust in Times of Uncertainty." *BMJ Leader* 5: 266–69. https://bmjleader. bmj.com/content/early/2020/09/29/leader-2020-000271.

Case 15.3 Questions

1. How has the COVID-19 pandemic changed the culture of trust for healthcare leaders?

2. What specific steps should healthcare leaders take to ensure that trust is apparent when a work crisis occurs?

3. How do the concepts of trust and hope intersect?

NOTE

1. The opening vignette in this chapter represents the contributions that military officers bring to healthcare leadership and the healthcare field. It highlights the importance of trust in the military and its applicability to civilian leadership. Attendees at American College of Healthcare Executives events (especially the annual Congress on Healthcare Leadership) see and learn from many of these military leaders.

   The vignette is based on a true story. Healthcare leaders in the armed forces do not work in a top-down, command-and-control environment. Obviously, a certain amount of discipline and authority exists in the military, but the dynamic is nothing like many believe. Military healthcare leaders have to cultivate a high trust level while developing the same competencies as civilian healthcare executives. My work with leaders in the Medical Service Corps, the Medical Corps, and the Army Nurse Corps over the past 35 years tells me they are exceptional leaders. I thank them and applaud their service, sacrifice, and dedication.

REFERENCES

Cuddy, A. 2015. *Presence: Bringing Your Boldest Self to Your Biggest Challenges.* New York: Little, Brown and Company.

Cuddy, A. J. C., M. Kohut, and J. Neffinger. 2013. "Connect, Then Lead." *Harvard Business Review.* Published July. https://hbr.org/2013/07/connect-then-lead.

Kotter, J. 1996. *Leading Change.* Boston: Harvard Business School Press.

Kouzes, J. M., and B. Z. Posner. 2003. *Credibility: How Leaders Gain and Lose It, Why People Demand It*. San Francisco: Jossey-Bass.

Lencioni, P. 2002. *The Five Dysfunctions of a Team: A Leadership Fable*. San Francisco: Jossey-Bass.

Merriam-Webster, Inc. 2014. Merriam-Webster's collegiate dictionary. Springfield, Mass: Merriam-Webster, Inc.

Office of News and Public Information. 2009. "Voluntary and Regulatory Measures Are Needed to Reduce Conflicts of Interest in Medical Research, Education, and Practice." The National Academies. Published April 28. www8.national academies.org/onpinews/newsitem.aspx?RecordID=12598.

Robbins, S. P., and T. A. Judge. 2013. *Essentials of Organizational Behavior*, 12th ed. Upper Saddle River, NJ: Prentice Hall.

Rubenstein, D. 2021. Personal communication with author, November 30.

Schawbel, D. 2016. "Amy Cuddy: How Leaders Can Be More Present in the Workplace." *Forbes*. Published February 16. www.forbes.com/sites/danschawbel/2016/02/16/amy -cuddy-how-leaders-can-be-more-present-in-the-workplace /#4d39bef166ce.

Scholtes, P. R. 1998. *The Leader's Handbook: Making Things Happen, Getting Things Done*. New York: McGraw-Hill.

SUGGESTED READINGS

Afsar, B., and W. A. Umrani. 2020. "Does Thriving and Trust in the Leader Explain the Link Between Transformational Leadership and Innovative Work Behaviour? A Cross-sectional Survey." *Journal of Research in Nursing* 25 (1): 37–51.

Ahern, S., and E. Loh. 2021. "Leadership During the COVID-19 Pandemic: Building and Sustaining Trust in Times of Uncertainty." *BMJ Leader* 5: 266–69.

Anderson, C., and S. Brion. 2014. "Perspectives on Power in Organizations." *Annual Review of Organizational Psychology and Organizational Behavior* 1: 67–97.

Cook, A., A. Zill, and B. Meyere. 2020. "Observing Leadership as Behavior in Teams and Herds—An Ethological Approach to Shared Leadership Research." *The Leadership Quarterly* 31 (2): 101296.

Crandall, D. (ed). 2006. *Leadership Lessons from West Point*. San Francisco: Jossey-Bass.

Gardner, W. L., E. P. Karam, M. Alvesson, and K. Einola. 2021. "Authentic Leadership Theory: The Case for and Against." *The Leadership Quarterly* 32 (6): 101495.

Homan, A. C., S. Gündemir, C. Buengeler, and G. A. van Kleef. 2020. "Leading Diversity: Towards a Theory of Functional Leadership in Diverse Teams." *Journal of Applied Psychology* 105 (10): 1101–1128.

Murphy, K. R. 2020. "Performance Evaluation Will Not Die, but It Should." *Human Resources Management Journal* 30: 13–31.

Pfeffer, J. 1992. *Managing with Power: Politics and Influence in Organizations*. Boston: Harvard Business School Press.

Saxe-Braithwaite, M., and S. Gautreau. 2020. "Authentic Leadership in Healthcare Organizations: A Study of 14 Chief Executive Officers and 70 Direct Reports." *Healthcare Management Forum* 33 (3): 140–44.

Simha, A., and J. Pandey. 2021. "Trust, Ethical Climate and Nurses' Turnover Intention." *Nursing Ethics* 28 (5):714–22.

Singh, P. 2020. "Why COVID-19 Pandemic Builds a Convincing Case for Investing in 'Young Physician Leaders (YPL).'" *Journal of Family Medicine and Primary Care* 9 (11): 5432–34.

CHAPTER 16

Conflict Management

Although conflict can be uncomfortable, it is not unhealthy, nor is it necessarily bad. The question is not "How can people avoid conflict and eliminate change?" but rather "How can people manage conflict and produce positive change?"

—Peter G. Northouse (2021)

NEWLY HIRED JACK Lewis is a vice president of nursing clinical quality and education. Among his many responsibilities are nursing education and supervision of the clinical nurse specialists (CNSs). During his orientation, Jack rotated through various patient care units, talking with the managers and staff about his goals for improved patient safety and quality and a more comprehensive and coordinated nursing education program. Throughout his visits, he was well received by all staff. One week after his visit to surgery, he received the following e-mail from Margaret Strong, the vice president of surgical nursing. Margaret reports to Mike Volkman, the chief operations officer, and not to Lisa Apolinario, the chief nursing officer who is Jack's boss:

Jack,
I appreciate your enthusiasm for nursing quality and education. I must tell you that surgical nursing is different from the

rest of nursing at the hospital. Surgery does not have a need for your services. I have talked to Mike and Lisa, and it has been decided that the CNSs who work in surgery will now be under my direct supervision effective immediately. Please do not plan any nursing education or quality improvement programs for surgery because we intend to continue to use our own courses. Thank you for your attention to this matter.

Margaret

CONFLICT IS THE natural byproduct of the human thought process. It is present in us and is exacerbated by our interactions. The workplace, especially where decisions are made and implemented, hosts various kinds of conflict. How big a conflict becomes and how fast it spreads depend on the number of people involved, the situation's degree of difficulty, and the power structure in place.

Healthcare management is a breeding ground for conflict, as its issues span from operational to strategic and all points in between and even beyond. Such conflicts require leaders to be engineers of consent. That is, they must invite others to suggest solutions, guide that discussion, build consensus, and manage the discord that arises.

A conflict management guideline will help the leader and management team in this regard. Such a document, however, was shunned for years by many organizational leaders. They knew it was a critical instrument, but they offered myriad excuses for not creating one, including lack of time and few incidents of conflict. Fortunately, in 2009, The Joint Commission issued a mandate: All hospitals and health systems must develop and put into practice a guideline for managing conflict in leadership

> When engaging in conflict with peers, be careful not to allow your words or actions to cross into areas that might be perceived as unethical. In the heat of the moment, the lines between effective politicking and office sabotage can blur quickly, so leaders should have a mental checklist that they go through when they engage with a colleague.
>
> —Carson F. Dye and Brett D. Lee (2016)

teams. Recognizing that leadership conflicts can endanger human lives, The Joint Commission (2015, 106) states: "Conflict commonly occurs even in well-functioning hospitals and can be a productive means for positive change. However, conflict among leadership groups that is not managed effectively by the hospital . . . has the potential to threaten health care safety and quality. Hospitals need to manage such conflict so that health care safety and quality are protected. To do this, hospitals have a conflict management process in place."

HOW CONFLICT IS BENEFICIAL

Conflict is not fundamentally good or bad. After all, conflict represents our ability to reason, to work through a maze of possibilities and impossibilities. Also, it signifies the diversity of our perspectives, interests, and experiences. However, conflict can cause difficulty when not properly addressed.

In team functions, conflict also presents benefits, such as the following:

- *Ends complacency.* Conflict opens team members' eyes. They begin to see obstacles, inefficiencies, outdated practices, improprieties, and the like.

- *Starts dialogue.* Conflict almost always triggers a discussion—often heated and often generating more conflict. The once-quiet majority (or minority) then adds its voice to the conversation. Everyone really has something to say.

- *Activates a plan.* Conflict typically causes action; the action planned often is the solution to the conflict.

- *Forces participation.* The progression of conflict among team members often means that the conflicting parties will work together on the solution.

The ultimate problem with conflict is that it intimidates many people. Thus, it is seldom addressed—and inappropriately at that. Typically, minor conflicts—those that have no lasting implications—are ignored because they usually resolve themselves. However, over time, even minor conflicts (if persistent and repetitive) have the potential to turn major and corrupt and disrupt the team's performance and purpose.

THE CONCEPT IN PRACTICE

Following are strategies for preventing and responding to team conflicts.

Create a Conflict Management Policy

The first step toward conflict management is acknowledging that conflict inevitably occurs when intelligent, opinionated people converge. The second step is developing rules so that when a conflict does occur, all members can debate, deliberate, and compromise accordingly. These rules should be reviewed regularly by all members, and new members must be informed of their existence. Exhibit 16.1 is an example of conflict management guidelines.

Root Out the Potential Causes of Conflict

Meeting format and length, team size and composition, and member assignments and responsibilities are petri dishes for conflict. The leader should observe these areas for potential and hidden troubles that render the team ineffective. For example, if the team meets too often, team members are not given the time to do their work. Similarly, if vocal members dominate every team discussion, the rest of the group may harbor resentment for not having the chance

Exhibit 16.1 Conflict Management Guidelines

1. *Declare the conflict.* Not all discussions during group interaction are conflict oriented. When a struggle ensues, however, someone must inform everyone that a conflict has arisen so that proper procedures can be followed. Although this kind of statement may sound trite, it can become a powerful tool for managing conflict appropriately.

2. *Give the reason for the conflict.* Although disagreements and arguments are normal and necessary, they should not be initiated out of caprice or malice. Strife, hostility, and animosity must still be avoided at all cost, but if they do surface the reason (or reasons) for them must be stated.

3. *Clarify the issues of the conflict.* A neutral group member or one who is not directly embroiled in the conflict must be elected to clarify contentions and interpret ambiguities. All members must actively participate in the discussion or debate and specify in detail their issues. Although members are entitled to express their personal concerns or emotional responses, facts (not opinions) must govern the debate.

4. *Address one issue at a time.* To ensure appropriate and thoughtful consideration of all issues, only one issue at a time must be considered. Many people prefer to save their issues and raise them all during debates, but that practice should not be allowed or tolerated. All members should address their concerns as they occur.

5. *Require all members to participate in the debate.* No party in the dispute is allowed to "pull in his head" during the conflict. All members must give their opinion and not cower behind others on their side.

6. *Be fair.* Members must keep their "weapons" appropriate to the level of the fight. In other words, no personal attacks are allowed in a strictly professional discussion, and each party is given an opportunity to respond to accusations and defend itself.

7. *Declare that the conflict is over.* All members must know that the debate has ended and an outcome has been reached. The outcome agreement should be specifically defined so that no confusion, which could escalate into another conflict, will arise later.

to talk, which discourages their participation. See exhibit 16.2 for more causes of conflict.

The point here is that a leader can be more proactive in managing conflict if she knows where it usually starts.

Adopt a Format That Works for the Team

Team members should help establish a format for the meetings. This way, they are more apt to uphold it. For example, each meeting is run by a team member, who also creates the agenda, invites guests if needed, distributes necessary materials before the meeting, leads the discussions, and so on. No matter the format suggested, the leader should make every effort to adopt one that promotes involvement, reduces cynicism, and benefits the attendees.

Exhibit 16.2 Reasons for Conflict

- Incompatible personalities or value systems
- Overlapping or unclear job boundaries
- Competition for limited resources
- Inadequate communication
- Interdependent tasks (e.g., one person cannot complete his assignment until others have completed their work)
- Organizational complexity (i.e., the greater the decision-making layers and special requirements, the greater the conflict)
- Unreasonable or unclear policies, standards, or rules
- Unreasonable deadlines or extreme time pressure
- Collective and consensus decision making
- Unmet expectations
- Unresolved or suppressed tension

Source: Adapted from Kreitner and Kinicki (2012).

Practice Directspeak

Management teams whose members challenge one another's thinking develop a more complete understanding of the choices, create a richer range of options, and ultimately make the kinds of effective decisions necessary in today's competitive environments.

—Kathleen Eisenhardt, Jean Kahwajy, and L. J. Bourgeois III (1997)

Directspeak, a term I coined for speaking directly and clearly, is a straightforward manner of communicating without being insensitive. Directspeak does not work everywhere, but it thrives in team settings in which trust prevails, because every member of these teams knows that confrontations are never meant to be personal attacks. See exhibit 16.3 for a guide to Directspeak. CEOs or team leaders must be aware that some team members are uncomfortable with this technique, toe the line to avoid offending others, and are not active participants in debates. Conversely, some members are strong-willed and more verbal, which may intimidate the mild-mannered members. What results is another conflict: a personality conflict.

Exhibit 16.3 How to Practice Directspeak

Do	Don't
Speak with precision and clarity	Speak with vagueness and ambiguity
Make sure the debate takes place in the room	Allow the debate to take place in the hallway
Invite all questions	Make some questions off-limits
Keep discussion impersonal	Allow personal smears
Begin with the end in mind	Make us guess where you're going
Say something if you feel strongly about it	React strongly later in the conversation
Ask for clarification if needed	Assume or wait for a later time
When asked a question, answer it directly	Take the long way around to the "yes," "no," or "I don't know"

Prohibit Personal Attacks

Strong personalities (and hence opinions) can usher in conflict. One way to minimize personality-induced conflict is to keep the discussion focused on the issues, not the people. The leader should step in when inappropriate comments are introduced. Spirited debates are invigorating, especially if they do not include personal attacks. When team members veer off topic, the leader (e.g., CEO) could get up and jot down on the flip chart the goals of the discussion. His movement alone—not to mention that fact that he is pointing out the meeting's objectives—is often enough to rein in the chaos.

Choose a Collaborative Approach

As mentioned in chapter 14, the five usual reactions to conflict are as follows:

1. Avoid the other party and thus the conflict
2. Give in to the demands of the other party
3. Compete, with a goal to win
4. Compromise or strike a deal
5. Collaborate, with a goal to achieve

These responses illustrate the sink-or-swim mindset among team members.

Avoidance is valid only when the conflict is too minor to merit full-time consideration—that is, when the problem will resolve itself without intervention. Giving in or surrendering is tied to the system of bartering favors (see chapter 15). Although well employed by teams, bartering is a temporary fix and could lead to more conflict if not executed appropriately. Competition, sometimes called *forcing*, creates an all-or-nothing environment in which team members do everything possible to defeat their perceived enemies. In this sense, team meetings become a personal battlefield where members show off their achievement to gain more power. Compromise, while democratic, stalls conflict resolution because it relies on too many people and too many variables.

Collaboration usually bests all other responses. It is a mature approach, not merely a reaction, to conflict that yields long-term benefits. The leader should verbalize her support of collaboration and put in place goals and activities that require inter-disciplinary partnerships.

A very popular research tool called the Thomas-Kilmann Conflict Mode Instrument (TKI) presents a solid model for understanding conflict. Essentially, it suggests that people's behavior when interacting stems from one of two basic dimensions—their desire to satisfy their own concerns (measured by their degree of personal assertiveness) or their willingness to satisfy the other person's concerns (measured by their degree of cooperativeness). Exhibit 16.4 shows this relationship.

> Teams must agree on how they will work together to accomplish their purpose and goals. Real team members always do equivalent amounts of real work beyond and between meetings where things are discussed and decided. Over time, a team's working approach incorporates a number of spoken or unspoken rules that govern contribution and membership.
>
> —Douglas K. Smith (1996)

The TKI suggests that five conflict styles emanate from this dynamic: competing (satisfying your own concerns), accommodating (sacrificing your concerns to meet the concerns of others), avoiding (ignoring the conflict), collaborating (finding a solution that is fully win-win for both parties), and compromising (finding a solution that is a partial win-win for both parties). Leaders can learn much about conflict by studying these concepts. Sample TKI assessments can be found on the Internet and are excellent tools for team building.

Visualize the End of the Conflict

Conflict has a beginning. That's the bad news. The good news is it also has an end. By visualizing the ideal outcomes of a conflict, the team is also generating ideas to prevent and manage it. For example, if the desired or visualized outcome is regular and relevant

Exhibit 16.4 Thomas-Kilmann Conflict Mode Instrument

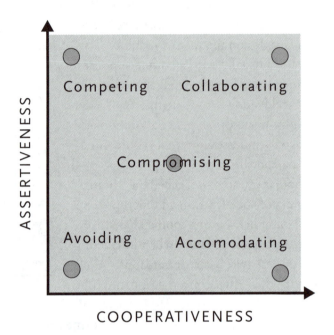

Source: Adapted from Thomas and Kilmann (2022). www.kilmanndiagnostics.com/ overview-thomas-kilmann-conflict-mode-instrument-tki.

communication between physicians (through the chief medical officer) and the C-suite, then the team could work backward, analyzing the causes of the conflict, brainstorming practical solutions, developing action steps, and assigning responsibilities for implementing those steps. Although conflicts do end, the end still has to be closely monitored to ensure that the same conflicts do not resurface.

CONCLUSION

To a strong team, conflict is a temporary foe but a permanent ally. To a weak team, it is a predator. Regardless of its role, conflict is an inevitable occurrence in organizational life. Teams must understand that it is under their control.

Self-Evaluation Questions

❑ How does my team manage conflict? Is our approach working? If not, why not?

❑ What is my personal conflict management style? Is it working?

❑ Does my team suppress conflict? Why?

❑ Has my team established a conflict management policy? Was it developed for the team's sake, or to comply with requirements of The Joint Commission?

❑ How has conflict affected me personally?

Cases and Exercise

Case 16.1

Professor William Bligh, a retired ship captain, writes the following on the board:

- Power and influence
- Bigger is better
- Anger
- Emotional intelligence
- Bargaining
- Bullying
- You scratch my back and I'll scratch yours
- Scorekeeping

Then he addresses the class: "Write a ten-page paper about how each of these concepts contributes to team conflict.

(continued)

(continued from previous page)

I expect to see your papers in two days. Class dismissed."
Give thought to what the students might prepare. How
might the answers from a class of older, part-time students
in a master's of health administration program be different
from those given by people in a full-time residential program
where most students are in their early twenties?

Consult the following books to gain a better understanding of team conflict:

Fisher, R., and W. L. Ury. 2011. *Getting to Yes: Negotiating
Agreement Without Giving In*, 3rd ed. New York: Penguin.

Patterson, K., J. Grenny, R. McMillan, and A. Switzler. 2005.
*Crucial Confrontations: Tools for Resolving Broken Prom-
ises, Violated Expectations, and Bad Behavior*. New York:
McGraw-Hill.

The Arbinger Institute. 2020. *The Anatomy of Peace: Resolving
the Heart of Conflict*, 3rd ed. Oakland, CA: Berrett-Koehler
Publishers.

Wisdom, J. 2020. *Millennials' Guide to Management & Leadership: What No One Ever Told You About How to Excel as a
Leader*. New York: Winding Pathway Books.

Case 16.2

Jessica, Brianna, Ruth, and Zachary are assistant vice presidents
in a large teaching hospital. Every month, they gather with their
mentor, Dr. Lon Right, to talk about the challenges they face
on the job and the trends in management and leadership. This
month, they are discussing the book *Crucial Confrontations*.

Dr. Right. On the basis of our reading, what should be the ultimate goal in resolving conflict?

Jessica. To resolve the conflict and get compromise on the matter. Get the parties to meet halfway and then move on.

Brianna. I totally disagree. Compromising often means that you get poor results. Solving conflict does not mean you should give up on your key principles.

Zachary. I can see both sides. The real goal of conflict management, though, is to mount the debate but to do it in a respectful manner. Get the issue on the table, agree clearly on what the end goal is, and then hammer out the solution.

Ruth. In my view, practically all conflict is a classic power struggle. Human beings resolve these power struggles through fighting for their right to be heard. Compromises don't always happen, but what the book teaches us is how to negotiate with others so that we don't damage the relationships we worked hard to build.

Case 16.2 Questions

1. Is the ultimate goal of conflict management winning an argument, preserving a relationship, compromising on a solution, or all of these?

2. What lessons from this chapter and from *Crucial Confrontations* can be applied to your conflict management efforts?

(continued)

(continued from previous page)

Exercise 16.1

Read the vignette in the beginning of the chapter and answer the following questions:

1. What kind of conflict is present in this situation?

2. What are the short- and long-term effects of this conflict on the two nurse leaders involved, their chief executives, and the education of the CNSs?

3. What should Jack's next step be?

4. What organizational structure issues exist that gave rise to this conflict? How may they be resolved?

5. The vignette illustrates an age-old story of strife between line and staff. What are some ways that these stresses can be avoided?

REFERENCES

Dye, C. F., and B. D. Lee. 2016. *The Healthcare Leader's Guide to Actions, Awareness, and Perception*, 3rd ed. Chicago: Health Administration Press.

Eisenhardt, K. M., J. L. Kahwajy, and L. J. Bourgeois, III. 1997. "How Management Teams Can Have a Good Fight." *Harvard Business Review* 75 (4): 77–85.

Joint Commission. 2015. *Hospital Accreditation Standards*. Oak Brook Terrace, IL: The Joint Commission.

Kreitner, R., and A. Kinicki. 2012. *Organizational Behavior*, 10th ed. Burr Ridge, IL: McGraw-Hill Education.

Northouse, P. G. 2021. *Leadership: Theory and Practice*, 9th ed. Los Angeles: SAGE Publications.

Smith, D. K. 1996. *Taking Charge of Change: 10 Principles for Managing People and Performance*. New York: Addison-Wesley.

Thomas, K. W., and R. H. Kilmann. 2022. "An Overview of the Thomas-Kilmann Conflict Mode Instrument (TKI)." Accessed November 28. https://kilmanndiagnostics.com /overview-thomas-kilmann-conflict-mode-instrument-tki/.

SUGGESTED READINGS

Gardner, W. L. 2019. "Riddle Me This: What Do Top Management Team Boundary Spanning, Team Conflict Trajectories, Team Creativity, Faultlines, Grit, and Global Virtual Teams, Have in Common? Answer: Outstanding 2019 *GOM* Articles." *Group & Organization Management* 45 (6): 747–61.

Johansen, M. L., and E. Cadmus. 2016. "Conflict Management Style, Supportive Work Environments and the Experience of Work Stress in Emergency Nurses." *Journal of Nursing Management* 24 (2): 211–18.

Johnson, S. L., D. M. Boutain, J. H. C. Tsai, R. Beaton, and A. B. de Castro. 2015. "An Exploration of Managers' Discourses of Workplace Bullying." *Nursing Forum* 50 (4): 265–73.

Kim, S., E. Buttrick, I. Bohannon, R. Fehr, E. Frans, and S. E. Shannon. 2016. "Conflict Narratives from the Health Care Frontline: A Conceptual Model." *Conflict Resolution Quarterly* 33 (3): 255–77.

Larson, L., and L. A. DeChurch. 2020. "Leading Teams in the Digital Age: Four Perspectives on Technology and What They Mean for Leading Teams." *Leadership Quarterly* 31 (1): 101377.

Rudolph, C. W., R. S. Rauvola, D. P. Costanza, and H. Zacher. 2020. "Generations and Generational Differences: Debunking Myths in Organizational Science and Practice and Paving New Paths Forward." *Journal of Business and Psychology* 36: 945–67.

Schaubhut, N. 2007. *Technical Brief for the Thomas-Kilmann Conflict Mode Instrument.* Psychometrics. Accessed November 28, 2021. www.psychometrics.com/wp-content/uploads /2015/02/tki-technical-brief.pdf.

Urick, M. J., E. C. Hollensbe, S. S. Masterson, and S. T. Lyons. 2017. "Understanding and Managing Intergenerational Conflict: An Examination of Influences and Strategies." *Work, Aging and Retirement* 3 (2): 166–85.

Wong, C. A., P. Elliott-Miller, H. Laschinger, M. Cuddihy, R. M. Meyer, M. Keatings, C. Burnett, and N. Szudy. 2015. "Examining the Relationships Between Span of Control and Manager Job and Unit Performance Outcomes." *Journal of Nursing Management* 23 (2): 156–68.

Yeung, D. Y., H. H. Fung, and D. Chan. 2015. "Managing Conflict at Work: Comparison Between Younger and Older Managerial Employees." *International Journal of Conflict Management* 26 (3): 342–65.

PART IV

EVALUATION

CHAPTER 17

Assessing Team Values

*For teams to be successful, the organizational culture
needs to support member involvement.*

—Peter G. Northouse (2021)

THE MESSAGE OF this book is simple: The leader and the team
(separately and together) must subscribe to a set of values that can
support and enhance effectiveness and success now and in the future.

What are your team values? Does your team discuss these values?
Are these values embedded in the norms and activities of the team?
What team behavior and practice will you change or improve to
live by these values?

This chapter explores the values that drive team functions and
performance. It guides you in assessing how well your leadership
team—specifically its members—upholds the team and other values.

KEY VALUES FOR ASSESSMENT

Team members should regularly assess the team's values. This activity reveals areas of deficiency and curtails harmful practices. Taplin,
Foster, and Shortell (2013, 280) state, "For leaders to help create and
support effective teams, they must know what conditions encourage

effective functioning of a particular type of team in a particular setting."

The following list, along with the questions posed after each item, may be used to start a values discussion with the team. Team members may compare and contrast their answers and then offer suggestions for improvement.

Competence

Basic competencies are expected of every leadership team. (For an extended list of leadership competencies, see Dye and Garman 2015.) Specifically, team members must possess a triumvirate of skill types—technical, decision-making, and interpersonal. Each of these skills is critical for a leadership role, but together they strengthen the leader and make her a sustainable member of the team. The team member does not have to possess expert-level abilities, but she must be able to harness each skill at any time.

For example, if a team member has great technical acumen (e.g., finance, technology, business savvy) but lacks interpersonal skills, she may avoid opportunities to socialize with other team members, display behaviors that alienate her staff and other team members, fail to share or communicate information, and not participate in general discussions or team-building exercises. Similarly, if a team member has plenty of interpersonal charms but no decision-making instinct or technical abilities, he may not be able to perform the basic business responsibilities of a leader—let alone a team member.

> To engage people in strategies and create better business results, organizations require discussions that are authentic and real. Most companies and teams don't know how to have these conversations.
>
> —Jim Haudan
> (J. Haudan, personal communication, December 5, 2021)

Ask yourself: Does the team value competence? Do members of my team possess a triumvirate of skills, at least? If not, what improvements are needed?

Awareness

In an effective team, members are aware of each other's roles and responsibilities as well as the team's purpose, standards (or norms), and goals. Moreover, each member keeps abreast of current and future initiatives of the team. In this environment, all team members share information, discuss matters openly, and offer recommendations.

> It is helpful if team leaders understand the conditions that contribute to or enable team excellence.
>
> —Peter G. Northouse (2021)

Ask yourself: Are all team members aware of our collective purpose, goals, and norms as well as each other's roles and responsibilities? If not, what improvements are needed?

Active Participation

Awareness comes from active participation in all that the team does, including meeting discussions, planning activities, goals and standards development, decision-making, and role assignments. Even when not all members are directly involved or needed in a team activity, cooperative members are still considered participants because they attend meetings, volunteer their time and talent, express and listen to opinions and ideas, give feedback, contribute to the camaraderie, and support collaboration.

Participation is crucial in attaining buy-in. That is, if team members are involved in any team activity from the start, they tend to commit to the initiative and encourage others to follow suit.

Ask yourself: Do members of my team actively participate in our activities and initiatives? If not, what improvements are needed?

Cohesiveness

Team cohesiveness reduces personal animosity and organizational politics among members. It also increases the possibility that team goals will be achieved. Although cohesiveness presents several disadvantages, such as groupthink and low tolerance for change, it leads the way to cooperation and collaboration.

> **Ask yourself:** Is my team cohesive? If so, is my team aware of the danger of groupthink? If not, should we discuss it?

Commonality

A shared goal, values, or even profession is sometimes enough to bond people together. If the commonality is a shared goal, the effort put into achieving that objective is maximized, as everyone is working toward the same vision. Having commonality also means that team members may require less explanation and convincing about an initiative and the ensuing process. One negative aspect of commonality is that it could lead to the formation of cliques, which harm the cohesiveness of the team.

> **Ask yourself:** Does my team have a commonality? If so, how is it helpful? If not, what improvements are needed?

Commitment

When team members are committed (which is often brought about by cohesiveness and commonality), they work harder, set aside personal agendas, and contribute readily to team efforts. Simply put, committed members are highly engaged. This level of engagement generates thoughtful questions, creative and multifaceted solutions, and ambitious but feasible objectives. More important, the undertaking to which the members are committed results in desired outcomes.

> **Ask yourself:** Is my team committed to our purpose, goals, and tasks? If not, what improvements are needed?

Communication

Communication (including sharing of information and meeting discussions) enables the team to move forward. For work purposes, communication informs decision-making, defines parameters (e.g., deadlines, goals, expectations, tasks), clarifies responsibilities, and prevents misunderstanding, to name a few functions. For interpersonal purposes, communication eases member interactions, assists with conflict resolution, and strengthens cohesiveness. Team communication—formal and informal, written and oral—should be regular, open, candid, and accurate.

The use of dyads in leadership is a significant topic for any healthcare leader hoping to adapt her organization to the clinical integration world. The subject is covered comprehensively in Kathleen Sanford, FACHE, and Stephen Moore's *Dyad Leadership in Healthcare: When One Plus One Is Greater Than Two* (2015). Sanford and Moore draw on their experiences creating clinical dyads to describe how this style of management can help healthcare organizations foster physician leadership—while managing the gaps in physician training—through collaboration with other managers. This book, plus Alan Belasen's *Dyad Leadership and Clinical Integration: Driving Change, Aligning Strategies* (2019), provide excellent insight into dyad structures.

Ask yourself: How well do my team members communicate with one another? Does our communication produce desired outcomes? If not, what improvements are needed?

Independence Versus Interdependence

Interdependence can be likened to cohesiveness in that it is good, but it has its limits. In other words, an interdependent team is naturally collaborative. The members are supportive of each other, and they can rely on each other to fill in gaps in skills, for example.

Too much interdependence can strip the individual members of their independence, which is dangerous in healthcare delivery. For example, an interdependent team usually makes decisions as a unit. If one member is unexpectedly gone, the rest of the people on the team may not know what to do or may not be empowered to exercise their skills or authority. This indecision is counterproductive and does not forward the team's function. This example works for both administrative and clinical teams.

Ask yourself: How interdependent is my team? To what extent do my team members rely on each other for support and input in decision-making? Are team members independent or empowered to make decisions? If not, what improvements are needed?

Camaraderie

Camaraderie is the goodwill among team members. It is the basis of active participation, cohesiveness, and communication. Team camaraderie develops when members spend time outside of the work context to get to know each other. Although it can form between members who have nothing in common, camaraderie is strongest when a commonality exists (and sometimes, being a member of the same team is common ground enough).

Ask yourself: Is there camaraderie among my team members? What do we do to maintain it?

High Energy

High energy makes the team more productive, creative, and participative. Energetic members anticipate team meetings and do not view them as a chore. Also, they are eager to receive new

> Once a team is created and its composition is established, the next team leadership function is to define the team's mission. This involves determining and communicating the organization's performance expectations for the team in such a way that they are broken down into tangible, comprehensible pieces. Once the team is clear about these expectations, the team leadership process focuses on establishing the team's mission or purpose.
>
> —Frederick P. Morgeson, D. Scott DeRue, and Elizabeth P. Karam (2010)

> Do not assume that any team members, even those who have been formal managers for years, know the vocabulary of *teamwork* or are experts in making a *team work*.
>
> —Kathleen Sanford and Stephen Moore (2015)

assignments and tasks, their minds already computing the details before they even begin.

Ask yourself: What is my team's energy level? Are my team members productive and eager? If not, what improvements are needed?

CONCLUSION

Every leadership team should periodically assess its values. If a team is productive and effective now (or "perfect"), imagine the even greater results it will achieve as it continues to lead by its values. Regular assessment of these values will help such a team sustain its success.

Ways to Boost Team Energy

- *Move a meeting to a different location, each time or occasionally.* A change of venue refreshes team member interests because it connotes a new beginning. Many retreats are effective solely because they take place outside of the office.

- *Celebrate team and individual accomplishments.* Festivities reverse moods positively, and good moods hike up energy levels.

- *Invite guest presenters.* Trained presenters inspire and rally people to act.

- *Take a break from routine.* This break does not need to be work related, but it should be fun and meaningful. For example, team members could volunteer at a homeless shelter or food pantry.

- *Bring more focus to virtual meetings.* If meetings are held virtually, consider ways to ensure focus, relevance, and personal sensitivity. Be certain there is a clear purpose for the meeting; encourage all to have their cameras on; consider the use of breakout rooms; and respect the fact that "personal" aspects such as pets or children may surface during the meeting.

Self-Evaluation Question

❑ As a team member, what values do I espouse that may support or impede my team's function?

REFERENCES

Belasen, A. 2019. *Dyad Leadership and Clinical Integration: Driving Change, Aligning Strategies.* Chicago: Health Administration Press.

Dye, Carson F., and Andrew N. Garman. 2015. Exceptional leadership: 16 critical competencies for healthcare executives, 2nd ed.. Chicago: Health Administration Press.

Morgeson, F. P., DeRue, D. S., & Karam, E. P. (2010). Leadership in teams: A functional approach to understanding leadership structures and processes. Journal of Management, 36(1), 5–39. https://doi.org/10.1177/0149206309347376.

Northouse, P. G. 2021. *Leadership: Theory and Practice*, 9th ed. Los Angeles: SAGE Publications.

Sanford, K. D., and Moore, S. L. 2015. *Dyad Leadership in Healthcare: When One Plus One Is Greater Than Two.* Philadelphia: Lippincott Williams & Wilkins.

Taplin, Stephen, Foster, Mary, and Shortell, Stephen. "Organizational Leadership For Building Effective Health Care Teams." The Annals of Family Medicine, May 2013, 11 (3) 279-281; DOI: 10.1370/afm.1506.

SUGGESTED READINGS

Goleman, D. 2002. *Primal Leadership: Realizing the Power of Emotional Intelligence.* Boston: Harvard Business School Press.

Hu, J., B. Erdogan, K. Jiang, T. N. Bauer, and S. Liu. 2018. "Leader Humility and Team Creativity: The Role of Team Information

Sharing, Psychological Safety, and Power Distance." *Journal of Applied Psychology* 103 (3): 313–23.

Karl, K. A., J. V. Peluchette, and N. Aghakhani. 2021. "Virtual Work Meetings During the COVID-19 Pandemic: The Good, Bad, and Ugly." *Small Group Research* 53 (3): 343–65.

Mukherjee, S., and Z. R. Mulla. 2021. "Empowering and Directive Leadership: The Cost of Changing Styles." *Business Perspectives and Research* 10 (2): 251–66.

Naylor, M. D., and E. T. Kurtzman. 2010. "The Role of Nurse Practitioners in Reinventing Primary Care." *Health Affairs* 29 (5): 893–99.

CHAPTER 18

Evaluating Team Effectiveness

Teamwork is an example of lateral decision making as opposed to the traditional vertical decision making that occurs in the organizational hierarchy based on rank or position in the organization.

—Peter G. Northouse (2021)

HOW DOES YOUR leadership team function? Is the team composition carefully put together, with an eye toward the organizational hierarchy? Are all team members involved in decision-making? Are your meetings always, sometimes, or never necessary? Is the team bound to a set of protocols?

Garman and I argue that for teams to be effective, five critical activities are needed (Dye and Garman 2015):

1. Get the best people for team roles.
2. Develop an orientation toward a common vision and collective goals.
3. Develop trust among team members (as discussed in chapter 15).
4. Develop cohesiveness between team members.
5. Help team members productively work through the inevitable conflicts that come with group interaction.

The team's structure (size, hierarchy, membership) and primary activities (decision-making, holding meetings, establishing team protocols) greatly affect its effectiveness, just as team values do. This chapter presents the components that a leadership team should assess on a regular basis.

TEAM STRUCTURE

Size

As mentioned in chapter 14, there is no ideal team size because every team has a different purpose, and this purpose dictates the number of members needed to make the team function well. However, there is such a thing as a team that is either too large or too small. Typically, a team that has 12 or more members is too large, while a team that has 4 or fewer members is too small. The problem with a large team is that decision-making is slow, as too many people are involved in the process. With a small team, on the other hand, the expertise and experience of members may be limited, forcing the team to look outside for reinforcement and advice.

A team made up of 6 to 11 members works efficiently. Here, values (e.g., collaboration, cooperation) are more readily shared and learned, decisions are reached faster, tasks are more equally distributed, and conflicts are easier to spot and manage.

> **Ask yourself:** Is my team too large or too small? When was the last time my team assessed its size? What are the advantages and disadvantages of resizing my team?

Hierarchy

Although humility is the virtue that prevents people from boasting about their accomplishments and even compels them to say "titles don't mean anything," it is not the same virtue that commands people to be truthful. The importance of titles and status in the organization cannot be minimized. They are important, especially to high-ranking leaders (those in the C-suite).

A leader's title is not merely a short description of her job responsibilities; it bears prestige and influence. As such, it should be given its proper place on the team's hierarchy. For example, an executive vice president (VP) should be ranked higher than an assistant VP, and the two positions should not be given equal decision-making capabilities. One practice that fuels an imbalance of power among the team is granting undeserved titles either as an enticement for certain individuals to participate in an initiative or as a reward for an accomplishment that makes the team look good.

> All the empowered, motivated, teamed-up, self-directed, incentivized, accountable, reengineered, and reinvented people you can muster cannot compensate for a dysfunctional system. When the system is functioning well, these other things are just foofaraw. When the system is not functioning well, these things are still only empty, meaningless twaddle.
>
> —Peter R. Scholtes (1998)

Ask yourself: Does my team recognize and respect the hierarchy among our members? Do we inappropriately bestow titles?

Membership

Membership on the leadership team is a coveted and highly esteemed post. Unfortunately, appointment to this team (or even an invitation to attend its meetings) is often perceived by employees either as a privilege of being a leader or as a sign of cronyism. This perception is often justifiable, given that some departments and interests have a disproportionately large representation on the team and at its meetings (see exhibit 18.1 for examples).

To combat this perception, each membership appointment and invitation to meetings must be assessed according to practical, unbiased criteria, such as the following:

- The person's expertise, training, and skills
- The person's position and responsibilities
- The position's importance to the work and diversity of the team
- The position's potential contribution to the goals of the team
- Other work-related reasons for membership or attendance

Ask yourself: How is membership on my team viewed? As a privilege? As a reward? As a form of recognition? Does my team invite guests to our meetings, and how do they contribute to the discussion? Does my team follow established criteria for membership and meeting participation?

TEAM ACTIVITIES

Decision-Making

Many teams are proficient in delaying (although not deliberately) decision-making. Some teams discuss issues repeatedly but reach neither solution nor compromise. Other teams, meanwhile, are paralyzed by fear that any decision will create a conflict among team members. Yet decision-making is a primary activity of a leadership team—an activity that cannot be delegated to another group or avoided without repercussions.

Often, the reason for this avoidance is the lack of a practical decision-making method. Specifically, basic components, such as the following, are missing:

- Facts and historical data about the issue at hand
- Brainstorming (for generating solutions and alternatives) and critical analysis tools and techniques (for examining ideas)

Exhibit 18.1 Examples of an Imbalance of Power in a Leadership Team

- The public relations director is a member. She is in charge of disseminating organizational information to all staff.

- Both the senior VP of patient care services and the VP of nursing are members. Both have nursing backgrounds and thus skew clinical discussions toward nursing issues.

- Although not VPs, the director of human resources and the chief information officer are members.

- The director of the medical staff regularly attends team meetings, but he is not a member.

- Structured discussion method
- Well-defined goals and responsibilities
- Clear deadlines
- Trained leader or facilitator
- Participative members
- Time commitment

Ask yourself: Does my team employ a decision-making method? If not, how do we make decisions? Is my team known to delay or avoid making a decision, and what are the consequences of such an action? How do we handle disagreement or conflict about a decision? What can my team do to improve its decision-making skills?

Holding Meetings

Virtual meetings (which became prevalent during the COVID-19 pandemic) present unique

In the typical senior working group, individual roles and responsibilities are the primary focal points for performance results. There is not incremental performance expectation beyond that provided by individual executives working in their formal areas of responsibility.

—Jon R. Katzenbach and Douglas K. Smith (1993)

challenges. While many leaders higher up in organizations became accustomed to meetings in front of the computer screen, those working in clinical areas did not have as many opportunities to do so. Regardless, for teams to effectively work through issues, there is a need to gather and discuss in person. Meetings, if well planned and well run, enable the team to think together and collectively make decisions. In addition, meetings are a key contributor to building camaraderie. Meeting attendees almost always have an opportunity before and after the meeting to socialize with each other.

The backlash against meetings, whether virtual or in person, points to poor planning. That is, people greatly dislike meetings because (1) they are time wasters, (2) they do not ensure anything will get accomplished, (3) they are scheduled one after another (or there are too many), and (4) they are a platform for ad nauseam discussions and show-offs.

Poor planning is the root cause of these complaints. This section offers strategies that can improve the major components of a meeting.

Necessity

Unfortunately, meetings have been so ingrained in the workplace that only few attendees question their purpose and relevance. The rest of us just show up. This conditioning is costly because while the leader is sitting in an unproductive and haphazard meeting, revenue-generating opportunities could be passing him by.

Here are two simple ways to determine if your attendance is necessary:

1. Review the minutes or notes from the last meeting and the agenda (if available) for the upcoming meeting.
2. Ask.

Ask yourself: Are all of our team meetings necessary? Have I questioned their relevance?

Objectives, Agendas, and Handouts

Objectives specify the purpose of the meeting. If a meeting is called just so the team can share information or updates but no discussions are expected, team members may request to send in their information (via e-mail perhaps) and be excused from attending. Although this option is not available to everyone, such as the meeting chair, it can free up time for those whose absence from the meeting will not make a difference.

Objectives are typically found on the meeting agenda. An agenda lists the items to be discussed in order of importance or according to the meeting format. Equipped with an agenda, team members can minimize digressions.

Handouts (e.g., financial statements, statistical reports, proposals) distributed before the meeting help attendees prepare their comments, questions, or suggestions. Fortunately, the protocol at most meetings now is that any item that comes with a handout will not be discussed if the materials are not disseminated ahead of time. Without this protocol, much of the meeting time is wasted on explaining background information.

> **Ask yourself:** Does my team distribute an agenda with clear objectives? Who determines the objectives? Do our meetings follow the agenda? Are our meetings structured so as to prevent side conversations, multiple discussions, and other interruptions? Do we require and distribute handouts or preparatory material?

Roles and Norms

As mentioned in chapter 14, each team member must have a role to play (e.g., conscience, historian, devil's advocate). Such roles must conform to the norms (standards and expectations) of the team. For example, if the CEO is the chair, he must come prepared, come on time, come to stay, come to listen, come to participate, and come to ensure order during the meeting.

1. *Composition.* Are criteria followed in assembling the team? Who establishes and evaluates the criteria? How many members does the team have, and does this size benefit or disadvantage the team? Are major departments evenly represented on the team? How are members replaced when they leave? Does the team have subgroups to facilitate decision-making and decisions, and if so, who assigns what members to serve on these subgroups?

2. *New-member integration.* How are new members integrated into the group? Do they go through a formal or informal orientation? When do the integration activities take place—before or after the member is introduced to the team? Who is responsible for ensuring that integration and orientation occur?

3. *Personality and style differences.* Is a structured tool—Myers-Briggs Type Indicator, Keirsey Temperament Sorter, or Hogan Personality Inventory—used to develop an understanding of different personalities and leadership styles? If not, how are these differences viewed and managed?

4. *Purpose, goals, and roles.* Who sets the purpose, goals, and roles for the team? Are all members involved in this process, and are these elements discussed by the team? Do all members have an understanding of each other's responsibilities and expectations?

5. *Protocols.* Are there rules and standards for decision-making, interactions, behaviors,

Ask yourself: What is my role, and does it abide by the norms that my team has set? What are my team's norms, and do we follow them closely? Do cliques or factions exist in my team? If so, do they have a different set of norms?

Time

Meetings are ravenous eaters of time. Flexible meetings are wasteful because they encourage too much deliberation and too little resolution. Although thoughtful discussions prevent risky undertakings, they are impractical in an environment pressured by constant change and quick fixes. The biggest time wasters are information-sharing meetings, which must not last longer than three hours. Although meetings in which strategies are developed and shaped must not have time limits, they should still be scheduled in advance and planned. Part of this planning is distributing a summary or minutes of the past meeting to refresh attendees. The minutes are also a great tool for initiating discussion.

Ask yourself: How long do our meetings last? Do we have a regularly scheduled, time-limited meeting, or is it often flexible? Who keeps the minutes, and when are they distributed? Are the minutes detailed or vague, and are they useful for the next meeting?

Format

Generate creative ideas by making the meeting participatory. This interactive format enhances the team's awareness of others' responsibilities and expertise, and it also displays team members' personalities, which could help develop commonality and camaraderie. Following are common (and often visual) approaches used during interactive discussions:

(continued from previous page)
and other components of team function? Who established them, and are they well known to and practiced by the team? What consequences are levied against those who disobey the rules?

6. *Conflict management.* What methods does the team employ to manage conflict? Is the team aware of the areas in which conflict may be introduced (e.g., decision-making, discussions, power structure)?

- *Parking lot.* Innovative ideas not directly relevant to the current topic often emerge during a discussion. The parking lot is a way to save those ideas for later consideration.

- *Multivoting.* Multivoting is useful when the agenda lists too many items for discussion or consideration. Each team member is given a set number of votes to pick the issues (listed on a flip chart) she deems most important. All votes are cast confidentially to prevent political ramifications for the voters. The issues that receive the greatest number of votes remain on the agenda, and the rest are taken out. Multivoting is a democratic process that gives all members—especially the silent ones—a chance to be heard.

- *Affinity diagram.* This technique helps the team to organize and prioritize ideas and information. Using sticky notes, team members jot down data or suggestions and affix them to a flip chart. These notes are then arranged according to themes or categories. For example, "Use Twitter to create buzz about the new, green maternity ward," could be grouped under "marketing and communication."

- *Process mapping.* Process mapping alerts the team to the intricacies (i.e., responsibilities, tasks, measures, objectives) of a specific workflow. This technique is helpful when modifying an existing process and when creating a new one.

Ask yourself: Are our meetings interactive and fun? If not, have we considered changing the format? What kind of participatory methods do we use?

> High-performing teams are those with members whose skills, attitudes, and competencies enable them to achieve team goals. These team members set goals, make decisions, communicate, manage conflict, and solve problems in a supportive, trusting atmosphere in order to accomplish their objectives.
>
> —W. Gibb Dyer Jr., Jeffrey H. Dyer, and William G. Dyer (2013)

Etiquette

Professional conduct must be expected in every professional setting. Distracting and rude behaviors (e.g., side conversations, flippant remarks) should not be tolerated during a meeting. Unfortunately, such behaviors (including the following examples) can be observed in leadership team meetings:

- Reading material unrelated to the team agenda to tune out an ongoing presentation
- Constantly stepping out to attend to a crisis or to take a break
- Constantly interrupting the facilitator or chair to ask a question, elucidate a point, complain, or argue
- Arriving late and unprepared
- Dominating the discussion and speaking out of turn
- Displaying dissent and impatience through body language, such as yawning, eye rolling, pounding on the table, and walking out

- Antagonizing a speaker or an idea with sarcastic comments and jokes
- Telling offensive (e.g., racist, sexist, elitist) jokes and anecdotes

The team, as a unit, should establish a code of conduct for meetings, post it in a visible setting or distribute it to all team members, and require all members to follow it. This code should include a clear statement about the consequences of not abiding by the rules. The team should also periodically discuss and evaluate the code.

Ask yourself: Has my team established etiquette guidelines? Generally, are my team members respectful? How does my team typically address inappropriate or distracting behaviors? What sanctions have been established for such cases?

Participation

Constant absence and nonparticipation may also fall under rude and distracting behavior. A team member who is not actively engaged impedes or slows down the team's work. In addition, conflicts of interest may arise when only part of the team is involved and represented in the decision-making.

The team could draw quiet members into the discussion by using various methods, one of which is the nominal group technique (NGT). NGT's process is as follows:

1. Identify the problem.
2. Ask all members to offer at least one solution.
3. Write down, on a flip chart, all the ideas as they are suggested.
4. Discuss, clarify, and evaluate every idea on the list. Eliminate those that are repetitive or not feasible.

5. Compile a final list of solutions as agreed on by the team.
6. Ask all members to vote on each solution on the basis of its significance to their priorities. Each member gets one vote.
7. Rank the solutions according to the number of votes received.
8. Select the solution that garnered the top spot.

> **Ask yourself:** How engaged are my team members? Does my team encourage everyone to participate? What kind of tools does my team use to support an all-member discussion?

Wrap-Up

End the meeting right. Many meetings last so long that, by the end, participants are so eager to leave that they fail to hear the last minutes of the discussion. The final minutes of any meeting should be the strongest because at this time the leader can rally support for the issues discussed and motivate the team to follow through. The team leader must conclude the meeting by providing a short summary (one or two sentences) of the issues discussed, the responsibilities assigned, and the steps that need to be taken before the next meeting.

> **Ask yourself:** How does my team end our meetings? Do members leave exhausted and overwhelmed with too much information? How do we remind members of the decisions made and the next steps?

Establishing Team Protocols

All team members should be involved in developing the protocols that govern its behaviors, interactions, activities, decisions, and all other dealings. Equal participation by all members ensures that the protocols are not just created but also obeyed.

Following is an example of a decision-making protocol established by the entire team.

1. *Decisions must be made by all members, not just by a subset.* Because some teams are too large, their leaders rely on a subgroup to deliberate on issues and make decisions. As a result, members outside of this subset may feel disrespected and could start a conflict. Conversely, members of the subgroup may feel arrogant and superior to the rest of the team. Although using a small group is a practical alternative to a lengthy all-member deliberation, it can harm team cohesiveness. If decisions must be made by a subset, the reasons must be explained to and discussed by the entire team. This way, everyone is aware of the intentions, and a rift is less likely to develop.

2. *A decision-making process must be determined for the issue on hand.* Will a vote be taken? If so, will the decision be determined by a majority? Are some members' votes given more weight than others'? By discussing the process in depth, the team can avoid the Abilene paradox: A family made a long trip to Abilene, simply because one person suggested the location and the others believed that everyone agreed. As the family members returned from Abilene, they discovered that none of them had wanted to go to Abilene in the first place.

3. *Divergent or nontraditional ideas must not be discouraged.* Unique perspectives can strengthen decision-making, introducing innovative concepts, problems, and consequences that the team may not have considered before.

4. *Team member expertise should not cause an imbalanced decision.* Teams have the tendency to allow clinical decisions to be guided solely by the chief nursing officer or the chief medical officer. Members without such training can also offer meaningful and creative approaches.

5. *Proper decorum and courtesy must always be practiced.* Respect and honor in debate and deliberation are essential to effective team outcomes.

CONCLUSION

Inefficiencies can easily creep into the smallest details of a team. Regular monitoring and evaluation ensure that the structure and activities of the team still function in its favor. After all, an inefficient team cannot produce a successful outcome, let alone sustain itself. See appendixes C and D for leadership team evaluation tools.

Self-Evaluation Questions

❑ What is the composition of my team? Does the membership evenly represent the major areas in the organization?

❑ How are our team meetings conducted? Do we abide by certain rules of conduct during the meeting?

❑ What is our decision-making process? Are my team members involved in discussions?

❑ Has my team established team protocols? Do we follow these protocols?

Exercises

According to an excellent article by Reader and colleagues (2009), there is a growing literature on the relationship between teamwork and patient outcomes in intensive care, providing new insights into the skills required for effective team performance. Review the article with other clinical leaders and determine what specific factors contained in the article might enhance team effectiveness. The article can be found at https://citeseerx.ist.psu.edu/viewdoc/download?doi=10.1.1.1056.7888&rep=rep1&type=pdf.

A recent article by Kyriacou and colleagues shows the relationship between patient safety and team climate. The article can serve as an excellent guide for discussion. The article can be found at: https://www.cureus.com/articles/70330-correlation-between-teamwork-and-patient-safety-in-a-tertiary-hospital-in-cyprus.

REFERENCES

Dye, C. F., and A. N. Garman. 2015. *Exceptional Leadership: 16 Critical Competencies for Healthcare Executives*, 2nd ed. Chicago: Health Administration Press.

Dyer, W. G. Jr., J. H. Dyer, and W. G. Dyer. 2013. *Team Building: Proven Strategies for Improving Team Performance*, 5th ed. San Francisco: Jossey-Bass.

Katzenbach, J. R., and D. K. Smith. 1993. *The Wisdom of Teams: Creating the High-Performance Organization*. Boston: Harvard Business School Press.

Northouse, P. G. 2021. *Leadership: Theory and Practice*, 9th ed. Los Angeles: SAGE Publications.

Reader, T. W., R. Flin, K. Mearns, and B. H. Cuthbertson. 2009. "Developing a Team Performance Framework for the Intensive Care Unit." *Critical Care Medicine* 37 (5): 1787–93.

Scholtes, P. R. 1998. *The Leader's Handbook: Making Things Happen, Getting Things Done*. New York: McGraw-Hill.

SUGGESTED READINGS

Bartsch, S., E. Weber, M. Buttfen, and A. Huber. 2021. "Leadership Matters in Crisis-Induced Digital Transformation: How to Lead Service Employees Effectively During the COVID-19 Pandemic." *Journal of Service Management* 32 (1): 77–85.

Bowman, B. A., A. L. Back, A. E. Esch, and N. Marshall. 2020. "Crisis Symptom Management and Patient Communication Protocols Are Important Tools for All Clinicians Responding to COVID-19." 2020. *Journal of Pain and Symptom Management* 60 (2): e98–e100.

Buljac-Samardzic, M., K. D. Doekhie, and J. D. H. van Wijngaarden. 2020. "Interventions to Improve Team Effectiveness Within Health Care: A Systematic Review of the Past Decade." *Human Resources for Health* 18 (2).

Collins, C. G., C. B. Gibson, N. R. Quigley, and S. K. Parker. 2016. "Unpacking Team Dynamics with Growth Modeling: An Approach to Test, Refine, and Integrate Theory." *Organizational Psychology Review* 6 (1): 63–91.

Friedrich, T. L., J. A. Griffith, and M. D. Mumford. 2016. "Collective Leadership Behaviors: Evaluating the Leader, Team Network, and Problem Situation Characteristics That Influence Their Use." *Leadership Quarterly* 27 (2): 312–33.

Günzel-Jensen, F., A. K. Jain, and A. M. Kjeldsen. 2016. "Distributed Leadership in Health Care: The Role of Formal Leadership Styles and Organizational Efficacy." *Leadership.* Published May 12. http://lea.sagepub.com/content/early/2016/05/11/1742715016646441.abstract.

O'Donavan, R., and E. Mcauliffe. 2020. "A Systematic Review of Factors That Enable Psychological Safety in Healthcare Teams. *International Journal for Quality in Health Care* 32 (4): 240–50.

Reader, T. W., R. Flin, and B. H. Cuthbertson. 2011. "Team Leadership in the Intensive Care Unit: The Perspective of Specialists." *Critical Care Medicine* 39 (7): 1683–91.

Stoverink, A. C., B. L. Kirkman, S. Mistry, and B. Rosen. 2020. "Bouncing Back Together: Toward a Theoretical Model of Work Team Resilience." *Academy of Management Review* 45 (2): 395–422.

Whittaker, G., H. Abboudi, M. S. Khan, P. Dasgupta, and K. Ahmed. 2015. "Teamwork Assessment Tools in Modern Surgical Practice: A Systematic Review." *Surgery Research and Practice*. Published September 30. http://www.hindawi.com /journals/srp/2015/494827/.

CHAPTER 19

Self-Evaluation at All Career Stages

Navigating effectively through life, creating a meaningful purpose in it, and ultimately, reflecting yourself requires an organized perspective on life's structure.

—Michael P. McNally (2015)

TASHA RHONA, A search consultant, and her close friend Rebecca Boling-Rodriguez are on the phone regarding a recent job disappointment.

REBECCA. The search consultant just called to tell me I didn't get the CEO job. I have no idea why. I pushed him to give more details but he said it was close, but there was nothing I could have done to change the outcome. Apparently, I didn't make any mistakes in the interview process. Frankly, I have the experience and the skills. My interviews with the physicians went very well, or so I thought. In fact, two doctors approached me after the medical executive committee interview just to say they were looking forward to working with me. At the final interview, which felt like a welcome-to-the-club dinner meeting, the board chair and vice chair asked if I could think of any areas I needed special help or guidance with . . .

TASHA. How did you answer that?

REBECCA. With a no! What else am I supposed to say?

TASHA. Let's calm down here. In your 20-plus-year career, this was the first time you actually competed in a job search. You found your previous jobs via individuals with whom you had worked before. How could you have really known how to prepare for an interview? I can't tell you why they passed on hiring you, but I can tell you what they might have been looking for. Are you ready to hear that?

REBECCA. I have a feeling you'll tell me anyway.

TASHA. When was the last time you did a self-evaluation of your skills, your style, your values—the whole nine yards?

REBECCA. Why? Is that important?

VALUES-DRIVEN LEADERS ARE self-assessors. They understand that they cannot expect others to speak, think, and act according to principles if they do not demand the same things of themselves. Thus, these leaders study their own moves and thought processes, with the dual intention of personal improvement and professional achievement.

All leaders—early, mid-, and late careerists—can benefit from evaluating their performance or practice in various areas related to their respective career stages.

ALL CAREERISTS

Personal Mission Statement

A personal mission statement is the road map of any careerist, pointing to the desired destination and preventing the person from veering off course. This statement should answer the following questions:

- What is my purpose in life?
- What is my ultimate personal goal?
- What is my ultimate professional goal?
- What do I enjoy doing most?
- How and where do I make the most impact?
- How would I like my obituary to read? (Although morbid, this question forces you to think about your legacy.)

Writing this statement is daunting, taxing, frustrating, and awkward at first, but this tension eases after several drafts. Exhibit 19.1 provides examples of personal mission statements.

Reviewing the statement after a certain time is beneficial. Doing so will ensure that the document (1) is kept alive through daily deeds and words and (2) is revised to reflect the leader's values and goals. After several years, the statement can serve as a reminder of accomplishments and shortcomings. Some seasoned leaders have saved the mission statements they wrote when they were new to the field. One executive pulls out his old mission statements and self-evaluation notes annually. Revisiting them helps him find the "true north" of his personal life and career.

Ask yourself: Have I written a personal mission statement?

Personal and Professional Style

The Kuder Career Assessment or the Strong Interest Inventory are among the most commonly used tools for assessing career interests

Exhibit 19.1 Sample Personal Mission Statements

Sample 1

My faith and my family are the most important things in my life. I want to be remembered by my family as a loving spouse and a caring parent. I want my children to remember that I did do an effective job of balancing work and home. I want my spouse to be comfortable with my desire to make a difference in healthcare.

I will end up compromising these values if I take a bigger, better job with more prestige. I do not want to do this. Therefore, I must be cautious in being tempted by these kinds of jobs. I will enjoy serving in an organization where I can make a personal impact without neglecting my children and spouse.

Although I want to be a CEO, I understand that the trade-off with my family is not worth that price. So, I will try to serve my CEO so effectively that he will include me in more of his decision making and give me greater authority, and I will gain greater fulfillment. This will give me much of the satisfaction typically enjoyed by CEOs.

I will try to work in organizations that respect and support work/family balance. I will try to show this same respect for my division managers.

At the end of my life, I would like to be remembered as a person who was effective in balancing both family and career and one who did not allow work and career to take over.

Sample 2

I entered healthcare to serve others. As a clinician, I studied the art and science of healing. I want to keep this healing mission the central focus of my working life. I want others to know me as a person who always puts patients first. I will be a good steward of the skills given me and will work to get others around me to develop and sustain the passion for patient care that I possess.

I want to work in organizations that put missions first and margin second. I do not want to be affiliated with organizations that are not committed to high quality. I do not want to work in the for-profit health sector.

---

and proclivities. Other assessments provide insight into personal and professional styles and behaviors. Validated instruments such as the Hogan Personality Inventory; the Hogan Development Survey; and the Hogan Motives, Values, and Preferences Inventory provide in-depth insight into personality as it relates to the workplace. These inventory tools are applicable to the skills and styles expected of workers today, and they reflect the leadership competency systems that many organizations have begun to develop. Search consultant firms also employ assessment instruments to evaluate candidates.

> **Ask yourself:** Am I aware of my personal and professional style? Do I use assessment tools, or do I rely on feedback alone?

Values

Constant review of values is imperative, as they affect priorities, behaviors, mindset, and performance. Team or executive retreats, performance reviews, self-reflection exercises, and mentor meetings are forums for thinking about and discussing these values.

Unfortunately, stories about senior executives who have committed unethical acts have dominated the news in recent years. Such incidents exemplify that (1) no one is immune to the seductive power of high office and (2) many careerists—from new to veteran—verbally support great values but do not understand how to live those values or why they must do so.

Especially at senior management levels—at which increases in revenues, market share, and physician and customer satisfaction rates are the primary focus—values-based concepts tend to be viewed as window dressing.

Personal values drive many professional values. In this way, a deficiency in one is a deficiency in another. For example, a careerist who values self-interest tends to form or join a clique, sabotage cohesiveness and collaboration, and refrain from participating in initiatives that do not directly benefit him.

> **Ask yourself:** What are my values? Are they aligned with those of my organization? If not, what is the difference, and is it hurting my chances of achieving my goals?

Continuing Education

Education should not stop with the completion of a graduate degree. In fact, such a degree is only an entrance ticket. Learning should be a lifelong pursuit because it makes the careerist more marketable, more in touch with current trends and practices, and more able to overcome challenges. Continuing education (both degree and nondegree programs) is offered by various entities, including professional associations, public agencies, private companies, and colleges and universities. Many such offerings are designed for working adults, as evinced by the proliferation of webinars, distance learning, night and weekend classes, and accelerated programs. The most accessible and inexpensive forms of learning are reading healthcare-related publications and discussing trends with colleagues.

Ask yourself: How do I keep up with changes in healthcare, in the management field, and in my role? What can I do to expand my knowledge and skill base? Is my organization supportive of continuing education? If not, what other avenues of learning may I explore?

EARLY CAREERISTS

Mentor Relationship

An early healthcare careerist undoubtedly has a lot to learn. Who better to serve as teacher than a practicing healthcare leader? Graduate health administration curricula and professional management courses put much emphasis on the technical (including financial), administrative, and human resources aspects of leadership, but they often fail to cover behavior and ethics standards. A mentor can fill in for the new careerist the gaps that exist between education and practice, including interpersonal expectations. In addition, a mentor can introduce the new careerist to resources, provide advice and insight, clarify nuances, serve as a sounding board, and urge improvement.

> The secret of joy in work is contained in one word—excellence. To know how to do something well is to enjoy it.
>
> **—Pearl S. Buck (1964)**

Ask yourself: Do I have a mentor? What kind of relationship do I have with my mentor? Is this mentoring relationship beneficial to my career growth? If not, how may I improve it?

The Unexpected

Everything will be unexpected to the new careerist, especially in a fast-changing field such as healthcare. Preparation is the best response to the unexpected. It makes the person think quickly and creatively, retain interest and focus, and be less intimidated by the unknown. For example, an early careerist is far less reluctant to try an untested, risky idea if she has done her research, spoken with experts and other experienced staff, weighed the pros and cons, designed a backup and response plan, and communicated the information she has with her supervisees. This way, if the idea develops an unexpected glitch later on, the glitch will not cause a major disturbance for those involved.

Ask yourself: How well do I prepare for any activity? How do I respond to the unexpected?

Strengths and Weaknesses

An early careerist must be aware of his abilities and limitations, as this knowledge puts him in control of what can be enhanced, what can be mastered, and what can be delegated (although this option only works for nonrequired responsibilities such as volunteering on a team). For example, if the person knows he is not good with numbers, he can attend budgeting and finance classes, ask others for help in understanding the concepts, and seek opportunities for practicing or applying the skill. Awareness of a personal limitation humbles a person, but it also serves as an impetus for improvement.

Early careerists can benefit from knowing what their leaders expect. One CEO distributes the following list of knowledge, skills, and abilities she demands from her team:

- Concise communication
- Focus on results
- Listening skills
- Strategic thinking
- Consistent and appropriate behavior
- Drive and initiative
- Persuasion
- Customer and team orientation

Ask yourself: What are my strengths and weaknesses? Am I committed to improving and mastering my skills? Do I understand the perils of my weaknesses?

Broad Perspective

Many early careerists tend to focus on only one organizational function—strategic planning, financial analysis, operations, human resources, or some other specialty. Although this practice enables the careerist to master a certain discipline, it curbs creativity and narrows perspective. During the first years, the early careerist should be a generalist, learning all the functions and their interrelationships. An early careerist is expected to ask questions and listen intently.

Everyone else feels obliged to share his knowledge and contribute to the early careerist's development. Nobody loses in this type of exchange.

> **Ask yourself:** Do I shadow, ask questions of, and forge relationships with people with diverse knowledge and specialties? How much do I know about the inner workings of my job and others' jobs? How may I widen my understanding and perspective?

Organizational Politics

Early careerists are primarily focused on gaining project experience. As such, they tend to be oblivious to the political undercurrents surrounding them. These power struggles are often common knowledge among staff, who suffer the consequences, such as red tape, slow decision-making, and multiple layers of approval. The early careerist should pay attention to signs of conflict and political upheaval, such as the following:

- Sudden departure of a well-liked, high-performing leader
- Distribution of multiple memos with divergent messages
- Side negotiations and secret campaigns
- Frequent "special" and closed-door meetings
- Increased backroom gossiping and theorizing
- Sudden cuts in budget, staff, and other resources
- Disruptions of routine
- Diminished morale
- Hierarchical or structural changes

> **Ask yourself:** Am I aware of the political nuances in my organization? How do I find out about them?

Diligence

For an early careerist, every assignment is a test of skills, patience, persistence, and potential. Thus, the careerist must validate, double-check, corroborate, proofread, and reference every piece of information, as any errors and omissions can be viewed as the result of sloppy work. This diligence helps the careerist develop great habits, which are the root of effective performance.

Ask yourself: Is my work meticulous? If not, what can I do to improve?

Job Opportunities

Some early careerists spend five to six years in their first jobs without considering (or experiencing) a promotion, a lateral move to a different department, or a position in another organization. Part of the reason may be loyalty or complacency, but more often than not the reason is fear. At this early stage, careerists should only fear stagnation and burnout, not the possibility of a job opportunity.

Staying in one place for a long time is admirable; in fact, many successful leaders retire from the same organizations that originally hired them. However, today's healthcare environment thrives on change and newness, demanding its leaders to follow suit.

One way to pursue change (and prevent burnout) is to apply for job opportunities. This process, including interviewing, enables the careerist to tout her strengths, assess her weaknesses, articulate her goals, discover her earning and career potentials, learn about the job market, and interact with professionals in another workplace. In addition, the process sharpens the careerist's communication and negotiation skills and presents a fresh perspective.

> Behold the turtle. He only makes progress when he sticks his neck out.
>
> —James Bryant Conant (quoted in Hershberg 1993)

Ask yourself: How long ago did I apply for another job inside or outside my organization? Am I confident enough of my knowledge, skills, and abilities to pursue a promotion, a lateral move, or a job opening in a different institution? Do I think the application process (even if I don't intend to leave my job) is beneficial or harmful to my career growth, and why?

MIDCAREERISTS

Complementary Work and Home Life

"Busy" is the most succinct description of a midcareerist's workday, which can stretch for more than 14 hours at times. These long days, not to mention occasional weekend events, wreak havoc on personal time and relationships.

The tug of war between personal and professional life is a stressor faced by most, if not all, midcareerists. Although some are skilled at balancing these pursuits, many others struggle, leading to bad tendencies such as impatience, intolerance, arrogance, selfishness, and negative attitudes.

Ask yourself: What can I do to live a balanced life? How is the imbalance in my life affecting my work, my relationships, and my future goals? To whom can I turn for help in this regard?

360-Degree Feedback

The 360-degree feedback instrument is the surest way to obtain frank comments from an array of people. The main reason for this is that the tool ensures confidentiality to participants, taking away the commenters' fear of reprisal. This tool, and similar feedback tools, is helpful to the midcareerist's development because the assessments come from those who work directly or have regular contact with the person. In addition, the tool evaluates a broad aspect of the careerist's performance.

> **Ask yourself:** How often do I get feedback, and what tool do I use? Is the feedback I receive constructive or destructive? Do I promote the use of feedback to effect positive change? If not, why?

Networking

Networking breeds innovative ideas and fresh perspectives. Expanding their professional networks is most beneficial to midcareerists because at this stage they have been in the field long enough to have repeatedly tried the same strategies but not long enough to have become cynical about novel approaches. In addition, networking gives midcareerists another source of data and information, feedback, recommendations, and advice—all of which are essential to the work they do.

> **Ask yourself:** What networking opportunities do I pursue? In what ways are they helpful?

Mentoring and Teaching Opportunities

Mentoring is beneficial to both parties involved. It allows the mentor to

- contribute to someone else's career development and growth;
- share insights into the implicit, unwritten, and unspoken rules of organizational life;
- offer advice on professional decisions that have the potential to turn into mistakes with long-lasting consequences;

- celebrate someone else's victories and provide counsel and comfort in that person's defeats;
- gain satisfaction and pride from being a vital resource, an advocate, a confidant, and a friend; and
- give back to (and do one's part for) the healthcare community.

The questions that a protégé poses can also prompt the mentor to reevaluate her own career path or choices. For example, one former CEO admits that she returned to being a chief operations officer after her protégé asked if she liked what she was doing. This question made the former CEO realize that she missed running day-to-day operations and the enjoyment she gained from that role.

Mentoring is fundamentally equal to teaching. Teaching, however, is structured, abides by rigid schedules, and requires much preparation. Practitioners are valuable additions to the faculty of any graduate program in health services administration because they strengthen the credibility of these programs. Many students prefer to learn from teachers who have field experience and who have applied (or created) methodologies explored in textbooks and other course materials. More important, students gain much insight from teachers who have actually failed and succeeded at making real-world, organization-wide decisions.

Teaching provides ample rewards for midcareer practitioners, including the following:

- Opportunities to learn about (or at least become familiar with) new trends, forecasts, best practices, general and specific concerns, and public opinions—both inside and outside the field
- Opportunities for self-reflection, values reassessment, and reevaluation of career choices
- Forums for discussing healthcare-related news, history, customers, operational challenges, strategic approaches, and similar topics

- Regular lessons in humility, open-mindedness, diverse perspectives and expectations, relationships, and values

Both mentoring and teaching enhance the mid-careerist's performance levels, preparing him for his next role.

Ask yourself: Am I a mentor or a teacher? If so, what advantages does each role present? If not, have I considered mentoring and teaching opportunities? Do I have a mentor or teacher who has been part of my growth?

LATE CAREERISTS

Retirement Planning

For active and busy late careerists, thinking about retirement can be traumatic for several reasons. First, their level of control will diminish. Second, the pace of their everyday lives will slow down. Third, the number of their associates will dwindle. Fourth, and most important, their sense of productivity and contribution will shrink. Regardless of such trepidations, retirement is inevitable and thus must be faced accordingly.

The late careerist must develop clear plans (for home and work purposes) for her departure and communicate those plans with her family and staff. Financial preparation is imperative, but it is not the sole element of a robust retirement plan, which should include a next-career transition plan.

The plans of some retired CEOs include the following elements:

Further Development Opportunities

The American College of Healthcare Executives provides extensive career services and support. Its online service, CareerEDGE, is a unique, interactive, comprehensive tool for planning and managing a career. Additional resources can be found at https://www.ache.org/career-resource-center.

- A personal mission statement for the retirement years
- A phased plan for the next, less-rigorous occupation, such as being an instructor

Note that retirement planning is markedly different from succession planning. The latter is a structured, multilevel development process, while the former is a personal transition exercise.

> **My Creed**
>
> To have no secret place wherein
> I stoop unseen to shame or sin;
> To be the same when I'm alone
> As when my every deed is known;
> To live undaunted, unafraid
> Of any step that I have made;
> To be without pretense or sham,
> Exactly what men think I am.
>
> —Edgar A. Guest (1911)

Ask yourself: How am I preparing—intellectually, financially, physically, socially, and emotionally—for my retirement? Are my family and staff aware of my plans?

Attitude Toward Younger Colleagues and Aspiring Leaders

Some late careerists question the values (including commitment) and contributions of "today's generation," regarding young workers with cynicism and skepticism. This negative attitude runs counter to the values espoused by the late careerist and harms team morale. Hearing it is also offensive, even when said in jest. Seasoned leaders have accomplished too much to tarnish their reputation by making petty remarks.

Ask yourself: How do I regard the younger generation? Am I welcoming, or am I curmudgeonly? How do my colleagues respond to this attitude, and how are they affected?

Self-Tributes

Self-tributes are a documentation of not only the late careerist's achievements but also the positive changes to the organization, the community, and the lives of many people. Writing this tribute is not an exercise in egomania; rather, it is an exercise in self-affirmation—that is, it serves as a reminder that your personal sacrifices eased others' hardships, that you instituted improvements that saved lives and livelihood, or that your tireless advocacy and support led to progress in the community and the organization. After all, no one knows all the good that has been done better than the person who made it happen.

Ask yourself: What will people remember about me? Have I written a self-tribute? If not, what will I include in this document?

CONCLUSION

Finding time for self-assessment is more easily said than done. But doing so is not impossible, especially when a strong commitment to improvement exists. Self-evaluation and self-reflection are routine practice for successful leaders because they understand that even the most ideal people can be "consistently inconsistent"—that is, everyone falls victim to saying one thing but doing another. If we are not aware of this tendency, we cannot begin to remedy it. This book offers not only a detailed explanation of this tendency but also a strong remedy.

Self-Evaluation Questions

❑ Have I ever formally, using assessment tools, evaluated my leadership successes and failures?

❑ How well do I live by my values? Do I expect those around me to live by their values?

❑ What is my legacy?

Exercise: Impact of COVID-19 on Career Management

Review one of the following articles and discuss how the issues addressed affect career management.

Akkermans, J., J. Richardson, and M. L. Kraimer. 2020. "The Covid-19 Crisis as a Career Shock: Implications for Careers and Vocational Behavior." *Journal of Vocational Behavior* 119: 103434.

Mahmud, M. S., M. U. Talukder, and S. M. Rahman. 2021. "Does 'Fear of COVID-19' Trigger Future Career Anxiety? An Empirical Investigation Considering Depression from COVID-19 as a Mediator." *International Journal of Social Psychiatry* 67 (1): 35–45.

Sklar, D. P. 2020. "COVID-19: Lessons from the Disaster That Can Improve Health Professions Education." *Academic Medicine: Journal of the Association of American Medical Colleges* 95 (11): 1631–33.

REFERENCES

Buck, P. S. 1964. *The Joy of Children.* New York: J. Day.

Covey, S. R. 1990. *The Seven Habits of Highly Effective People: Powerful Lessons in Personal Change.* New York: Fireside Press.

Guest, E. A. 1911. *Just Glad Things.* Detroit.

Hershberg, J. G. 1993. *James B. Conant: Harvard to Hiroshima and the Making of the Nuclear Age.* New York: Knopf.

McNally, M. P. 2015. *Reflect Yourself: Exploring, Assessing, Understanding, and Improving Your Life.* Tucson, AZ: Wheatmark Publishing.

Shaw, G. B. 1906. *Mrs. Warren's Profession: A Play in Four Acts.* London: Archibald Constable and Co.

PART V

ADDITIONAL PERSPECTIVES ON LEADERSHIP

CHAPTER 20

Inclusive Leadership

Carla Jackie Sampson, PhD, FACHE

CLEO MARS, CHIEF human resources officer, glanced at her slide deck before she began her presentation. She was about to seek support from her colleagues for yet another new diversity initiative. The last two efforts resulted in several hires at various levels within the organization over the past five years. The turnover rate for diverse hires was compelling—almost 50 percent within the first year and 85 percent after two years of employment.

Mars had conducted the exit interview with Dr. Jacinta Mazza, the senior VP of Clinical Informatics, whom the recruiters had headhunted from New York City. Dr. Mazza had impressive credentials as a foreign-trained physician with a master of science in nursing and a PhD in computer science. In addition, this hire had finally added several dimensions of diversity to the senior leadership team—Black, Latinx, foreign-born, LGBTQIA, atheist, veteran. However, they resigned after just nine months into the role. What was worse, they were leaving without a new job offer.

Toward the end of the interview, Dr. Mazza had said, "Health System ABC was not serious about diversity and inclusion. This was all a numbers game when real lives—mine and my partner's—were at risk." When pressed for more information, Dr. Mazza said, "I have never felt like I belong here. I am exhausted from trying to fit into a place that does not see me as a whole person but as an oddity that somehow checks several diversity boxes. I resent that I am treated this way, yet I am also expected to be the whisperer of all things diversity?" Mars was confused about what to make of those statements at the time, knowing Dr. Mazza's solid qualifications and relevant experience.

Mars cleared her throat to signal her readiness to begin the presentation with her colleagues on the senior leadership team. This discussion was the only item on the agenda. She hoped it signaled to her colleagues how the effort to achieve a vital transformation should be perceived.

PRIOR TO THE COVID-19 pandemic, social justice advocates pointed to disparities in infant and maternal mortality to support the need for racially concordant care (Greenwood et al. 2020). However, this body of research in health disparity includes control factors that are themselves the product of myriad systemic bias issues (Asch et al. 2021). COVID-19 morbidity and mortality statistics have underscored the same stark inequities (Owen, Carmona, and Pomeroy 2020). One solution is to assure that healthcare staff reflects the population served, and in so doing, the organization will be prepared to deliver racially concordant care. While this seems to suggest that we need more diversity on the frontlines, the place to begin welcoming diversity is at the top—with inclusive leadership.

DIVERSITY IS INCLUSION AND BELONGING

Far too often, organizations attempt to address the critique of not enough visible diversity in their ranks with hiring initiatives to increase the diversity of persons included in their staff. However, concentrating on selecting from a diverse pool or hiring a diverse candidate is insufficient for inclusive organizations and, ultimately, true diversity (Webb 2017). This approach makes it seem to others like these hires were not based on qualifications or competencies and excludes these employees as they face discrimination within an unwelcoming culture. A focus on diversity metrics and the presence of historically underrepresented persons creates the wrong impressions for the dominant group (Dover, Major, and Kaiser 2016).

Sometimes organizations include implicit bias training for existing employees. Indeed, implicit bias (sometimes referenced as *unconscious bias*) training has been popular to counteract any subliminal conditioning that leads each of us to make judgments about or be fearful or suspicious of people who are not like us. This training makes employees aware of these potential barriers to collegiality, but it is only a start. Healthcare leaders wanting to improve diversity in the ranks cannot assume that implicit bias training for existing staff can address perceived deficits in the organization's culture. These stand-alone or tandem efforts are not sustainable because by focusing on the resulting diversity metrics (however defined), they miss the key factors in the diversity equation: inclusion and belonging (Agarwal 2019).

DIVERSITY IS MULTIDIMENSIONAL AND INTERSECTIONAL

Diversity is more than what we can see. There are numerous dimensions to diversity, some visible, and some not. They include personalities, thinking styles and patterns, communication styles, language, nationality, creed, religion, personal habits, life experience, race, ethnicity, age, and gender identity or expression, to name a few. A list of these dimensions is included in exhibit 20.1. These aspects of identity overlap and are interdependent, giving each person a unique story and sometimes putting them at a disadvantage. Often, those affected are fully aware of the disadvantages of existing as a minority in a majority population. These diverse individuals develop a facade knowing that this is the burden—an emotional tax—they must bear for being different. And while they may be calm outwardly, they actively question whether their perception of an experience was invalidating to these efforts to fit in, to belong. That distance between knowing psychological safety should exist and experiencing that safety is the challenge with belonging. Until they feel safe, these persons are not fully engaged as their authentic selves and continually question whether they really belong or are merely being tolerated.

Exhibit 20.1 Diversity Dimensions

	Diversity Dimension
Personality	Introversion/extraversion, interests, communication preference, thinking styles, values, morals/ethics, intelligence, thinking frames and patterns
Internal	Age, race, ethnicity, gender, gender identity, sexual orientation, physical ability, physical qualities, nationality, familial nationality, language
External	Marital/relationship status, caretaker status, family status, appearance, work experience, geographic origin and location, educational background, religion, group identity and affiliations, class, military experience, relationships, life experiences, generation
Organizational Role	Seniority, union affiliation, management status, job function, job classification, professional preparation/role, career stage

Organizations that seek to become more inclusive require a transformation of the organizational culture that is driven by leaders who develop the primary competency for this journey—inclusive leadership. It cannot be just yet another initiative, not an equal employment opportunity or other compliance effort, but a transformation of all organizational processes that govern every aspect of employee relationships, driven by the actions of inclusive leaders who willingly, enthusiastically, and patiently implement and nurture this vision (Shore and Chung 2021).

> *Stereotypes* describe notions, beliefs, or expectations about a group of persons. They might include expectations about appearance, abilities, conduct, or personality traits. Stereotypes about dimensions of diversity may be negative or positive. However, these notions are inappropriate simply because all individuals do not conform to perceptions about how groups or individuals should behave, look, or act.
>
> Black, indigenous, and people of color (BIPOC); women; and other persons with marginalized dimensions of diversity bear the burden of appearing in majority spaces as a representative of whom they should be as deemed by the majority. The challenge becomes more than twofold. First, they alone must work to contradict the stereotypes held about the people they are presumed to represent while subjugating other elements of their personal story to fit in with the majority. Second, they are often called upon to complete additional, unpaid service to build a bridge to other minority populations, which then detracts physically, emotionally, and temporally from the work they were hired to do—an *emotional tax*.

WHAT IS INCLUSIVE LEADERSHIP?

At its core, inclusive leadership is about fairness—treating people based on their uniqueness. It is about learning the personal story, valuing that story, accepting that individual as they are, and as part of the group. It is about cherishing the points of difference and treasuring the dissimilar perspectives and lenses each person brings (Bourke and Titus 2020). By this approach, we develop trust—the most indispensable ingredient in an inclusion and belonging recipe.

Inclusive leadership builds on the leadership values espoused in other chapters of this text. It describes the leadership traits and competencies necessary to create the inclusive spaces required to attract and retain diverse talent within all ranks in the organization.

It is committed to creating these spaces for people to be and feel like they belong (Alexander 2020). And as we work to develop the next generation of healthcare leaders, we must develop and model inclusive leadership as an essential skill. If not, we exclude historically underrepresented talent, and we will not have diverse talent who can perform at their best. Even worse, piecemeal efforts or even well-developed strategies to address these gaps may still result in a lack of representation at the highest levels of healthcare leadership.

INCLUSIVE LEADERSHIP IN PRACTICE

In popular literature, many metaphors are used to describe the differences among justice, equity, and equality, and the differences among diversity, inclusion, and belonging. Some examples include pie sharing, conference room seats, glass ceilings, having a voice, driving in traffic, dance party invitations, running a race, and watching a game from the sidelines. Nonetheless, achieving positive human capital and organizational outcomes at any level demands keen situational awareness from those with the power to disrupt the status quo, champion and support sustained change efforts, set realistic expectations, and tactfully navigate the conflicts that will arise when everyone no longer uses the same frames of reference or sings the same tune. Inclusive leaders develop interpersonal trust, consider diverse perspectives, expertly resolve the resulting conflicts, and practice situational leadership. These competencies are shown in exhibit 20.2.

What About the Business Case for Diversity?

Scholars at Harvard University and Morehouse College have suggested that while it is a noble cause, the business case for diversity could be exploitative to the marginalized groups that diversity initiatives seek to include (Ely and Thomas 2020). Adding diverse employees simply to leverage their potential for design thinking, creative problem-solving, or innovation potential is not enough. They argue that organizations must do more. The right conditions must be created to welcome these differences and effectively manage the conflicts that arise with such inclusion.

Exhibit 20.2 Inclusive Leadership Competencies

Develop interpersonal trust:

- Use honesty to explore commonalities and differences. Learn about perspectives not yet encountered.

Develop human capital:

- Seek equitable outcomes and provide support to diverse team members so that they thrive along with the unit.

Consider diverse perspectives and resolve conflicts:

- Use empathy to understand needs, consider these different lenses, mediate the conflicts and boldly navigate issues arising in the absence of groupthink.

Practice situational/adaptive leadership:

- Leverage an expansive mental frame to deploy an appropriate approach to best support the innovation possible from thriving diverse teams.

Source: Adapted from Tapia and Polonskaia (2020).

Inclusive leaders take action along personal, interpersonal, team, and organizational dimensions, as illustrated in exhibit 20.3. Inclusive leaders understand that they are held to a high standard and are expected to model appropriate behavior, which goes well beyond the expected organization, state, and federal compliance requirements. These leaders actively intervene in the presence of exclusionary actions to help achieve an equitable outcome.

Inclusive Conversations and Collaboration

None of this work to build inclusive spaces can be successful without open and inclusive conversations with marginalized persons of all visible and nonvisible dimensions. Inclusive conversations

Exhibit 20.3 Multidimensional Inclusive Leadership in Action

Dimension	Inclusive Leadership Awareness of Human Need	Inclusive Leadership in Action
Personal	• To feel seen and heard, have a voice, and know that they are respected, welcomed, and valued to feel psychologically safe. • Can show up as their authentic selves to contribute fully.	• Demonstrates sensitivity to difference and understands the impact of their words and actions on others. • Open to a plethora of experiences to be curious about dimensions of diversity to model inclusive action and behaviors. • Is self-aware of attitudes and biases held.
Interpersonal	• Fairness, meaning interaction with colleagues, recognition of differences, cultural acceptance, sharing.	• Active listening. Understands and adapts to different work styles and thinking. • Treats others respectfully and according to their wishes and is open to changing preferred styles to meet these wishes. • Can intervene sensitively when exclusive behavior is demonstrated.
Team	• Fairness, cooperation, and collaboration, authenticity, engagement, acknowledgment, equity, inclusive decision-making.	• Forms diverse teams. • Encourages innovation and creativity. Embraces diversity as a value. • Celebrates diverse input. • Learns/practices different styles of conflict resolution as appropriate.

| Organization | • Access to shared information, opportunities, and resources.
• Supportive and inclusive culture.
• Formal policies. | • Transparency.
• Challenges prejudice and injustice.
• Advocates for fair treatment and accommodation for different abilities.
• Committed and actively involved in diversity, inclusion, and belonging work as part of personal and organizational values. |

Source: Adapted from Turnbull et al. (2010).

seek to bridge the divide across differences with the goal of an equitable outcome.

These conversations are grounded in an enhanced mutual understanding, which is a necessary building block for the psychological safety required for inclusion (Ajayi-Hackworth 2020). Chapter 6 explains these tenets for true collaboration. Exhibit 20.4 outlines how to approach an inclusive conversation.

Inclusive Meetings

Unfortunately, the standard office meeting is often one venue where attacks on inclusion go unnoticed. These attacks, called *microaggressions*, undermine the cultural shift required for inclusion. Microaggressions are fleeting, yet they are common. They may surface in words or behaviors that could be unintentional but still convey disparaging, hateful slights that are based on stereotypes. For example, a well-meaning colleague may mention to an Asian colleague "You must be good at math," or to a Black colleague "You are very articulate" or to a female colleague "You get so emotional." Thus, inclusive leaders must be mindful of the following pitfalls:

Exhibit 20.4 The Inclusive Conversation

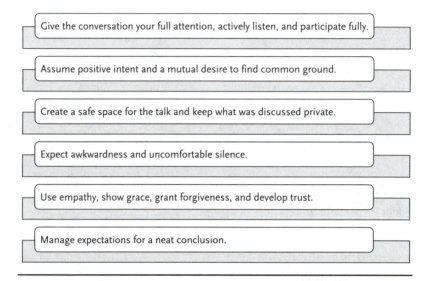

Give the conversation your full attention, actively listen, and participate fully.

Assume positive intent and a mutual desire to find common ground.

Create a safe space for the talk and keep what was discussed private.

Expect awkwardness and uncomfortable silence.

Use empathy, show grace, grant forgiveness, and develop trust.

Manage expectations for a neat conclusion.

Source: Adapted from McDaid (2020) and Winters (2020).

- Failing to send meeting materials in advance, especially when there are team members for whom English is not their first language
- Failing to send meeting materials in advance for team members who are introverts or contemplative thinkers
- Mansplaining
- Allowing creative ideas to be disparaged
- Accepting a restated idea without attribution to the colleague with the original idea
- Asking or expecting BIPOC or LGBTQ+ persons to speak for all others in their perceived diverse group
- Allowing others to complain about different accents or rates of speech, or to correct regional pronunciation differences
- Allowing interruptions/talking over others
- Omitting diverse team members from important relevant meetings

Inclusive leadership can be practiced at all levels of the organization to establish an inclusive culture in which all members thrive. This work requires consistent investment, commitment, and accountability, and results in diversity throughout the organization. Only then will the myriad benefits of diversity with inclusion redound to the organization as a whole, its various units, and its stakeholders.

> Inclusive leaders must also be mindful of off-site settings that are selected for work assignments or after the workday is complete that may be exclusive for colleagues. Notable examples include golf courses (for non-golfers and differently abled), bars (for religious team members), and dinner parties (for caregivers or colleagues with young families).

To achieve an inclusive organizational culture, leaders must reflect on their commitment to embark on this journey—a new paradigm. To begin, develop the following practices:

1. Demonstrate an unwavering and visible commitment to diversity, equity, inclusion, and belonging (DEIB); challenge the norms; and make inclusion part of a personal mission. (See chapter 19 on the personal mission.)

2. Develop humility and know that mistakes will be made during the work to create spaces and audiences for omitted voices.

3. Be acutely aware of personal biases and actively avoid them when they surface.

4. Be curious about others, actively listen to personal stories, and develop empathy (not sympathy) to understand these different perspectives.

5. Develop an intelligence about other cultures and continue learning about what is unfamiliar, but not from a position of superiority.

6. Collaborate proactively with diverse team members.

7. Work continuously to resolve conflicts, and develop psychological safety to get closer to the goal of effective, diverse teams (Bourke and Titus 2020).

Self-Evaluation Questions

❑ How inclusive are the members of the leadership team in my organization?

❑ Review your organization's guiding statements of mission, vision, and values.

❑ What signals do they send to external stakeholders about your commitment to inclusion and belonging?

❑ What message do they convey to internal stakeholders?

❑ Consider which accepted organizational practices at your organization (orientations, social activities, meetings, town halls, etc.) could be deemed exclusive for diverse team members.

Case and Exercises

Case 20.1

Consider the vignette at the beginning of this chapter.

1. During the exit interview, Dr. Jacinta Mazza was upset that she was asked to be the "whisperer of all things diversity." What did she mean?

2. What does Cleo Mars, the chief human resources officer, say to her C-suite colleagues in her talk?

3. How might Mars advance her new ideas?

Exercise 20.1

Diverse employees bear yet another burden: They live in fear of their mistakes being magnified as an example of why they do not belong or were hired to meet a quota and are wholly unqualified. They often work arduously to be "twice as good only to get half as far." This inequality is heightened when they witness a celebration of mediocrity among members of the majority. Using information from a reliable source, determine whether this describes perfectionism. If so, what are the dangers of perfectionism for employee well-being?

Exercise 20.2
1. What stereotypes do you hold? How have you become aware of these stereotypes?

2. Take the implicit bias assessments at https://implicit.harvard.edu/implicit/.

Exercise 20.3
1. Complete the LinkedIn Learning course Skills for Inclusive Conversations at https://www.linkedin.com/learning/skills-for-inclusive-conversations/six-steps-to-inclusive-conversations?autoAdvance=true&autoSkip=false&autoplay=true&resume=true.

REFERENCES

Agarwal, D. P. 2019. "Belonging in the Workplace: A New Approach to Diversity and Inclusivity." *Forbes*, August 26. https://www.forbes.com/sites/pragyaagarwaleurope/2019/08/26/belonging-in-the-workplace-a-new-approach-to-diversity-and-inclusivity/#7bf197717a66.

Ajayi-Hackworth, F. 2020. "The Buzz: Psychological Safety and Race Discussions." The Inclusion Solution, October 8. http://www.theinclusionsolution.me/the-buzz-psychological-safety-and-race-discussions.

Alexander, N. S. 2020. "A Point of View: Why Belonging Is #UpNext for Diversity and Inclusion." The Inclusion Solution, January 22. https://www.theinclusionsolution.me/a-point-of -view-why-belonging-is-upnext-for-diversity-and-inclusion/.

Asch, D. A., M. N. Islam, N. E. Sheils, Y. Chen, J. A. Doshi, J. Buresh, and R. M. Werner. 2021. "Patient and Hospital Factors Associated with Differences in Mortality Rates Among Black and White US Medicare Beneficiaries Hospitalized with COVID-19 Infection." *JAMA Network Open* 4 (6): e2112842.

Bourke, J., and A. Titus. 2020. "The Key to Inclusive Leadership." *Harvard Business Review*, March 6. https://hbr.org/2020/03 /the-key-to-inclusive-leadership.

Dover, T. L., B. Major, and C. R. Kaiser. 2016. "Members of High-Status Groups Are Threatened by Pro-diversity Organizational Messages." *Journal of Experimental Social Psychology* 62 (2016): 58–67.

Ely, R. J., and D. A. Thomas. 2020. "Getting Serious About Diversity: Enough Already with the Business Case." *Harvard Business Review*, November–December. https://hbr.org/2020/11 /getting-serious-about-diversity-enough-already-with-the -business-case.

Greenwood, B. N., R. R. Hardeman, L. Huang, and A. Sojourner. 2020. "Physician–Patient Racial Concordance and Disparities in Birthing Mortality for Newborns." *Proceedings of the National Academy of Sciences* 117 (35): 21194–21200.

McDaid, E. 2020. "How to Have Inclusive Conversations at Work." *Leader's Edge*, June 1. https://www.leadersedge.com /brokerage-ops/how-to-have-inclusive-conversations-at-work.

Owen, W. F., R. Carmona, and C. Pomeroy. 2020. "Failing Another National Stress Test on Health Disparities." *JAMA* 323 (19): 1905–06.

Shore, L. M., and B. G. Chung. 2021. "Inclusive Leadership: How Leaders Sustain or Discourage Work Group Inclusion." *Group & Organization Management* May 2021. doi:10.177/1059601121999580.

Tapia, A., and A. Polonskaia. 2020. *The 5 Disciplines of Inclusive Leaders: Unleashing the Power of All of Us.* Oakland, CA: Berrett-Koehler Publishers.

Turnbull, H., R. Greenwood, L. Tworoger, and C. Golden. 2010. "Skill Deficiencies in Diversity and Inclusion in Organizations: Developing an Inclusion Skills Measurement." *Academy of Strategic Management Journal* 9: 1–14.

Webb, M. 2017. "Hiring Diverse Candidates Is Not Enough—It's About Keeping Them." *Forbes*, October 30. www.forbes.com /sites/maynardwebb/2017/10/30/hiring-diverse-candidates -is-not-enough-its-about-keeping-them/#2a024c15b7c1.

Winters, M. F. 2020. *Inclusive Conversations: Fostering Equity, Empathy, and Belonging Across Differences.* Oakland, CA: Berrett-Koehler Publishers.

SUGGESTED READINGS

Adichie, C. N. 2009. "The Danger of a Single Story." TED Talk, October 6. https://www.ted.com/talks/chimamanda_ngozi_ adichie_the_danger_of_a_single_story?language=en.

Bourke, J. 2016. "The Six Signature Traits of Inclusive Leadership: Thriving in a Diverse New World." Deloitte Insights, April 14. https://www2.deloitte.com/us/en/insights/topics/talent/six -signature-traits-of-inclusive-leadership.html.

Burns, T., J. Huang, A. Krivkovich, I. Rambachan, T. Trkulja, and L. Yee. 2021. "Women in the Workplace 2021." McKinsey Insights, September 27. https://www.mckinsey.com/featured-insights /diversity-and-inclusion/women-in-the-workplace.

Human Rights Campaign Foundation. "Talking about Pronouns in the Workplace." Accessed April 26, 2022. https:// hrc-prod-requests.s3-us-west-2.amazonaws.com/files/assets /resources/TalkingAboutPronouns_onesheet_FINAL.pdf.

Kahneman, D. 2011. *Thinking, Fast and Slow*. New York: Farrar, Straus and Giroux.

Winters, M. F. 2020. *Inclusive Conversations: Fostering Equity, Empathy, and Belonging Across Differences*. Oakland, CA: Berrett-Koehler Publishers.

READINGS RELATED TO WOMEN PHYSICIANS

Carnes, M., C. M. Bartels, A. Kaatz, and C. Kolehmainen. 2015. "Why Is John More Likely to Become Department Chair Than Jennifer?" *Transactions of the Clinical and Climatological Association* 126: 197–214.

Lochner, J., and V. Gilchrist. 2021. "Women in Academic Family Medicine." *Family Medicine* 53 (2): 89–91.

Shlian, D. 2021. "Tips from Women Physician Leaders for Future Women Physician Leaders." *Journal of Medical Practice Management* 37 (1): 365–66.

Wehner, M. R., K. T. Nead, K. Linos, and E. Linos. 2015. "Plenty of Moustaches but Not Enough Women: Cross Sectional Study of Medical Leaders." 2015. *BMJ* 351: h6311.

CHAPTER 21

Physician Leadership Issues

Margot Savoy, MD, FAAFP, FABC, FAAPL, CPE, CMQ

What got you here won't get you there.

—Marshall Goldsmith and Mark Reiter (2007)

If you want to go fast, go alone;
but if you want to go far, go together.

—Zambian proverb

HISTORICALLY, WHEN YOUNG aspiring physicians described their dream career, they typically mentioned caring for others and helping them become (or remain) healthy. Aspirations of becoming the CEO of an accountable care organization, department chair at a university health system, or even medical director of a medical clinic were rarely mentioned. As the demand for physician executives and leaders rises, growing numbers of medical students looking to be competitive for residency and career prospects are seeking secondary degrees—notably master's degrees in physician and executive business administration, quality improvement, and population health management. According to the American Medical Association

Wearily, Jack slumps into his chair and glances at the stacks of paper on his desk. He leans back, reflecting on his feelings and trying to drum up the energy to tackle another late night at the office. He was so excited to take on this leadership role as medical director. At the time it seemed like fitting recognition for a job well done. He never had any aspiration of being a physician leader, but ignoring a problem has never been his modus operandi.

Five years ago, when Jack joined his practice, it quickly became clear to him that someone had to do something. Low morale, high patient turnover, and overall dissatisfaction were hampering the practice's ability to be successful. He was the most recent in a revolving door of clinicians. Determined to be the last, he pushed up his sleeves and got busy doing the hard (and often thankless) work, ultimately turning the practice around.

Over the past five years, the practice's patient panel doubled and then doubled again while quality and patient satisfaction improved. Jack's staff love working for him and brag constantly about how kind he is. Patients rave that he is not just an advocate—he is *their* advocate. And Jack takes pride in knowing that he would indeed fight the world if it came between his patient and the care he prescribed. Health system leaders thrilled with the practice's turnaround and seeing opportunities to translate his success across the medical group offered the perpetual "Top Doc" the opportunity to become the medical group's medical director. Jack eagerly jumped into the role, making rapid changes across the group within his first month. Over

(Murphy 2017), in 2011 only 7.7 percent of medical students pursued a degree in addition to their medical degree; however, by 2017 nearly 10 percent of students were enrolled in dual degree programs.

Transition to value-based care structures, increased interest in quality improvement and population health, and enlarging employed physician networks have each played a part in this boom of physician leadership opportunities. Lured by the opportunity to make a wider and more lasting change in the delivery of healthcare, a desire to escape the demanding pressures of full-time clinical care or teaching and the higher salary, many physicians will seriously consider making the transition from clinician to executive leadership.

All healthcare leaders can expect challenges navigating their health systems through an increasingly VUCA world. VUCA is managerial shorthand for *volatile, uncertain, complex,* and *ambiguous* (Bennett and Lemoune 2014). The rapid pace of clinical transformation, information technology and digital health, emerging diseases, and constantly changing payment models suggest that VUCA medicine is likely here to stay. While healthcare needs the knowledge and skills physicians can bring to the boardroom, physician leaders must be prepared to face the largest challenge to their success in these new roles—the very training they received as physicians. To optimize their success, physicians stepping into new roles need to be aware of their limitations and be equipped with strategies, skills, and resources to ensure they are prepared to be the effective, competent, and capable leaders their teams deserve. Far too often this is not the situation, and while their astute clinical acumen is often what got the physicians the opportunity to lead, it isn't what will keep them in the role moving forward.

CHALLENGE ORIGIN STORY

Many physician leaders feel like Jack does at some point in their career. They are truly at a loss for why they have hit a wall for doing what has worked for them their entire careers. If we are honest with them, we would tell them that they were indeed gaslighted by their medical training. (Gaslighting refers to manipulating someone by psychological means into questioning their own sanity.) Every step of the more than 20,000 hours of the journey to becoming a physician rewards and advances individuals for being exceptionally excellent, autonomous, and resilient decision-makers.

(continued from previous page)
time Jack's enthusiasm began to fade as he found himself facing significant resistance to change from his peers.

Take today, for example. After weeks of late nights spent carefully planning and researching alone in his office, Jack could barely wait to reveal the new optimal patient flow slated to be implemented next week. It worked wonders in his practice, and he was certain it could make the other practices more efficient and reduce wasted time and resources. Yet at the business meeting his proposal was met with audible groans, mumbling, eye rolls, and head shakes. He even overheard someone call him "nothing more than a suit with a white coat" and another complain that he has "no idea what it is like working on the front lines." Frustrated, hurt, and disappointed, Jack announced a delay on the implementation date and abruptly ended the meeting.

Now, as he sits in his office watching the sun set and seeing all those who poked holes in his plans head home, he realizes he feels very alone. "This can't be my new life," Jack mumbles to himself as he stares blankly at the slide deck on the computer screen. "What am I doing wrong?"

The admission process weeds out the people who do not profess a deep desire to dedicate their lives to practicing altruistic medicine and putting their patients before all others, including themselves. Being smart and dedicated to learning is enough to gain admittance to medical school, but the education process quickly grooms medical students to have all the answers on cue or risk shameful public humiliation.

After directly competing to be selected for limited slots in top-notch residency programs, resident physicians are typically rewarded for solving problems without relying on others, including their physician educators. Behind the scenes, though, everyone on the care team may feel more comfortable openly sharing their insights and thoughts. Ultimately, if things go wrong, the physician is thrust forward as the leader. Physicians in this situation face two options: save the day, or experience terrifying loneliness in the shadow of a reprimand via lawsuit threatening their livelihood and putting their personal and professional reputation at stake. This educational conditioning leads physicians to shoulder the leadership burden and responsibility alone. Unfortunately, when the "lone wolf" or "superhero" role is brought into a leadership setting, the outcome is often not only unfulfilling for their future teams but also detrimental to their own health.

THE DOWNSIDE OF THE CHALLENGE

Having leaders who willingly take full responsibility for the team's performance, accept nothing less than the best, and voluntarily run into difficult headwinds seems on the face like a win for healthcare team. Valuable to a point, when consistently applied inappropriately, these altruistic traits will eventually lead to significant issues for both the physician leader and the team.

The Quest for Perfection Leads to Burnout and Moral Injury

We want the person who is directing our life-saving care to be meticulous, thorough, and exacting. From the beginning we intentionally select students who are painstakingly perfect on paper and during an interview. The highest achieving among the high achievers who never truly stumble, working second jobs in labs while balancing their other extracurricular activities, are often not well equipped to manage failure. This perfection expectation does not let up, because medicine is a space that consistently has little tolerance for complications or undesired outcomes, let alone errors.

Imprinted early in training with the negative consequences of being seen as weak—needing help or lacking knowledge—most physicians turn inward when faced with less than perfect outcomes. As Dike Drummond (2015) points out, the physician training that conditions doctors to be successful overdevelops traits (exhibit 21.1) that ultimately drive the physician to burnout. He names two "prime directives" that guide physician thinking: "The patient comes first" and "Never show weakness" (Drummond 2015). Given that humans are fallible, this unsustainable need to maintain the façade of perfection drives negative behaviors such as hiding opportunities to create systemic changes that could prevent others from making the same mistake later or failing to leverage coaching to improve personal performance.

Initially this overdependence on self-reliance may appear to work well, but eventually the physician leader will exceed their ability to identify the true underlying issue, objectively identify next steps, or create a path toward a new outcome. For some this can set off a spiral of self-doubt, anger, and disillusion with the field.

For other physician leaders, this can show up as burnout out or even moral injury. According to Dean, Talbot, and Dean (2019, 28), "moral injury occurs when we perpetrate, bear witness to, or fail to

Exhibit 21.1 Unhealthy Traits Reinforced Through Medical Education

Trait	How It Shows Up
Workaholic	Your only response to challenges or problems is to work harder.
Superhero	You feel like every challenge or problem sits on your shoulders and you must be the one with all the answers.
Perfectionist	You can't stand the thought of making a mistake—*ever*—and hold everyone around you to the same standard.
Lone ranger	You must do everything yourself and end up micromanaging everyone around you.

Source: Drummond (2015).

prevent an act that transgresses our deeply held moral beliefs." With such a strong emphasis on putting patients first embedded during physician training, the transition into the business side of medicine can be startling and upsetting. Seeing firsthand "how the sausage is made" can shatter a deeply held belief of the purity of medicine and the doctor–patient relationship. Now held to metrics that extend beyond the doctor–patient interaction, it ceases to be acceptable to make decisions solely on patients' individual interests.

The physician leader must learn to accept the additional stakeholder interests while being placed in the role of translating and driving the management activities that implement these changes. For some it can feel like a betrayal of the fundamental premise of the oath they swore to uphold at the start of their career. This discomfort and need to hold two at times conflicting protecting roles- patient advocate and organization guardian, can lead to cognitive dissonance.

Cognitive dissonance was first described by psychologist Leon Festinger, who published his theory in his 1957 book, *A Theory of*

Cognitive Dissonance. Cognitive dissonance is the state of having inconsistent thoughts, beliefs, or attitudes, especially as relating to behavioral decisions and attitude change (Festinger 1962). Put another way, it is described as the outcome of a person performing (or not performing) an action that contradicts personal beliefs, ideals, and values.

Cognitive dissonance also can arise when a physician leader is confronted with new information that contradicts his or her beliefs, ideals, and values. This disconnect can show up in many feelings and behaviors, such as confusion, anxiety, stress, shame, embarrassment, or even regret. Over time, if unable to resolve the internal conflict, the physician leader might internalize these negative feelings, leading to decreased self-worth and confidence. Ultimately, to create resolution the physician leader will need to change her behavior, attitude, or belief (Festinger 1962). Each of these choices presents a substantial challenge to overcome for those who are not properly equipped with emotional intelligence, self-awareness skills, and an adequate support system. Yet, as noted earlier, all of these tend to be counterintuitive to the physician who was conditioned to never show weakness and hold firm to self-determination, self-reliance, and perfection.

Physician leaders may feel this moral injury even more acutely when they have a support system that is mostly made up of other physicians. Initially supportive of a member of their peer group being elevated into a leadership position, this endorsement can often collapse. Physician peers are often hopeful that their peer who becomes a leader will bring their voices to the table, leading to necessary and overdue changes to the healthcare leadership team. Without the larger view of the complexity and underlying issues driving the

> In the health care context, that deeply held moral belief is the oath each of us took when embarking on our paths as health care providers: Put the needs of patients first. That oath is the lynchpin of our working lives and our guiding principle when searching for the right course of action. But as clinicians, we are increasingly forced to consider the demands of other stakeholders—the electronic medical record (EMR), the insurers, the hospital, the health care system, even our own financial security—before the needs of our patients. Every time we are forced to make a decision that contravenes our patients' best interests, we feel a sting of moral injustice. Over time, these repetitive insults amass into moral injury.
>
> —Dean, Talbot, and Dean (2019)

decisions, these peers can continue to press for centering the physician voice on behalf of their patients even when it comes at the expense of the organization's basic viability. Over time it is not uncommon for those networks to erode as the physician leader begins the delicate balancing act of being "one of us" versus "one of them." This leaves the physician leader in the particularly vulnerable position of being excluded from both sides—too uncomfortable to share their challenges with the nonphysician management team and unable to share with the peer physician network who now could view the physician as "one of the suits" or, even worse, lose faith in the physician's suitability to lead for having shown weakness in the face of a challenge.

A Shared Vocabulary Is Lacking

Having a shared language and vocabulary is fundamental to successful communication and collaboration. When team members are unable to communicate effectively, the resulting miscommunications can lead to errors, causing erosion of trust and cohesiveness (Thomas and McDonagh 2013).

Medical training teaches physicians to communicate using a shared lexicon in standard styles that effectively convey critical information. The red rash becomes a collection of erythematous macules and papules. The belly button is now properly called the umbilicus. Because the physician is surrounded by academics, even routine words such as *significant* and *sensitivity* take on new contextual meanings. Clinicians learn to organize a complex patient story into a synopsis integrating what the patient shared, what was found on examination, and the resulting diagnostic conclusions. Physicians are even taught to be sensitive to their patient's language needs, from dialect to reading level, to ensure they understand the medical care they are receiving.

Yet when physicians step into the business leadership space, the rules, communication expectations, and even the lexicon change dramatically. Bombarded by jargon, abbreviations, and concepts foreign to them, many new frontline physicians feel isolated, confused, and unable to participate fully in their new roles. To be heard and advance the programs that align with physician interests, physician leaders must learn to master the financial and economic-based language and point of view and present their patient-centered programs in terms of business cases, cost savings opportunities, or shared savings models. Simultaneously, physician leaders need to be adept at linking the business and financial descriptions, approaches, and terms to the key motivating factors that are likely to drive sustainable clinician change such as improving patient outcomes (e.g., decreasing mortality, increasing mobility, and reducing pain) (Pagán and Saloner 2015).

As healthcare becomes more complex, both business and physician leaders are being challenged to expand their vocabulary to incorporate the lexicons and core concepts from information technology, systems engineering and quality improvement, and population health.

THE UPSIDE OF THE CHALLENGE

Being a "lone wolf" or "superhero" does bring some advantages, especially in a confident, charismatic leader. Leaders who effectively leverage a top-down approach can ease team anxiety by quickly getting results. This style can restore confidence and a clear sense of direction for a team that has been

The Patient-Centered Medical Home: A Success in Shared Language?

Dugan Maddux, MD, FACP, highlights the patient-centered medical home as a successful model for creating a shared language between clinicians and business leaders that creates alignment that leads to successful outcomes. He notes that "PCMH successful efforts focus on health outcomes, patient and provider experience of care, expense reduction, and hospital and ER utilization. As a model of care, PCMH articulates and values clinical outcomes side by side with return on investment (ROI). The PCMH model, which supports multidisciplinary-team-based clinical care, has been embraced by primary care physicians and physician organizations" (Maddux 2015).

Kennedy and colleagues explored the patient's perspective on the PCMH and found that while inadequacies remain, patients were able to identify how the medical home helps them reach their health goals, and recognize the physicians' and nurses' commitment to providing them with high-quality healthcare and overall satisfaction with the care they receive (Kennedy et al. 2013).

feeling a leadership void or unclear direction. Even when the leader's initial decision is a misstep, the speed and nimbleness of a single decision-maker means that any corrective action can be implemented efficiently as well.

In times of crisis this command-and-follow approach is often preferred. Without the burden of collaboration, there is no hand-wringing over who is in charge or where the decisions are made. There is no desire for extensive discussion in the middle of a cardiac arrest. The most experienced person in the room takes the lead and quickly assigns tasks so everyone in the room is clear about their roles and expectations without losing time unnecessarily. It would be inappropriate to hold a meeting to reach a collaborative decision about whether the team should begin cardiopulmonary resuscitation. When a practice is failing, the team may also be willing to support a leader who appears to have the answers and can guide them safely out of the imminent danger. For physicians, it is often easy to step into this leadership role of giving orders and having others follow them. They have been well-trained to wield a hammer, and all the initial issues are clearly nails. The difficulty comes later when the physician is promoted based on his or her skill with the hammer and encounters practices that present a vast array of non-nail issues.

MANAGING THE CHALLENGE

The solution to managing this challenge is deceptively simple: develop emotional intelligence and self-awareness. Learn to leverage a

---

Challenge in Action (continued)

Jack is demonstrating workaholic, lone wolf, and superhero tendencies. Although his top-down, coercive approach appeared to be successful with his practice team when they were in crisis mode, this approach seems misguided, heavy-handed, and out of touch to the other practices. He failed to engage the other practices or their informal leaders to develop relationships and build trust. This meant he could not see that unlike in his practice, the other practices don't see an urgent need to change and are comfortable with their current practices. Unfortunately, his response to these oversights—doubling down on the same style and skills by trying to work harder—is unlikely to realize the success he seeks.

What steps could Jack take to shift this downward spiral?

range of leadership styles and approaches. Embrace inclusion and team-based approaches. Reframe failure as learning agility. Recruit a deep support bench.

Develop Emotional Intelligence and Self-Awareness

The term *emotional intelligence* was coined in the 1990s by Salovey and Mayer (1990), who described a form of social intelligence that involves the ability to monitor one's own and others' feelings and emotions, to discriminate among them, and to use this information to guide one's thinking and action. Later David McClelland and Daniel Goleman expanded the belief that both emotional and social factors are important and further developed the concept identifying five primary domains of emotional intelligence, which are shown in exhibit 21.2 (McClelland 1961, Goleman 1995; Goleman, Boyatzis, and McKee 2002).

Goleman (1998) compared star performers with average ones in senior leadership positions and found that nearly 90 percent of the differences in their profiles was attributable to emotional intelligence factors rather than cognitive abilities. Early researchers were uncertain if emotional intelligence is an innate trait similar to intelligence or whether it is a skill set that can be developed. It is now widely accepted that although we may naturally exhibit some adeptness in Emotional Quotient (EQ; sometimes abbreviated EI) skills, anyone can improve their EQ with deliberate and intentional practice. Leaders who choose to invest in their own EQ ability are rewarded with improvement in their personal effectiveness as a leader. Helpful books that explore more about EQ and leadership are shared in exhibit 21.3, but for most leaders simply reading a book will be insufficient to make and maintain the changes necessary without a coach or peer support.

Exhibit 21.2 Five Domains of Emotional Intelligence

Domain	Description	Categories
Self-awareness	Ability to recognize and understand your moods, emotions and drives and their effect on others	Emotional Self-Awareness, Accurate Self-Assessment, Self-Confidence
Self-management/ regulation	Ability to control or redirect disruptive impulses and moods; ability to suspend judgment allowing to think before acting	Emotional Self-Control, Transparency/Trustworthiness, Adaptability, Achievement, Initiative, Optimism, Conscientiousness
Motivation	Passion to work for reasons beyond money or status; pursuing goals with energy and persistence	Sustained Motivation, Adaptable, Sense of Urgency
Social awareness/ Empathy	The ability to understand the emotional make-up of others and skill in treating people according to their emotional reactions	Empathy, Organizational Awareness, Service Orientation
Relationship management	Proficiency in managing relationship and building networks; finding common ground and building rapport	Inspirational Leadership, Influence, Developing Others, Change Catalyst, Conflict Management, Building Bonds, Teamwork and Collaboration, Communication

Source: Goleman (1998).

Exhibit 21.3 Selected Books about Developing Emotional Intelligence

- *Leadership: The Power of Emotional Intelligence*
  Daniel Goleman

- *Becoming a Resonant Leader: Develop Your Emotional Intelligence, Renew Your Relationships, Sustain Your Effectiveness*
  Annie McKee, Richard Boyatzis, and Frances Johnston

- *The Emotionally Intelligent Manager: How to Develop and Use the Four Key Emotional Skills of Leadership*
  John Mayer, David Caruso, and Peter Salovey

- *At the Heart of Leadership: How to Get Results with Emotional Intelligence*
  Joshua Freedman

- *Emotional Intelligence 2.0*
  Travis Bradberry and Jean Greaves

- *Thinking Fast and Slow*
  Daniel Kahneman

Leverage Leadership Styles and Approaches

While physician leaders are often initially identified by their outstanding clinical acumen or impressive leadership of a small team of like-minded individuals (e.g., a clinical department or practice), many are unaware of the techniques or skills they used to achieve their success. This makes it difficult for them to replicate their successes efficiently, and they may be unaware of additional options for approaching the issues facing them.

Ideally, the physician leader understands the underlying basis for both her and her team's motivation. David McClelland's three needs theory (exhibit 21.4) provides a model that describes the impact of the needs for achievement, affiliation, and power on leadership and management. Introduced in 1961, McClelland's book *The Achieving Society* outlines these three motivators, which

Exhibit 21.4 McClelland's Three Needs Theory of Motivation

Affiliation
- Wants to belong to the group.
- Wants to be liked, and will often go along with whatever the rest of the group wants to do.
- Favors collaboration over competition.
- Doesn't like high risk or uncertainty

Achievement
- Has a strong need to set and accomplish challenging goals.
- Takes calculated risks to accomplish their goals.
- Likes to receive regular feedback on their progress and achievements.
- Often likes to work alone

Power
- Wants to control and influence others.
- Likes to win arguments.
- Enjoys competition and winning.
- Enjoys status and recognition.

Motivation

Source: McClelland (1961).

are learned over time though life experiences (McClelland 1961). These drivers remain constant without regard to gender, culture, or age. Successful leaders can quickly and accurately identify and align the team's motivation with their own to advance the organization's goals. They can identify what type of leader their team needs them to be at the moment to achieve the optimal outcome, and can flex their style to match.

This leadership nimbleness is rooted in a robust foundation in and comfort with emotional intelligence. Goleman (2000) was not only instrumental in advancing EQ research in workplace settings, but he also explored how leaders leverage EQ in different ways to achieve results from their teams. Ultimately, he identified six executive leadership styles (exhibit 21.5) that have predictive effects on the team being led. While the initial impulse may be to identify

Exhibit 21.5 Six Executive Leadership Styles

Leadership Style	Modus Operandi	Descriptor	Works Best
Coercive	Demands immediate compliance	"Do as I say."	In a crisis, to kick-start a turnaround, or with problem employees
Authoritative	Mobilizes people toward a vision	"Come with me."	When changes requires a new vision, or when a clear direction is needed
Affiliative	Creates harmony and builds emotional bonds	"People come first."	To heal rifts in a team or to motivate people during stressful circumstances
Democratic	Forges consensus through participation	"What do you think?"	To build buy-in or consensus, or to get input from valuable stakeholders
Pacesetting	Sets high standards for performance	"Do at my pace."	To get quick results from a highly motivated and competent team
Coaching	Develops people for the future	"Try this."	To help an employee improve performance or develop long-term strengths

Source: Goleman (2000).

which style is "right," the reality is that a successful leader is skilled in all six styles and facile with choosing the appropriate approach to apply for the team at a given moment.

As noted earlier, being a top-down leader has its place in the physician leader arsenal either during a crisis situation when the coercive style immediately points the team in the appropriate direction or through an authoritative style mobilizing the team to a clear vision set out by the leader. When used inappropriately, however, both styles can undermine the team culture, causing demotivation and failure to achieve optimal outcomes. On the other hand, choosing an affiliative style, putting people first and seeking to create harmony and bonds in the midst of a crisis, may help team members feel seen but fail to provide them clear guidance and direction during a critical moment. This also can lead to negative consequences for the leader and the team. Formal leadership and management training will help the physician leader learn which styles come most naturally to them plus expose them to behaviors and actions that can give the team the support and leadership they need to thrive (Price-Dowd 2020).

Embrace Inclusion and Team-Based Approaches

Inclusiveness means more than gathering a wide range of people to work with you on your team. To be effective, multidisciplinary teams must be more than diverse. Leveraging the collective capabilities of each team member—pulling from their unique life experiences shaped by their gender, racial, or cultural heritage; age; disability; or other unique characteristics—is important. Yet if those members do not feel safe, valued, or included as a member of the team, no one will ever hear those perspectives. Leaders have a great effect on whether team members feel seen and valued, and fortunately, like EQ, inclusive leadership is skill that can be learned. Juliet Bourke and Andrea Titus (2019) surveyed 4,100 employees and identified six traits that are exhibited by inclusive leaders, shown in exhibit 21.6.

Exhibit 21.6 Six Traits of Inclusive Leaders

Trait	Description
Visible commitment	They articulate authentic commitment to diversity, challenge the status quo, hold others accountable, and make diversity and inclusion a personal priority.
Humility	They are modest about capabilities, admit mistakes, and create the space for others to contribute.
Awareness of bias	They show awareness of personal blind spots as well as flaws in the system and work hard to ensure meritocracy.
Curiosity about others	They demonstrate an open mindset and deep curiosity about others, listen without judgment, and seek with empathy to understand those around them.
Cultural intelligence	They are attentive to others' cultures and adapt as required.
Effective collaboration	They empower others, pay attention to diversity of thinking and psychological safety, and focus on team cohesion.

Source: Bourke and Titus (2019).

Although these traits may seem obvious, Bourke and Titus (2019) point out that many leaders have no insight into whether their team truly sees them as inclusive, what behaviors demonstrate inclusiveness, or how to most effectively ensure their commitment to inclusiveness was recognized. For example, one potential disconnect was employees ignoring grand gestures of inclusiveness and instead relying on how the leader behaves in smaller daily interactions. Another disconnect was leaders being comfortable with the majority of employees feeling psychologically safe and included without appreciating that unless everyone in the organization feels a sense of belonging, fairness, and respect, they have not yet achieved truly inclusive leadership (Bourke and Titus 2019).

A notable blind spot for physician leaders is the appearance of favoritism. Most physicians are promoted into leadership roles after years of service in a particular department, section, or practice. Their informal network of peers may be skewed to a particular setting or specialty, leading others to question their ability to be fair or balanced in decision-making. When choosing members for teams, leaders typically rely on familiar networks, which unintentionally gives the appearance that some team members' inputs are more valued than others'. Failure to seek out leaders from other disciplines, such as business leaders, nursing leaders, or other allied health leaders, can limit the team's ability to uncover the full range of opportunities and solutions.

Physician leaders can actively improve their inclusiveness by making some intentional changes to their daily routine (Bourke and Titus 2019). With an open mind and willingness to explore blind spots, strengths, and opportunities for improvement, physician leaders should do the following:

- Seek feedback from all team members about how your level of inclusiveness is perceived.
- Share your personal inclusion narrative with the team, publicly highlighting not only that inclusiveness is important to you but also why.
- Be intentional about seeking out diverse opinions, experience, and inputs.
- Look for unintended favoritism.
- When forming teams or looking to appoint new leaders, avoid relying solely on your personal experience.
- Identify the skills or knowledge you need on the team and then gather recommendations and nominations from a wide pool across the organization.
- Focus on daily habits and behaviors that demonstrate your commitment to inclusiveness.

Reframe Failure as Learning Agility

Perfectionism and fear of failure do not simply limit the individual physician leader when there is an error or mistake. They stifle creativity, innovation, or willingness to remain curious and open to alternative possibilities. Physician leaders face a steep climb to return to the carefree days of unbridled creativity and innovation. After years of training in disaster avoidance in clinical care, the physician's natural response to a problem is to generate a thorough list of all the things that could potentially go wrong and to create a plan that neutralizes or eliminates the undesired outcomes. While this approach leads to exquisite differential diagnosis lists and often saves lives, focusing solely on mitigating risks and preventing errors distracts the physician leader from innovating, imagining, or inventing solutions.

Successful physician leaders demonstrate the capacity for rapid, continuous learning from experience known as *learning agility* (Valcour 2015). Characteristics of agile learners include a willingness and ability to unlearn things when novel solutions are required; openness to new experiences; and willingness to experiment, actively seek feedback, reflect systematically, desire to acquire new skills, and master new situations (Valcour 2015).

According to Peter Sims (2012b), "entrepreneurs and designers think of failure the way most people think of learning," and expert entrepreneurs must "must make lots of mistakes to discover new approaches, opportunities, or business models." In his 2012 book *Little Bets: How Breakthrough Ideas Emerge from Small Discoveries*, Sims describes how across industries the most creative and adaptive organizations not only tolerate failure as a learning process but also actively encourage failing often and quickly and investing the learning into creating novel approaches, tools, and products (Sims 2012a).

> Agile learners value and derive satisfaction from the process of learning itself, which boosts their motivation as well as their capacity to learn from challenging developmental experiences.
>
> —**Monique Valcour (2015)**

Susan Peppercorn (2018) points out that "it's when you feel comfortable that you should be fearful, because it's a sign that you're not stepping far enough out of your comfort zone to take steps that will help you rise and thrive." She goes on to suggest four steps leaders can take to move through their fear of failure:

- Redefine failure to be more realistic about what is a small win versus a failure to meet a lofty goal.
- Craft your language around goal setting to focus on approach and not avoidance goals.
- Create a checklist of what you are afraid to do and what you fear will happen if you do it.
- Include the potential benefits of the attempted effort and the cost of inaction to create a more holistic view of your fear in context.

Finally, Peppercorn asserts that by focusing on learning, leaders will gain value no matter the outcome, making the fear of failing much more acceptable.

Recruit a Deep Support Bench

Beside a successful physician leader is a network of support including peers, role models, mentors, sponsors, and coaches. During different career stages a leader may rely more heavily on one group over another, but over a career each of these key players brings a level of accountability and support necessary to help the physician leader through challenges, setbacks, and stagnation to achieve personal growth and success (Sharma et al. 2019). A brief description of these roles is provided in exhibit 21.7 (Gotian 2020).

These critical relationships require active management, development, and cultivation. Not all initial pairings are successful or remain relevant over time. Leaders should be comfortable diplomatically

Exhibit 21.7 Physician Leader Support Team

Role	Description
Peer	Someone who has similar knowledge and experiences as you and is willing to be in a mutually beneficial relationship.
Role Model	Someone who has traits you admire and wish to emulate.
Mentor	Someone who talks *with* you about your career, goals, plans, and aspirations. They help you refine your plan, suggest people you should talk to, opportunities you should partake in, and obstacles you should be aware of.
Coach	Someone who talks *at* you as you try to perfect something very specific.
Sponsor	Someone who talks about you when you are not in the room. They nominate you for the choice committees, awards, and promotions.

Source: Adapted from Gotian (2020).

exiting these situations as their needs change. Straus and colleagues (2013) studied successful and failed mentoring relationships to identify common characteristics of each. Failed mentoring relationship characteristics included poor communication, lack of commitment, personality differences, perceived (or real) competition, conflicts of interest, and the mentor's lack of experience. Characteristics of successful mentoring relationships include reciprocity, mutual respect, clear expectations, personal connection, and shared values.

A physician leader who neglects to build and maintain relationships runs the risk of feeling professionally isolated, lonely, and burned out. One solution is to reimagine Balint groups, traditionally used to explore challenging physician–patient interactions, as a way to build processional networks and safe spaces (Frey 2020).

As Jack turned his attention to the computer screen, his phone rang. Mark, a more seasoned physician leader in the organization, was on the line. Mark was in the physician lounge earlier and overheard physicians complaining about Jack and his "cluelessness." Knowing Jack and his dedication to the team, Mark was surprised to hear the complaints. Then he recalled, with a brief blush of embarrassment, how difficult his early transition from peer to physician leader had been.

Mark decided to reach out. Jack, initially horrified and embarrassed that Mark was aware of his disastrous meeting, was relieved to hear Mark volunteer a story about his early physician leadership experience. The two talked about opportunities for Jack to consider, starting with including some of the key informal leaders in the planning stage to hear additional insights, garner support and allies, and improve the initiative before rolling it out. Mark connected Jack to the health system's emerging leadership program where he can learn more about his own style and how to effectively influence others and engage with multidisciplinary leaders from across the health system. Jack thanked Mark for reaching out and asked if he could contact him in a week or so share how things are going.

For women and other underrepresented groups in medicine, mentorship alone is insufficient for career advancement, yet opportunities for sponsorship are limited and remain difficult to attain (Ayyala, Skarupski, and Bodurtha 2019). This is problematic because while organizations can match high potential leaders with potential sponsors, no one can force someone to wield their power on behalf of their potential protégés. For members from underrepresented groups, getting promoted into senior positions, stretch assignments, and mission-critical roles becomes even more difficult (Ibarra and von Bernuth 2020). One proposed solution to this challenge is to reframe sponsorship into fewer high-stakes interactions (exhibit 21.8) for the sponsor by removing the "all or nothing mentality" currently used (Ibarra 2019).

CONCLUSION

Physician leaders bring valuable insight and skill to the C-suite and boardroom. Making the transition from full-time clinician to physician leader or executive requires more skill and preparation than is gained in traditional medical training. When a physician joins the leadership team, some attributes of a successful physician may

Exhibit 21.8 Reimagining the Spectrum of Potential Leadership Support Relationships

Mentor → Strategizer → Connector → Opportunity Giver → Advocate

Source: Adapted from Melanson (2009).

need to be rebalanced to allow for maximum effectiveness. Building and using EQ effectively, learning basic jargon and concepts, curating a team of supports who can provide candid feedback, guidance, and sponsorship help ensure a smoother transition into the leadership space.

REFERENCES

Ayyala, M. S., K. Skarupski, and J. N. Bodurtha. 2019. "Mentorship Is Not Enough: Exploring Sponsorship and Its Role in Career Advancement in Academic Medicine." *Academic Medicine* 94: 94–100.

Bennett, N., and G. J. Lemoune. 2014. "What VUCA Really Means for You." *Harvard Business Review*, January–February. https://hbr.org/2014/01/what-vuca-really-means-for-you.

Bourke, J., and A. Titus. 2019. "Why Inclusive Leaders Are Good for Organizations, and How to Become One." *Harvard Business Review*, March 29. https://hbr.org/2019/03/why-inclusive-leaders-are-good-for-organizations-and-how-to-become-one.

Dean, W., S. Talbot, and A. Dean. 2019. "Reframing Clinician Distress: Moral Injury Not Burnout." *Federal Practitioner* 36

(9): 400–402. [Published correction appears in *Federal Practitioner* 36 (10): 447.]

Drummond, D. 2015. "Physician Burnout: Its Origin, Symptoms, and Five Main Causes." *Family Practice Management* 22 (5): 42–47.

Festinger, L. (1957). A theory of cognitive dissonance. Evanston, Ill: Row, Peterson.

Festinger, L. 1962. "Cognitive Dissonance." *Scientific American* 207 (4): 93–102.

Frey, J. J. 3rd. 2020. "A New Role for Balint Groups in Overcoming Professional Isolation and Loneliness." *International Journal of Psychiatry in Medicine* 55 (1): 8–15.

Goldsmith, M., and Reiter, M. 2007. *What Got You Here Won't Get You There: How Successful People Become Even More Successful*. New York, NY: Hyperion.

Goleman, D. 2000. "Leadership That Gets Results." *Harvard Business Review* March–April: 78–90.

———. 1998. "What Makes a Leader?" *Harvard Business Review* 76 (6): 93–102.

———. 1995. *Emotional Intelligence: Why It Can Matter More Than IQ*. New York: Bantam Books.

Goleman, D., R. E. Boyatzis, and A. McKee. 2002. *Primal Leadership: Realizing the Power of Emotional Intelligence*. Boston: Harvard Business School Press.

Gotian, R. 2020. "Why You Need a Role Model, Mentor, Coach and Sponsor." *Forbes*, August 4. https://www.forbes.com/sites/ruthgotian/2020/08/04/why-you-need-a-role-model-mentor-coach-and-sponsor/?sh=2529e1787c48.

Ibarra, H. 2019. "A Lack of Sponsorship Is Keeping Women from Advancing into Leadership." *Harvard Business Review*, August 19. https://hbr.org/2019/08/a-lack-of-sponsorship-is -keeping-women-from-advancing-into-leadership.

Ibarra, H., and N. von Bernuth. 2020. "Want More Diverse Senior Leadership? Sponsor Junior Talent." *Harvard Business Review*, October 9. https://hbr.org/2020/10/want-more -diverse-senior-leadership-sponsor-junior-talent.

Kennedy, B. M., S. Moody-Thomas, P. T. Katzmarzyk, R. Horswell, W. P. Griffin, M. T. Coleman, J. Herwehe, J. A. Besse, and K. H. Willis. 2013. "Evaluating a Patient-Centered Medical Home from the Patient's Perspective." *Ochsner Journal* 13 (3): 343–51.

Maddux, D. 2015. "Spanning the Great Divide: Translating Medicine and Business into a Common Language." Accumend Physician Solutions, September 28. https://acumenmd.com /blog/spanning-the-great-divide-translating-medicine-and -business-into-a-common-language/.

McClelland, D. C. 1961. *The Achieving Society*. Princeton, NJ: Van Nostrand.

McClelland, D. C. (1973). Testing for competence rather than for 'intelligence'. American Psychologist, 1973, Volume 28, Issue 1, pp 1-14.

Melanson, M. A. 2009. "The Mentoring Spectrum." *US Army Medical Department Journal* October–December: 37–39. PMID: 20073362.

Murphy, B. 2017. "Considering a Dual Degree? Those Who Did It Share the Pros, Cons." American Medical Association, September 6. www.ama-assn.org/residents-students/medical -school-life/considering-dual-degree-those-who-did-it-share -pros-cons.

Pagán, J. A., and B. Saloner. 2015. "Do You Speak My Language? When Patient Care Meets Cost-Effectiveness." *American Journal of Accountable Care* 3 (2).

Peppercorn, S. 2018. "How to Overcome Your Fear of Failure." *Harvard Business Review*, December 10. https://hbr.org/2018/12/how-to-overcome-your-fear-of-failure?ab=at_art_art_1x1.

Price-Dowd, C. F. J. 2020. "Your Leadership Style: Why Understanding Yourself Matters." *BMJ Leader* 4: 165–67.

Salovey, P., and J. D. Mayer. 1990. "Emotional Intelligence." *Imagination, Cognition and Personality* 9 (3): 185–211.

Sharma, G., N. Narula, M. M. Ansari-Ramandi, and K. Mouyis. 2019. "The Importance of Mentorship and Sponsorship: Tips for Fellows-in-Training and Early Career Cardiologists." *JACC: Case Reports* (2): 232–34.

Sims, P. 2012a. *Little Bets: How Breakthrough Ideas Emerge from Small Discoveries*. London: Random House Business Books.

———. 2012b. "The No. 1 Enemy of Creativity: Fear of Failure." *Harvard Business Review*, October 5. https://hbr.org/2012/10/the-no-1-enemy-of-creativity-f.

Straus, S. E., M. O. Johnson, C. Marquez, and M. D. Feldman. 2013. "Characteristics of Successful and Failed Mentoring Relationships: A Qualitative Study Across Two Academic Health Centers." *Academic Medicine* 88: 82–89.

Thomas, J., and D. McDonagh. 2013. "Shared Language: Towards More Effective Communication." *Australasian Medical Journal* 6 (1): 46–54.

Valcour, M. 2015. "4 Ways to Become a Better Learner." *Harvard Business Review*, December 31. https://hbr.org/2015/12/4-ways-to-become-a-better-learner.

CHAPTER 22

Humans Working with
Humans to Heal Humans

Katherine A. Meese, PhD, and David A. Rogers, MD, MPHE

> *"What is one thing senior leadership could do*
> *to improve your experience at work?"*
>
> *"To feel that I am not expendable."*
>
> —Healthcare worker (July 2020)

THE HEALTHCARE LANDSCAPE is becoming ever more complex, with the rapid expansion of medical discoveries, advancing technologies, regulatory and reimbursement reforms, and the most dangerous pandemic in over a century. These industry pressures often demand so much attention from our leaders that managing them and adapting to them becomes the sole focus. Healthcare workers have long been known to sacrifice themselves in the care of others. When these two dynamics come together, it creates a ripe environment for distraction from the core business of healthcare, which is and always has been *humans working with humans to heal humans*. As leaders, we focus on the complexities of financial and operational performance, and the dedication and sacrificing nature of our workforce allows us to get away with it until things are very broken.

NO MARGIN, NO MISSION?

It is nearly impossible to have any exposure to healthcare management and leadership education without hearing the phrase "no margin, no mission." The phrase originated from Sister Irene Krauss, a trailblazer in healthcare and founding executive of the Daughters of Charity National Health System, a $3 billion, 17-state multihospital system at the time (Thomas 1998). Sister Irene believed that healthcare was a ministry, not an industry, and the underserved remained her passion and focus (Modern Healthcare 1996). She believed the key to this aim was financial stability—if one cannot afford to keep the doors open, they will not be able to help others (Thomas 1998). Her ability to pursue strong financial performance stood out in a time when hospitals were transitioning to a prospective payment format.

Under cost-plus, what the hospital spent to provide care was reimbursed in full, as well as a portion of capital costs (Barr 2016). This allowed hospitals to operate without the difficulty of financial scarcity, but they also were not incentivized for being prudent with their spending since all would be reimbursed, leading to ballooning costs of care. When prospective payment began, healthcare executives were faced with intense financial pressures that had never been experienced before, meaning they had to be more aggressive in the financial management of the organization (Hafferty and Light 1995). Undoubtedly, cuts would have to be made, which is always unpopular. If the hospital could not achieve a financial margin, then it could not keep the doors open and thus could not meet its mission of caring for patients and the community. The financial pressures have worsened, with declining reimbursements and healthcare reform making financial sustainability an ever-present challenge for for-profit and non-profit systems alike (Barr 2016; Malik, Kahn, and Goyal 2020).

The mantra of "no margin, no mission" has since transformed into the battle cry for making difficult choices for the sake of financial performance.

But what if the margin becomes the mission?

THE MCDONALDIZATION OF HEALTHCARE

Declining reimbursements and nationwide shortages of physicians and nurses have led to an environment of increasing scarcity in healthcare, where organizations are facing continuing pressures to do more with less (Alexander, Werner, and Ubel 2004). As a result, organizations have turned their attention to opportunities to increase patient volumes to ensure healthy revenues, with the mantra of "heads in beds" (Rosenthal 2018).

The application of Lean/Six Sigma has been used to increase patient throughput to drive greater revenues (de Koning et al. 2006). Providers are often expected to see patients every 15 minutes and also attend to a massive increase in paperwork and documentation requirements (Noseworthy 2019). The hyper sub-specialization of care has also led to clinicians performing smaller and smaller pieces of the patient's overall care, instead of participating in the broad range of activities required to achieve health and healing.

The concept of McDonaldization offers a framework to understand these trends in healthcare (Ritzer 2013). To understand this concept, we must first explore a brief evolution of modern workplace. Increasing efficiency was the goal of Frederick Winslow Taylor (1919). Taylor was known for closely monitoring workers and timing how long each task would take, then making corrections so that each step was completed in the minimal possible time. This movement toward scientific management became the basis for busy assembly lines, with workers quickly repeating a specific task ad infinitum (Drucker 2010). This form of working reduced the variety of tasks for workers during the day, diminished their autonomy, and drastically changed the way people engaged with their work. Despite early concerns about the negative consequences this system would have on workers, it was rapidly embraced in education, industry, and the government (Lepore 2018).

These organizational patterns in contemporary times have been described as McDonaldization (Ritzer 2013). If you have ever been to a busy McDonald's or other fast-food restaurant, you may have noticed that the work is highly divided, with each crew member completing discrete tasks, often quickly and repeatedly. Ritzer (2018) uses the concept of a fast-food restaurant to examine how these concepts continue to infiltrate our work environments today using the principles of efficiency, calculability, predictability, and control, citing many instances in which these categories have been introduced in healthcare (see Exhibit 22.1).

What Is the Result?

The sum of these changes has resulted in healthcare workers feeling less like humans helping humans heal, and more like machine components on an assembly line (Haque and Waytz 2012; Light and Levine 1994). These sentiments emerged during a survey of healthcare workers during the COVID-19 pandemic in July 2020 (see sidebar).

These sentiments fueled a massive burnout epidemic prior to the pandemic, with rates skyrocketing during the unprecedented challenges of working in healthcare during the worst global pandemic in a century. During the early phases of the pandemic, 71 percent of physicians, 89 percent of advance practice providers, and 90 percent of nurses reported high distress (Meese et al. 2021). These pressures combined have led to massive resignations from the healthcare workforce (Yong 2021).

The McDonaldization of healthcare is creating unhealthy and unsustainable work. What does a different path forward look like?

OPTIMIZING HEALTHCARE WORK THROUGH ENLIGHTED LEADERSHIP

There is nothing inherently wrong with seeking to improve efficiency in healthcare processes and pursue financial health. However, a focus on financial and operational performance becomes a problem when it

Exhibit 22.1 Concepts of McDonaldization

Concept	Definition	Nonhealthcare Examples	Healthcare Examples
Efficiency	Completing tasks with no wasted effort and minimal use of resources	UPS drivers plan routes to make mostly right turns (instead of left), saving millions of dollars in fuel	Primary care providers are allotted 15 minutes per patient encounter
Calculability	Placing a priority on using quantitative measures to evaluate work	Uber's system of driver and passenger ratings	The conversion of the patient encounter into relative value units
Predictability	Processes to ensure services will be the same over time and in different locations	Standardized training and ingredients worldwide to ensure a Starbucks latte tastes the same in Beijing and Birmingham	The use of best practices, a standardized surgical checklist, or ICD-10 documentation requirements
Control	Regulating the conduct of people in a system	Amazon watching delivery drivers with cameras to ensure they do not deviate from their delivery route	Automated "reminders" in the electronic health record to prompt providers and staff about policies or procedures

Source: Adapted from Ritzer (2018).

reduces the equally important focus on the humans within the organization, both provider and patient. The solution is enlightenment among leaders who can strike the right balance between gaining efficiency and adequate finances while designing work that promotes wellness and engagement. Decades of research have been conducted on human motivation and performance, which has revealed that humans' needs at work lie beyond the mere speedy repetition of routine tasks (Alderfer 1972; Herzeber 1968; Kouzes and Posner 2006; Pink 2009; Seligman 2011). These needs include things like task variety, autonomy, mastery, purpose and meaning, relatedness, good leadership, and opportunities for growth, as well as the ability to care for one's physical needs. Self-determination theory, job-demands resource model, and empowering leadership and job-crafting provide useful concepts for the optimal design of healthcare work (Bakker and Demerouti 2007; Demerouti 2014; Gagné and Deci 2005). These sentiments emerged during a survey of healthcare workers during the COVID-19 pandemic in July 2020 (see sidebar).

Self-Determination Theory

Self-determination theory postulates that humans have the basic needs of autonomy, competence, and relatedness, and the fulfillment of these needs promotes well-being (Ryan 2009). A recent application of self-determination theory provides definitions of these three basic constructs (Dreison et al. 2018). Autonomy is having freedom and choice in one's actions that might include latitude about how tasks are completed. Competence is the feeling that one is capable of performing the necessary tasks, and relatedness, or belongingness, is the need to form and maintain positive interpersonal relationships that might be marked by high levels of cohesion with trust between team members. An enlightened leader would be attentive to the presence of these three job features and attend to threats of competence through training and creating social connections through team development. Autonomy should be provided to the greatest extent possible appropriate to the individual worker and the task. The elements of self-determination theory are fundamental and therefore should be considered in the design or redesign of every job.

> **Have there been any positive changes during this time? (June–July 2020)**
>
> I feel that our staff and especially the clinical team has been able to adapt with the changes. Mostly individuals who have been present and continued to come to work during the pandemic. It has been positive to see some coworkers become more independent.
> —**Advance practice provider**
>
> Do think it has stirred the creative juices to find new ways and safer ways for workers and families to do tasks.
> —**Physician**
>
> I believe my coworkers and I have grown immensely as a team. We were forced to overcome huge obstacles and teamwork was the only way we could get through it.
> —**Nurse**
>
> I have seen people work together even helping out in other departments and that has been a major positive impact.
> —**Clinical support staff—social worker**

Job Demands Resources Theory

The job demands resource model conceptualizes workplace well-being as representing a state of balance between demands and resources. Imbalances, generally in the form of increasing demands, lead to strain and can ultimately result in burnout (Bakker and de Vries 2021). This model offers the advantage of being dynamic in nature, so leaders can use it to predict situations where worker well-being might be at risk and how this risk could be mitigated. Specifically, any increase in workplace demand increases strain, and it may be possible that this can be offset through the provision of additional support. More recent versions of this model have divided both demands and resources into two categories (Tims, Bakker, and Derks 2012). Challenge demands are those that involve effort but are perceived by the worker as offering the possibility of leading to personal gain or growth. Hindering demands are those seen as thwarting that growth. Structural resources are those inherent to the individual or provided by the organizational and social resources, include enhancing or increasing social connections with supervisors or colleagues. These expanded models show that there are many ways balance can be achieved and that demands are not always necessarily negative.

Empowering Leadership and Job Crafting

Among the myriad leadership approaches, those that involve attention to workers' needs are generally associated with increased worker well-being (Pearce and Sims 2002). A recent leadership form that offers some exciting prospects is empowering leadership that is marked by a leader who invites participation in decision-making, expresses confidence in the subordinate, enhances meaningfulness in work, and provides autonomy (Audenaert et al. 2020). Empowering leadership is distinct in that it challenges subordinates and offers the opportunity to develop them, which provides both the worker and the organization a long-term organizational benefit. Some positive outcomes of empowering leaders appear to occur through job crafting. Job crafting is the modification of work by the most highly motivated workers (Kim and Beehr 2020). These workers would make changes in their own work that lead to improved fit between themselves and their jobs, resulting in an increasing willingness to make future changes (Dubbelt, Demerouti, and Rispens 2019). Changes on the demand side of the model might include taking on a challenge demand or delegating a hindering demand. Increasing structural resources might involve gaining more administrative support, and increasing social resources might involve asking for supervisor feedback. One cautionary note about job crafting is that reducing hindering demands can be associated with reduced engagement. It remains unclear whether an empowering leader can guide employees to optimally job-craft.

HUMANS ARE THE MARGIN AND THE MISSION

Humans are at the center of both the margin and the mission. The COVID-19 pandemic has brought an alarming awareness to the healthcare industry. If you have no healthcare workers, you have no financial margin, no operational margin, and no mission.

At the beginning of the pandemic, healthcare organizations were mandated to cancel elective surgeries to reduce the spread of the virus and conserve intensive care unit beds and personal protective equipment, resulting in massive financial losses (Barnett, Mehrotra, and Landon 2020; Best et al. 2020).

Financial margin is only one way to conceptualize "margin," but we must expand our definition of the word (Swenson 2014). There are other margins we build into healthcare operations to allow us to absorb a shock to the system. We keep additional supplies on hand in the event of a natural disaster or supply chain disruption. We aim to keep a margin of extra blood in the blood bank so we can handle unexpected traumas that may come through our doors. We maintain a financial margin to ensure we can fix broken equipment and manage uncompensated care. These financial and operational margins are often closely measured, monitored, and managed—as they should be.

But What of the Human Margin?

Expenditures for staffing and compensation are typically the largest line items on a hospital's budget. As a result, staffing ratios are typically kept as lean as possible to ensure a financial margin while maintaining the minimum level of staffing to provide quality care (Kumar, Subramanian, and Strandholm 2002). These lean staffing ratios have led to increasing workloads and burnout of epidemic proportions (Shah et al. 2021). Further, they left us vulnerable to COVID-19. There were never enough people to absorb a shock to the system. We created no human margin for the unexpected. As reported by the Centers for Disease Control and Prevention (CDC) in May 2022, more than 900,000 healthcare workers have become sick and over 3,000 died while caring for our communities (CDC 2021). We had no human margin to absorb it. Furthermore, because the industry had accepted high levels of physician and nurse burnout as the norm, the humans we did have remaining had few emotional reserves left to withstand the unbelievable stress and uncertainty of working in a hospital during a pandemic, causing a mass exodus from the workforce (Dionisi et al. 2021; Willard-Grace et al. 2019). This further depleted our human margins that were unacceptably lean in the first place.

A walk through any modern, state-of-the-art hospital will leave us wondering whether the existential financial threat of "no margin, no mission" is real. Newly built towers, hotel-style amenities, fountains, and every latest technology are prevalent. How many of these purchases were made at the expense of better staffing? What good are these bells and whistles when there is no human margin to deliver on the mission of patient care?

While hospitals were required to cancel elective surgeries at the beginning of the pandemic to contain the disease, now they must cancel because there simply aren't enough people left to do the surgeries (Holpuch 2021). No human margin means no financial margin, and no mission.

What of the Mission?

A search of mission and vision statements of healthcare organizations reveals some common threads. They aim to provide excellent care or improve the health of their community, city, state, nation, or world. Healthcare organizations are often among the largest employers in their communities, which means that their workforce comprises a sizeable portion of the community they vow to care for (Meese et al. 2021). However, they cannot care for the health of the community without caring for the health and well-being of members of the community that work within their walls. The humans who work in healthcare are central to the mission, not a means to some other mission.

REFERENCES

Alderfer, C. P. 1972. *Existence, Relatedness, and Growth: Human Needs in Organizational Settings.* New York: Free Press.

Alexander, G. C., R. M. Werner, and P. A. Ubel. 2004. "The Costs of Denying Scarcity." *Archives of Internal Medicine* 164 (6): 593.

Audenaert, M., B. George, R. Bauwens, A. Decuypere, A.-M. Descamps, J. Muylaert, R. Ma, and A. Decramer. 2020. "Empowering Leadership, Social Support, and Job Crafting in Public Organizations: A Multilevel Study." *Public Personnel Management* 49 (3): 367–92.

Bakker, A. B., and J. D. de Vries. 2021. "Job Demands–Resources Theory and Self-Regulation: New Explanations and Remedies for Job Burnout." *Anxiety, Stress, & Coping* 34 (1): 1–21.

Bakker, A. B., and E. Demerouti. 2007. "The Job Demands–Resources Model: State of the Art." *Journal of Managerial Psychology* 22 (3): 309–28.

Barnett, M. L., A. Mehrotra, and B. E. Landon. 2020. "Covid-19 and the Upcoming Financial Crisis in Health Care." *NEJM Catalyst Innovations in Care Delivery* 1 (2).

Barr, D. 2016. *Introduction to US Health Policy: The Organization, Financing, and Delivery of Health Care in America*, 4th ed. Baltimore: John Hopkins University Press.

Best, M. J., E. G. McFarland, G. F. Anderson, and U. Srikumaran. 2020. "The Likely Economic Impact of Fewer Elective Surgical Procedures on US Hospitals During the COVID-19 Pandemic." *Surgery* 168 (5): 962–67.

Centers for Disease Control and Prevention (CDC). 2021. "Cases & Deaths Among Healthcare Personnel." https://covid.cdc .gov/covid-data-tracker/#health-care-personnel.

de Koning, H., J. P. S. Verver, J. van den Heuvel, S. Bisgaard, and R. J. M. M. Does. 2006. "Lean Six Sigma in Healthcare." *Journal for Healthcare Quality* 28 (2): 4–11.

Demerouti, E. 2014. "Design Your Own Job Through Job Crafting." *European Psychologist* 19 (4): 237–47.

Dionisi, T., L. Sestito, C. Tarli, M. Antonelli, A. Tosoni, S. D'Addio, A. Mirijello, G. A. Vassallo, L. Leggio, A. Gasbarrini, G. Addolorato, and Gemelli Against COVID-19 Group. 2021. "Risk of Burnout and Stress in Physicians Working in a COVID Team: A Longitudinal Survey." *International Journal of Clinical Practice* 75 (11).

Dreison, K. C., D. A. White, S. M. Bauer, M. P. Salyers, and A. B. McGuire. 2018. "Integrating Self-Determination and Job Demands–Resources Theory in Predicting Mental Health Provider Burnout." *Administration and Policy in Mental Health and Mental Health Services Research* 45 (1), 121–30.

Drucker, P. F. 2010. "The Coming Rediscovery of Scientific Managment." In *F. W. Taylor: Critical Evaluation in Business and Management*, edited by J. C. Wood and M. C. Wood, 351–58. New York: Routledge.

Dubbelt, L., E. Demerouti, and S. Rispens. 2019. "The Value of Job Crafting for Work Engagement, Task Performance, and Career Satisfaction: Longitudinal and Quasi-experimental Evidence." *European Journal of Work and Organizational Psychology* 28 3: 300–314.

Gagné, M., and E. L. Deci. 2005. "Self-determination Theory and Work Motivation." *Journal of Organizational Behavior* 26 (4): 331–62.

Hafferty, F. W., and D. W. Light. 1995. "Professional Dynamics and the Changing Nature of Medical Work." *Journal of Health and Social Behavior*, 132–53.

Haque, O. S., and A. Waytz. 2012. "Dehumanization in Medicine." *Perspectives on Psychological Science* 7 (2): 176–86.

Herzeber, F. 1968. "One More Time: How Do You Motivate Employees?" *Harvard Business Review* 81 (1): 87–96.

Holpuch, A. 2021. "Strained Massachusetts Hospitals Will Cut Back on Elective Procedures." *New York Times*, November 24, 2021.

Kim, M., and T. A. Beehr. 2020. "Job Crafting Mediates How Empowering Leadership and Employees' Core Self-evaluations Predict Favourable and Unfavourable Outcomes." *European Journal of Work and Organizational Psychology* 29 (1): 126–39.

Kouzes, J. M., and B. Z. Posner. 2006. *The Leadership Challenge*. Hoboken, NJ: John Wiley & Sons.

Kumar, K., R. Subramanian, and K. Strandholm. 2002. "Market and Efficiency-Based Strategic Responses to Environmental Changes in the Health Care Industry." *Health Care Management Review* 27 (3): 21–31.

Lepore, J. 2018. *These Truths: A History of the United States.* New York: W. W. Norton & Company.

Light, D. W., and S. Levine. 1994. "The Changing Character of the Medical Profession: A Theoretical Overview." In *The Corporate Transformation of Health Care*, 2nd ed., edited by J. W. Salmon. New York: Routledge.

Malik, A. T., S. N. Khan, and K. S. Goyal. 2020. "Declining Trend in Medicare Physician Reimbursements for Hand Surgery from 2002 to 2018." *Journal of Hand Surgery* 45 (11): 1003–1011.

Meese, K. A., A. Colón-López, J. A. Singh, G. A. Burkholder, and D. A. Rogers. 2021. "Healthcare Is a Team Sport: Stress, Resilience, and Correlates of Well-Being Among Health System Employees in a Crisis." *Journal of Healthcare Management*, 66 (4): 304–322.

Modern Healthcare. 1996. "Health Care Hall of Fame Past Inductees—Sister Irene Krauss." https://www.modernhealth care.com/awards/health-care-hall-fame-inductees-sister -irene-kraus.

Noseworthy, J. 2019. "The Future of Care—Preserving the Patient–Physician Relationship." *New England Journal of Medicine* 381 (23): 2265–69.

Pearce, C. L., and H. P. Sims. 2002. "Vertical Versus Shared Leadership as Predictors of the Effectiveness of Change Management Teams: An Examination of Aversive, Directive, Transactional, Transformational, and Empowering Leader Behaviors." *Group Dynamics: Theory, Research, and Practice* 6 (2): 172–97.

Pink, D. H. 2009. *Drive: The Surprising Truth About What Motivates Us*. New York: Riverhead Books.

Ritzer, G. 2018. *The McDonaldization of Society: Into the Digital Age*, 9th ed. Thousand Oaks, CA: SAGE Publications.

———. 2013. *The McDonaldization of Society*, 20th ed. Thousand Oaks, CA: SAGE Publications.

Rosenthal, E. 2018. *An American Sickness: How Healthcare Became Big Business and How You Can Take It Back*. New York: Penguin Books.

Ryan, R. 2009. "Self-determination Theory and Wellbeing." *Social Psychology* 88: 822–48.

Seligman, M. 2011. *Flourish: A Visionary New Understanding of Happiness and Well-being*. New York: Free Press.

Shah, M. K., N. Gandrakota, J. P. Cimiotti, N. Ghose, M. Moore, and M. K. Ali. 2021. "Prevalence of and Factors Associated with Nurse Burnout in the US." *JAMA Network Open* 4 (2): e2036469.

Swenson, R. A. 2014. *Margin: Restoring Emotional, Physical, Financial, and Time Reserves to Overloaded Lives*. Carol Stream, IL: Tyndale House.

Taylor, F. W. 1919. *The Principles of Scientific Managment*. New York: Harper & Brothers.

Thomas, R. M. J. 1998. "Irene Kraus, 74, Nun Who Led Big Nonprofit Hospital Chain." *New York Times*, August 27, 24.

Tims, M., A. B. Bakker, and D. Derks. 2012. "Development and Validation of the Job Crafting Scale." *Journal of Vocational Behavior* 80 (1): 173–86.

Willard-Grace, R., M. Knox, B. Huang, H. Hammer, C. Kivlahan, and K. Grumbach. 2019. "Burnout and Health Care Workforce Turnover." *Annals of Family Medicine* 17 (1): 36–41.

Yong, E. 2021. "Why Health-Care Workers Are Quitting in Droves." *The Atlantic*, November 16. https://www.the atlantic.com/health/archive/2021/11/the-mass-exodus-of -americas-health-care-workers/620713/.

CHAPTER 23

Leadership Matters—For Healthcare's Present and Future

Patrick D. Shay, PhD

T HE ANNUAL *HEALTHCARE TOMORROW* conference always gathered a diverse collection of healthcare professionals from across the city of Trinity Falls, including health administrators, physicians, clinical leaders, public health experts, and health services researchers. Attendees looked forward to hearing from prominent healthcare futurists in terms of what changes would confront and transform the healthcare landscape in the years and decades to come, and this year's conference was no exception.

After an afternoon workshop on the topic of how leaders can positively influence healthcare's future through moral and transformative leadership approaches, debate started to break out among a group of attendees who were reflecting on how the speaker's message applied to their own work. It started with a simple comment from a young healthcare entrepreneur, Alexis, who noted, "That message was great."

Davis, a seasoned hospital executive sitting next to Alexis, couldn't help but jump in: "You know, I hate to be the jaded pessimist and rain on your parade, but that was a waste of time."

"What do you mean? The leadership principles they shared are exactly the kinds of things I need to be doing if I'm going to effectively lead my team and help our start-up grow," Alexis replied.

Davis gave a derisive smile. "There's a reason they say nice people finish last. If you spend all your time being distracted by trying to hold on to some moral high ground, you'll end up getting lapped by the person who's willing to do what it takes to succeed. The reality is that there are plenty of folks on both sides of winning and losing that subscribe to this leadership stuff. In the end, what makes the difference is whether anyone can execute the job at hand, not whether someone followed some type of leadership recipe."

A third participant had been eavesdropping on Alexis and Davis's conversation and decided to weigh in as well. "I couldn't help but overhear you two, and I think you're both wrong. In today's world, leaders are just figureheads. We're all naive if we truly think that healthcare organizations in the future are going to be swayed by an individual's leadership values or philosophies."

"Come on, you're joking," Alexis replied. "You don't think leaders matter?"

"To be frank, I don't, not in the idealistic way you all seem to dream it does. We've spent all day here talking about what the future of healthcare is going to be, but let's be honest about who's really going to be calling the shots in the future: not the people themselves, but their organizations' algorithms and automated decision processes. The so-called leaders of those organizations will just be sitting around to make sure things stick to the script."

Alexis was stunned. "Leadership does matter; it has to. If not, why are we even here?"

INTRODUCTION

Throughout this book, the values and skills that characterize effective leaders have been convincingly presented and discussed, highlighting the importance of values-based leadership in today's complex and dynamic healthcare field. Yet, reflecting on how these values and skills connect with their own personal experiences, some may question to what degree these values and skills indeed matter. Do we see leaders who exhibit such qualities truly realize success, and do leaders who fail to adhere to these values fail to realize desired performance levels in return?

History is marked by examples of individuals who led high-performing organizations yet failed to embody values such as integrity, trust, compassion, or respectful stewardship. We see this represented in popular culture as well, with an abundance of examples of unsavory organizational leaders depicted in film and television, from Miranda Priestly in *The Devil Wears Prada* to Bill Lumbergh in *Office Space*. Of course, the frustrations surrounding the seeming success of those who treat others poorly are not new to modern society; Job, the biblical figure, famously lamented the prosperity of the wicked amid his own suffering. In the same way, we are often challenged to reconcile those instances in which a leader can seemingly enjoy success while behaving badly.

On the other hand, many of us can also think of examples of leaders who embody the values and characteristics described in this book but who have not enjoyed success. Despite being admired and adored leaders, their organizations, departments, or units have failed to meet performance expectations under their watch. This outcome begs the question: Is there a connection between leaders' adoption and adherence to these values and effective performance? Or do leaders merely serve as figureheads, and do the skills and characteristics they bring to their position have little effect in terms of organizational outcomes? Simply put, does leadership really matter?

To address these questions, this chapter looks to the extensive work of researchers who have examined the role of leadership in organizations. We begin by considering organizational theorists' perspectives on the part leadership plays in organizational phenomena, followed by a review of academic literature on the connection between leadership and healthcare organizational performance. The chapter concludes with a consideration of current conversations surrounding the role of leadership to help healthcare organizations navigate uncertainty, unpredictability, and complexity, both for today and tomorrow.

ORGANIZATION THEORY AND LEADERSHIP

Although it may seem an unappealing exercise reserved for scholars stuck in an ivory tower, organization theory offers important insights and considerable value for today's healthcare leaders. More than just an academic discipline, organization theory serves as a tool that draws from interdisciplinary thinking to allow us to better make sense of complex phenomena in the practical world, helping to simply explain and rationalize what we observe and experience while equipping individuals to be more effective leaders of the organizations they serve (Hatch 2018). In other words, engaging with organization theory is an exercise that provides value for all who are interested in healthcare organizations, practitioners and academics alike.

Within organization theory, scholars recognize that organizational phenomena occur at varying levels. As individuals and groups of individuals behave and work in an organizational setting, their personalities, activities, and other qualities affect the characteristics and outcomes of the overall organization. At the same time, these individuals and groups of individuals make up entire organizations, and organizational characteristics, properties, activities, and dynamics in turn influence organizational outcomes as well as the behaviors and actions of individuals. Across each of these levels, organization theory speaks to the role of leadership in organizational phenomena, offering a variety of perspectives with different approaches to consider the role of leaders. Although the terms *organization theory* and *organizational theory* will often be used interchangeably in different conversations, some use *organizational theory* to distinguish perspectives that are solely focused on macro (i.e., organizational and interorganizational) levels of analysis versus perspectives focused on micro (i.e., individual and group) levels of analysis, also referred to as *organizational behavior.* For the sake of clarity, this chapter's reference to *organization theory* encompasses the collection of varied perspectives at varying levels—micro and macro—that work to describe, understand, and explain the behaviors, processes, and phenomena both within and among organizations.

At the group and individual levels, organization theorists have sought to understand what characterizes effective leaders, developing a broad collection of theories over the past century that differentiate leaders from nonleaders as well as from one another. This includes a progression of different perspectives that have led to the evolved realization that leadership is not simply a title or innate gift for the privileged few, but rather is influenced by individual leaders' traits, behaviors, and responses to the situations presented to them (Walston 2017). Contemporary theories of leadership build on these past efforts while also emphasizing the complexity that is inherent in the role of leadership and the myriad factors that may affect the outcomes of leadership efforts. Concepts including transformational leadership, charismatic leadership, adaptive leadership, authentic leadership, collaborative leadership, ethical leadership, and servant leadership, among others, have been developed and emphasized by contemporary leadership scholars, bringing attention to the ways in which leaders can inspire, empower, foster trust, align values, change culture, and promote their followers' development (Borkowski and Meese 2021). Furthermore, contemporary theories challenge the traditional focus of leadership studies on the individual leader, calling for recognition of the diverse array of mechanisms that influence leadership dynamics, including situational, subordinate, structural, organizational, and environmental factors.

Across the development of perspectives on leadership within organization theory at the individual and group levels, scholars continually affirm the role of leaders to influence others and organizations through their conduct, decisions, interactions, communications, vision, and beliefs (Walston 2017). Similarly, at the broader organizational and field levels, organization theorists have examined leaders' impact on organizational life, specifically asking what role leaders play in shaping organizational structures, activities, strategies, and performance. These theories recognize that leaders cannot operate within a vacuum, but that their organizations are subject to, influenced by, and dependent on environmental forces and external factors (Hatch 2018). Furthermore, these perspectives vary in the degree to which they suggest the environment shapes organizational decisions and activities, with some theories emphasizing the leader's agency to influence organizational change and performance, while others recognize the deterministic power of the environment that can constrain leaders' abilities and decisions.

However, to assume that such theories inherently dismiss the role or effectiveness of leaders is an oversimplification. Even among scholars who view adaptive leadership as a romantic ideal limited by environmental powers and structural constraints or a social construct built artificially upon resources and institutional artifacts, organizational theorists see the work of the leader as consequential; leaders serve to create environments of trust, to foster critical social relationships, and to use organizational practices and tools to influence the organization's operations (Parry 2011; Peltonen 2016). In sum, whether expressed explicitly or implicitly, macro-level organization theorists and researchers convey a common conviction that leadership indeed does matter. Although their varied perspectives offer differing points of emphasis in recognizing the factors that influence organizational activity and outcomes, they recognize leaders as actors who engage external relationships, competitive markets, and industry trends in order to guide their colleagues, shape organizational culture, navigate environmental demands, and serve as agents of influence for their organizations (see exhibit 23.1).

Exhibit 23.1 A View of Leadership from Organization Theory

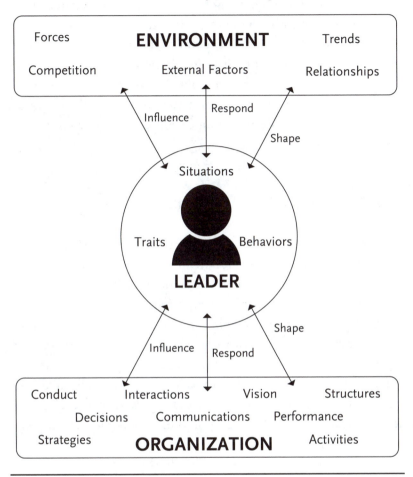

The extant literature offers a variety of perspectives on leadership in organizations, including different views of the role that leaders play, the constraints that affect leadership, the traits and behaviors that characterize effective leaders, the preferred leadership approaches for specific situations, and the complex mechanisms that influence leaders' decisions and performance. As organization theory has advanced to successively introduce, evaluate, and even synthesize these varied perspectives across different levels, scholars have gained a more nuanced view of leadership in organizations.

At the same time, we see a common thread across these different approaches when it comes to assessing leadership in organizations: It matters. Organizational theorists, despite their different perspectives and emphases, consistently point to the important role played by leaders, in turn affecting their organizations, the individuals they work with, and their external environment. Given such convictions within organization theory, we now turn to look at the empirical evidence of leadership's impact on organizational outcomes in the extant literature.

THE EVIDENCE ON LEADERSHIP

Many studies in general management literature have asked whether leadership makes a difference in organizational performance. Although some are quick to raise the argument that an entire organization's performance cannot be solely attributed to a single individual due to the complexity of organizations and the varied environmental, organizational, and historical factors that also contribute to organizational outcomes, research broadly supports the assertion that an organization's effectiveness is influenced and affected by its leadership across individual, group, and organizational levels (Parry 2011). Recent reviews of contemporary theories of leadership (e.g., transformational leadership, empowering leadership, ethical leadership, authentic leadership, servant leadership) that emphasize the importance of leaders' empathy, morality, and prosocial behaviors for enduring organizational success suggest that positive leadership behaviors connect to a wide variety of positive organizational outcomes, including job satisfaction, organizational commitment, organizational citizenship behaviors, well-being, employee health, and individual, team, and firm performance, among others (Eva et al. 2019; Hoch et al. 2018; Kim, Beehr, and Prewett 2018; Lemoine, Hartnell, and Leroy 2019; Mazzetti et al. 2019). The benefits of positive leadership behaviors can even be realized on a daily level, with such practices contributing to immediate positive outcomes (e.g., engagement, positive emotions, personal initiative, creativity) for both the leaders themselves and their organizational members (Kelemen, Matthews, and Breevaart 2020). Furthermore, studies consistently link an organization's culture to its performance, and they acknowledge the critical role that leadership plays in developing and sustaining a positive organizational culture (Hartnell et al. 2019; Kim and Toh 2019; O'Reilly, Chatman, and Doerr 2021).

Not only does research point to the relationship between effective leaders and desirable organizational outcomes, but it also points to a connection between poor leadership and poor performance, suggesting that leaders' failure to exercise effective leadership translates to negative organizational results. For example, destructive leadership practices are associated with outcomes such as job dissatisfaction, counterproductive work behaviors, and negative performance, among others (Mackey et al. 2021). Leaders who engage in abusive supervision—that is, either verbal or nonverbal hostile behaviors— have been associated with negative outcomes at individual, group, and organizational levels, including poor performance, low morale, withdrawal, depression, and psychological distress (Fischer et al. 2021; Mackey et al. 2017; Tepper, Simon, and Park 2017). Researchers also note that, although toxic leaders displaying "dark traits" such as Machiavellianism, narcissism, or psychopathy may seem to flourish in certain circumstances for a period, evidence suggests they "typically derail somewhere down the line" and "eventually fall from grace" (Furnham, Richards, and Paulhus 2013, 206).

In sum, the research on the relationship between leaders and their organizations' performance provides a clear verdict: Whether through positive or negative approaches, leaders make an impact on the organizations they serve. Yet, beyond the general management literature, our consideration of the skills and values essential to healthcare leaders begs the question of whether evidence of the importance and impact of leadership also extends specifically to healthcare organizations. Organizational scholars recognize the importance of specifically examining organizational phenomena and studying organization theory—including our understanding of leadership, its antecedents, its outcomes, and so forth—within healthcare settings, noting that the myriad challenges facing healthcare leaders (e.g., powerful professional groups, complex and uncertain work, multilevel interdependencies, variable performance criteria, continual technological advancements, widespread uncertainty, complex regulation, deep ethical concerns, conflicting demands from external stakeholders) make healthcare settings a unique and fertile ground for organizational research (Reay, Goodrick, and D'Aunno 2021). Thus, our driving question further narrows: Simply put, does leadership matter *in healthcare*?

The answer to that question, similar to the evidence generated in general management literature, is yes. We see evidence in healthcare-related studies pointing to the impact that leadership has on a variety of organizational outcomes and phenomena. Specifically, recent literature reviews provide clear support for leadership as a "strong predictor of organizational performance" (Mayo, Myers, and Sutcliffe 2021, 555). And not only do leaders matter in healthcare, but we also see evidence that high-performing leaders tend to be those who behave in positive ways. Healthcare leaders recognized as most successful and influential in their field are those characterized by positive traits, including humility, compassion, kindness, and generosity, while those viewed as unsuccessful and having a negative influence tend to be characterized as arrogant, condescending, self-focused, and eager to blame others (Kaissi 2018).

Healthcare in the twenty-first century has been characterized in part by an increased emphasis on quality of care and safety, which have emerged as chief concerns of healthcare providers today. Empirical evidence suggests that leaders play a key role in their organizations' realization of quality and safety outcomes. For example, leaders promoting laudable practices such as knowledge sharing, clear communication, participatory decision-making, and a consistent rhetoric emphasizing quality have been associated with key care outcomes including reduced readmissions, reduced hospital mortality, improved psychological safety to report errors, and an increased adherence to evidence-based practices (Leach et al. 2021; Mayo,

Myers, and Sutcliffe 2021; Sfantou et al. 2017). Furthermore, studies consistently point to a relationship between effective relational leadership practices and positive healthcare workforce outcomes such as improved nurse job satisfaction, productivity, safety climate, and effectiveness (Cummings et al. 2018; Sfantou et al. 2017). In contrast, studies of healthcare organizations with poor patient outcomes and quality of care suggest that struggling healthcare organizations commonly suffer from leaders who are disconnected, unsupportive, nontransparent, and foster a poor organizational culture (Vaughn et al. 2019).

Healthcare today is also characterized by growing emphases on team-based care and coordination, and the extant literature sees both topics as critical areas in which effective leadership can make a difference. For example, leaders involved in facilitating change (e.g., rewarding innovation, soliciting suggestions for change, and fostering a climate that allows for envisioning improved care) directly impact the relational coordination exhibited among care teams (Huber, Rodriguez, and Shortell 2020). Researchers also note that leadership in healthcare organizations is not reserved for those individuals occupying formal administrative or management positions. They point to the importance of leadership provided by doctors, nurses, and other clinicians across care teams, with effective leadership among members of the clinical workforce contributing to improved care coordination and patient outcomes (Daly et al. 2014). Across the extant literature, recent reviews conclude that leadership is "a core element for a well-coordinated and integrated provision of care, both from the patients and healthcare professionals" and regardless of care setting or duration of time (Sfantou et al. 2017, 73).

LEADERSHIP IN COMPLEXITY

Having examined the extant literature on healthcare leaders' impact on their organizations' performance, we see that leadership in healthcare indeed matters, and perhaps never more than within the climate we see facing health care today. The twenty-first century has presented myriad challenges that healthcare leaders both currently confront and anticipate for the future, including the following:

- Efforts to transform healthcare delivery systems from a reactive, volume-driven paradigm to a proactive, value-driven paradigm
- The advancement and potential disruption of new technologies, including artificial intelligence, precision medicine, virtual care, and cybersecurity threats
- The increased engagement and connectedness of society through social media
- Continued trends such as the increased consumerization, consolidation, globalization, and corporatization of healthcare
- The evolving needs of aging populations and increased patients struggling with chronic disease
- The increased awareness of wellness and mental health needs
- The shift to address population health needs by addressing social determinants of health and "upstream" care
- The impact of climate change and its effects on human health
- Disease threats such as pandemics, epidemics, bioterrorism, and antibiotic-resistant infections
- The changing dynamics and needs of the healthcare workforce, including ensuring the well-being and improved experiences of healthcare professionals
- The continual evolution of health policies and regulations to better control healthcare costs, improve care affordability, expand access, and advance the quality of care

- The imperative to address racial and ethnic disparities and inequities in healthcare, steadfastly pursuing increased diversity, equity, and inclusion throughout society (Berwick 2020; Lee and Cosgrove 2020; Mayo, Myers, and Sutcliffe 2021; Wagner 2020).

Recognizing these challenges and opportunities, what approaches will leaders need to effectively guide their organizations and serve their communities in the future healthcare landscape?

Scholars have characterized healthcare in the twenty-first century as volatile, uncertain, complex, and ambiguous—often referred to using the acronym VUCA—which places increased demands on healthcare leadership to understand the field, weigh possible responses and directions, and pursue emergent actions (Nembhard, Burns, and Shortell 2020; Rooke 2018). In short, a VUCA healthcare landscape requires healthcare leaders to engage in creative and effective problem-solving. Yet historically, healthcare professionals and leaders have operated within health systems that embrace linear thinking and reductionism as prevailing approaches to problem-solving, breaking down issues into their separate parts rather than allowing for a deeper consideration of complex relationships at work (Atun 2012; Khan et al. 2018; McNab et al. 2020). Furthermore, although approaches to creative problem-solving such as design thinking have received a fair degree of interest, their application in healthcare organizations and leadership remains relatively limited (Altman, Huang, and Breland 2018; Roberts et al. 2016). Recognizing this, numerous healthcare scholars, observers, and researchers have pointed to the importance of two approaches to problem-solving in particular—systems thinking and design thinking—that are seen as essential for tomorrow's healthcare leaders (Allwood et al. 2021; Mugadza and Marcus 2019; Shrier et al. 2020).

At a broad level, systems thinking applies complexity theory to provide a lens of viewing organizations and organizational phenomena as a series of interconnected elements pursuing specific functions or purposes, and it offers new vantage points from which we can better understand the complex problems we face and pursue more meaningful and effective solutions (Johnson and Rossow 2019; Peters 2014). Systems thinkers recognize that not only does healthcare face complex problems, but it also consists of healthcare organizations that are complex adaptive systems: entities with highly interdependent and dynamic elements that comprise a broader field of interrelated agents and units continually adapting and co-evolving with other organizations and the environment (Begun and Jiang 2020). As a result, the broader healthcare system and its interrelated elements do not follow linear behaviors or exhibit machine-like predictability, and for this reason, simple approaches to complex problems within a complex adaptive system often yield unintended consequences and minimally effective results (Khan et al. 2018; Peters 2014). Instead, meaningful solutions to the complex problems healthcare faces must take into account the many interrelated elements of the system, how they are interconnected, and what different functions and purposes they're individually pursuing.

Leaders possess the opportunity to apply a systems thinking and complexity science approach in guiding their organization to navigate change and solve complex problems, which in turn has been shown to stimulate innovation, facilitate collaboration, and support effective communication (Begun and Jiang 2020; Khan et al. 2018). Systems thinking directs leaders to embrace mindsets that favor exploration, action, mindfulness, curiosity, interconnections, collaboration, and diverse perspectives while fostering a willingness to pursue new directions, seek out surprises, and optimistically take experimental risks, receiving any setbacks as learning opportunities rather than end-of-the-road failures. Such approaches and mindsets proved critically important for healthcare organizations that effectively responded to the COVID-19 pandemic, and scholars suggest they are essential for leaders to navigate tomorrow's healthcare challenges (Begun and Jiang 2020; Gifford et al. 2021; Nembhard, Burns, and Shortell 2020; Sriharan et al. 2021; Stoller 2020). They are also mindsets that closely align with the principles promoted in design thinking.

Design thinking is a human-centered approach to problem-solving that emphasizes empathy, creativity, collaboration, and continual experimentation (Kelley and Kelley 2013). It guides participants to begin their problem-solving journey by first working to deeply understand the experiences and pain points of others, using empathy to gain underlying insights and more meaningfully and substantively define problems and needs. The design thinking approach then challenges participants to collaborate across diverse teams and applications, using the insights gained to reframe their perspectives and generate new ideas and creative directions. Design thinkers then take their ideas and embrace an iterative process of prototyping and testing potential concepts, continuously experimenting and gaining feedback to gain deeper insights, uncover new ideas, and better understand and address the problem. Through this approach, participants gain creative confidence and develop solutions that are more feasible, viable, and desirable (Kelley and Kelley 2013; Roberts et al. 2016). Design thinking guides its participants through an innovation journey that requires less risk and cost to innovate, generates increased buy-in, provides a better understanding of what truly matters, and ultimately leads to innovations that are more valued (Liedtka 2018). Within healthcare, design thinking has yielded more effective, usable, and satisfactory solutions, producing co-designed innovations that cultivate increased trust, including among patients, clinicians, and healthcare leaders (Altman, Huang, and Breland 2018; Shrier et al. 2020; Wheelock, Bechtel, and Leff 2020).

Design thinking prompts a variety of valuable mindsets for effective problem-solving, and although design thinking and systems thinking do not always use the same language, we can appreciate the similarities in the mindsets they promote and their complementary approaches to problem-solving (Mugadza and Marcus 2019). For example, design thinkers adopt a beginner's approach to let go of previously held assumptions, and they express passionate curiosity by continuously asking questions to seek fresh perspectives and insights, aligning with systems thinkers' values for curiosity and inquiry-based exploration. In design thinking, participants work to stretch their thinking and remain open to surprises and new ideas, and as previously noted, systems thinkers express a willingness to pursue new directions, monitor emergence, improvise, and seek out surprises. Design thinkers depend on the value of radical collaboration with others to unlock their creative potential, similar to how systems thinkers favor collaboration and pursue the benefits of diversity. Both approaches require leaders to remove their egos, as design thinkers engage in creative problem-solving with humility and empathy, welcoming constructive criticism and resisting the tendency to be possessive or defensive of ideas. Just as systems thinking encourages paradox, such as the dance between vision and detail or the expression of passionate detachment, design thinking requires innovators to balance divergent and convergent thinking as well as maintain a sustained focus on understanding the problem while simultaneously being continuously open to new directions. And, similar to systems thinking, design thinking maintains a bias for action and embraces failures as a necessary part of the learning and innovation processes that can ultimately accelerate transformation (see exhibit 23.2).

In the midst of complex challenges and a VUCA healthcare landscape, leaders play a critical role in providing direction, communication, and resources to navigate the problem-solving process. The extant literature on leadership, creativity, and innovation suggests that leaders have considerable influence on the creativity and innovation unlocked within their organizations, particularly when leaders participate in activities and behaviors that authentically encourage, empower, facilitate, and model creative problem-solving behaviors (Lee et al. 2020). Systems thinking and design thinking provide a powerful pathway for leaders to tap into such creative problem-solving potential, further underscoring the important role leaders play in healthcare organizations today. Although some may

Exhibit 23.2 Systems Thinking and Design Thinking Mindsets for Problem-Solving

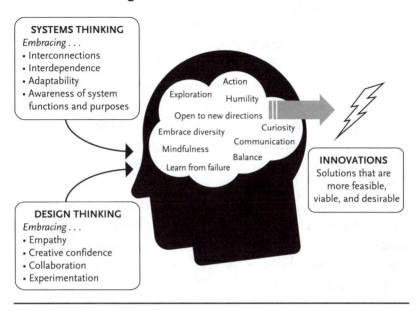

SYSTEMS THINKING
Embracing . . .
• Interconnections
• Interdependence
• Adaptability
• Awareness of system functions and purposes

Action
Exploration
Humility
Open to new directions
Curiosity
Embrace diversity
Communication
Mindfulness
Balance
Learn from failure

INNOVATIONS
Solutions that are more feasible, viable, and desirable

DESIGN THINKING
Embracing . . .
• Empathy
• Creative confidence
• Collaboration
• Experimentation

be tempted to go it alone and exercise leadership as an all-knowing hero, both systems thinking and design thinking provide an alternative paradigm for leaders to consider—one in which there is no single easy answer or silver bullet to be discovered, but instead where creative problem-solving is approached as a continuous journey, with limitless opportunities to leverage the power of diversity and unlock the creative potential of others, lead change, and foster innovation that better addresses system dynamics and societal needs (Johnson and Rossow 2019; Nembhard, Burns, and Shortell 2020; Roberts et al. 2016; Shrier et al. 2020).

CONCLUSION

This chapter began with a simple question: Does leadership actually matter? To address this question, we proceeded to consider the varied perspectives on leadership offered in organization theory, followed by an examination of evidence found in the extant literature of the impact of leadership on organizational outcomes. Collectively, both organization theory and empirical evidence provide clear support for the important role leadership plays in organizational life, including healthcare organizations.

However, as we think about the demands for leadership in an evolving, uncertain, unpredictable, and complex healthcare field, it's not sufficient to simply assent to the notion that leadership matters in healthcare. It certainly does, but such a sentiment also demands action, as leadership is critically needed to successfully meet today's myriad challenges to secure a better tomorrow. Healthcare leaders must "walk the talk" of effective leadership, adopting leadership values and skills that unlock the potential of the healthcare professionals, organizations, and systems they operate within to usher in the transformation of what's possible in healthcare. The values and skills highlighted throughout this book offer a roadmap for leaders to realize such a vision, fueling their growth to become the great leaders healthcare needs, both today and tomorrow.

REFERENCES

Allwood, D., S. Koka, R. Armbruster, and V. Montori. 2021. "Leadership for Careful and Kind Care." *BMJ Leader*, Published Online First: 1–5.

Altman, M., T. T. K. Huang, and J. Y. Breland. 2018. "Design Thinking in Health Care." *Preventing Chronic Disease* 15 (E117): 1–13.

Atun, R. 2012. "Health Systems, Systems Thinking and Innovation." *Health Policy and Planning* 27 (Suppl 4): iv4–iv8.

Begun, J. W., and H. J. Jiang. 2020. "Health Care Management During Covid-19: Insights from Complexity Science." *NEJM Catalyst Innovations in Care Delivery* 1 (5): 1–12.

Berwick, D. M. 2020. "Choices for the 'New Normal'." *JAMA* 323 (21): 2125–26.

Borkowski, N., and K. A. Meese. 2021. *Organizational Behavior in Health Care*, 4th ed. Burlington, MA: Jones & Bartlett Learning.

Cummings, G. G., K. Tate, S. Lee, C. A. Wong, T. Paananen, S. P. M. Micaroni, and G. E. Chatterjee. 2018. "Leadership Styles and Outcome Patterns for the Nursing Workforce and Work Environment: A Systematic Review." *International Journal of Nursing Studies* 85: 19–60.

Daly, J., D. Jackson, J. Mannix, P. M. Davidson, and M. Hutchinson. 2014. "The Importance of Clinical Leadership in the Hospital Setting." *Journal of Healthcare Leadership* 6: 75–83.

Eva, N., M. Robin, S. Sendjaya, D. van Dierendonck, and R. C. Liden. 2019. "Servant Leadership: A Systematic Review and Call for Future Research." *The Leadership Quarterly* 30 (1): 111–32.

Fischer, T., A. W. Tian, A. Lee, and D. J. Hughes. 2021. "Abusive Supervision: A Systematic Review and Fundamental Rethink." *The Leadership Quarterly* 32 (6): 101540.

Furnham, A., S. C. Richards, and D. L. Paulhus. 2013. "The Dark Triad of Personality: A 10 Year Review." *Social and Personality Psychology Compass* 7 (3): 199–216.

Gifford, R., B. Fleuren, F. van de Baan, D. Ruwaard, L. Poesen, F. Zijlstra, and D. Westra. 2021. "To Uncertainty and Beyond: Identifying the Capabilities Needed by Hospitals to Function in Dynamic Environments." *Medical Care Research and Review*, Published Ahead of Print: 1–13.

Hartnell, C. A., A. Y. Ou, A. J. Kinicki, D. Choi, and E. P. Karam. 2019. "A Meta-Analytic Test of Organizational Culture's Association with Elements of an Organization's System and its Relative Predictive Validity on Organizational Outcomes." *Journal of Applied Psychology* 104 (6): 832–50.

Hatch, M. J. 2018. *Organization Theory: Modern, Symbolic, and Postmodern Perspectives*, 4th ed. New York: Oxford University Press.

Hoch, J. E., W. H. Bommer, J. H. Dulebohn, and D. Wu. 2018. "Do Ethical, Authentic, and Servant Leadership Explain Variance Above and Beyond Transformational Leadership? A Meta-Analysis." *Journal of Management* 44 (2): 501–29.

Huber, T. P., H. P. Rodriguez, and S. M. Shortell. 2020. "The Influence of Leadership Facilitation on Relational Coordination Among Primary Care Team Members of Accountable Care Organizations." *Health Care Management Review* 45 (4): 302–10.

Johnson, J. A., and C. C. Rossow. 2019. *Health Organizations: Theory, Behavior, and Development*, 2nd ed. Burlington, MA: Jones & Bartlett Learning.

Kaissi, A. 2018. *Intangibles: The Unexpected Traits of High-Performing Healthcare Leaders*. Chicago: Health Administration Press.

Kelemen, T. K., S. H. Matthews, and K. Breevaart. 2020. "Leading Day-to-Day: A Review of the Daily Causes and Consequences of Leadership Behaviors." *The Leadership Quarterly* 31: 101344.

Kelley, T., and D. Kelley. 2013. *Creative Confidence: Unleashing the Creative Potential Within Us All.* New York: Crown Business.

Khan, S., A. Vandermorris, J. Shepherd, J. W. Begun, H. J. Lanham, M. Uhl-Bien, and W. Berta. 2018. "Embracing Uncertainty, Managing Complexity: Applying Complexity Thinking Principles to Transformation Efforts in Healthcare Systems." *BMC Health Services Research* 18: 192.

Kim, M., T. A. Beehr, and M. S. Prewett. 2018. "Employee Responses to Empowering Leadership: A Meta-Analysis." *Journal of Leadership & Organizational Studies* 25 (3): 257–76.

Kim, Y. J., and S. M. Toh. 2019. "Stuck in the Past? The Influence of a Leader's Past Cultural Experience on Group Culture and Positive and Negative Group Deviance." *Academy of Management Journal* 62 (3): 944–69.

Leach, L., B. Hastings, G. Schwarz, B. Watson, D. Bouckenooghe, L. Seoane, and D. Hewett. 2021. "Distributed Leadership in Healthcare: Leadership Dyads and Promise of Improved Hospital Outcomes." *Leadership in Health Services* 34 (4): 353–74.

Lee, A., A. Legood, D. Hughes, A. W. Tian, A. Newman, and C. Knight. 2020. "Leadership, Creativity, and Innovation: A Meta-Analytic Review." *European Journal of Work and Organizational Psychology* 29 (1): 1–35.

Lee, T. H., and T. Cosgrove. 2020. "Six Tests for Physicians and Their Leaders for the Decade Ahead." *NEJM Catalyst Innovations in Care Delivery* 1 (4).

Lemoine, G. J., C. A. Hartnell, and H. Leroy. 2019. "Taking Stock of Moral Approaches to Leadership: An Integrative Review of Ethical, Authentic, and Servant Leadership." *Academy of Management Annals* 13 (1): 148–87.

Liedtka, J. 2018. "Why Design Thinking Works." *Harvard Business Review* 96 (5): 72–79.

Mackey, J. D., B. P. Ellen III, C. P. McAllister, and K. C. Alexander. 2021. "The Dark Side of Leadership: A Systematic Literature Review and Meta-Analysis of Destructive Leadership Research." *Journal of Business Research* 132: 705–18.

Mackey, J. D., R. E. Frieder, J. R. Brees, and M. J. Martinko. 2017. "Abusive Supervision: A Meta-Analysis and Empirical Review." *Journal of Management* 43 (6): 1940–65.

Mayo, A. T., C. G. Myers, and K. M. Sutcliffe. 2021. "Organizational Science and Health Care." *Academy of Management Annals* 15 (2): 537–76.

Mazzetti, G., M. Vignoli, G. Petruzziello, and L. Palareti. 2019. "The Hardier You Are, the Healthier You Become. May Hardiness and Engagement Explain the Relationship Between Leadership and Employees' Health?" *Frontiers in Psychology* 9: 2784.

McNab, D., J. McKay, S. Shorrock, S. Luty, and P. Bowie. 2020. "Development and Application of 'Systems Thinking' Principles for Quality Improvement." *BMJ Open Quality* 9 (e000714): 1–10.

Mugadza, G., and R. Marcus. 2019. "A Systems Thinking and Design Thinking Approach to Leadership." *Expert Journal of Business and Management* 7 (1): 1–10.

Nembhard, I. M., L. R. Burns, and S. M. Shortell. 2020. "Responding to COVID-19: Lessons from Management Research." *NEJM Catalyst Innovations in Care Delivery* 1 (2).

O'Reilly, C. A., J. A. Chatman, and B. Doerr. 2021. "When 'Me' Trumps 'We': Narcissistic Leaders and the Cultures They Create." *Academy of Management Discoveries* 7 (3): 419–50.

Parry, K. W. 2011. "Leadership and Organization Theory." In *The SAGE Handbook of Leadership*, edited by A. Bryman, D. Collinson, K. Grint, B. Jackson, and M. Uhl-Bien, 53–70. Thousand Oaks, CA: SAGE Publications.

Peltonen, T. 2016. *Organization Theory: Critical and Philosophical Engagements*. Bingley, UK: Emerald Publishing.

Peters, D. H. 2014. "The Application of Systems Thinking in Health: Why Use Systems Thinking?" *Health Research Policy and Systems* 12 (51).

Reay, T., E. Goodrick, and T. D'Aunno. 2021. *Health Care Research and Organization Theory (Elements in Organization Theory)*. New York: Cambridge University Press.

Roberts, J. P., T. R. Fisher, M. J. Trowbridge, and C. Bent. 2016. "A Design Thinking Framework for Healthcare Management and Innovation." *Healthcare* 4 (1): 11–14.

Rooke, D. 2018. "Transformational Leadership Capabilities for Medical Leaders." *BMJ Leader* 2 (1): 3–6.

Sfantou, D. F., A. Laliotis, A. E. Patelarou, D. Sifaki-Pistolla, M. Matalliotakis, and E. Patelarou. 2017. "Importance of Leadership Style Towards Quality of Care Measures in Healthcare Settings: A Systematic Review." *Healthcare* 5: 73.

Shrier, L. A., P. J. Burke, C. Jonestrask, and S. L. Katz-Wise. 2020. "Applying Systems Thinking and Human-Centered Design to Development of Intervention Implementation Strategies: An Example from Adolescent Health Research." *Journal of Public Health Research* 9 (1746): 376–80.

Sriharan, A., A. J. Hertelendy, J. Banaszak-Holl, M. M. Fleig-Palmer, C. Mitchell, A. Nigam, J. Gutberg, D. J. Rapp, and S. J. Singer. 2021. "Public Health and Health Sector Crisis Leadership During Pandemics: A Review of the Medical and

Business Literature." *Medical Care Research and Review*, Published Ahead of Print: 1–12.

Stoller, J. K. 2020. "Reflections on Leadership in the Time of COVID-19." *BMJ Leader* 4: 77–79.

Tepper, B. J., L. Simon, and H. M. Park. 2017. "Abusive Supervision." *Annual Review of Organizational Psychology and Organizational Behavior* 4: 123–52.

Vaughn, V. M., S. Saint, S. L. Krein, J. H. Forman, J. Meddings, J. Ameling, S. Winter, W. Townsend, and V. Chopra. 2019. "Characteristics of Healthcare Organisations Struggling to Improve Quality: Results from a Systematic Review of Qualitative Studies." *BMJ Quality & Safety* 28: 74–84.

Wagner, S. L. 2020. *The United States Healthcare System: Overview, Driving Forces, and Outlook for the Future*. Chicago: Health Administration Press.

Walston, S. L. 2017. *Organizational Behavior and Theory in Healthcare: Leadership Perspectives and Management Applications*. Chicago: Health Administration Press.

Wheelock, A., C. Bechtel, and B. Leff. 2020. "Human-Centered Design and Trust in Medicine." *JAMA* 324 (23): 2369–70.

CHAPTER 24

Post-COVID Leadership

*The pandemic abruptly altered workplace culture and processes
in most industries. Personal interactions and meetings were
suddenly replaced by video conference calls and emails. We might
never return to the way we worked before the pandemic . . . and
perhaps we shouldn't. Rather than trying to recreate what was lost,
health care executives should consider looking at the opportunities
that have emerged for attracting and retaining employees.*

—Rahul Mehendale and Jen Radin (2021)

*We are well aware of the impact that the COVID-19 pandemic
has had on frontline healthcare workers. They have been
challenged with an ongoing lack of supplies and staff while trying
to manage tremendous surges in patient volume for months.
Many have been "repurposed" and asked to work in roles and
departments previously unfamiliar to them. We hear about
these stories on the news daily, but healthcare leaders have also
been quite challenged during this time. There is little talk on
the news about the tremendous impact this pandemic has had,
and will continue to have, on leadership moving forward.*

—Donna Prosser (2020)

*The pandemic has driven burnout among health care workers to crisis
levels, driving many stakeholders to call for systemic solutions to retain
critical personnel while preparing a new generation to take the field.*

—David Levine (2021)

I MUST BEGIN this chapter by proclaiming this strongly held personal belief: I believe that effective leadership is very much the same now as it was before the pandemic, the same as it was in the late twentieth century, the same as it was in the 1970s, and so forth. The behaviors of highly effective leaders are fairly consistent through the ages. This belief is not based on any research or evidence but is strictly anecdotal from my 40-plus years of working in healthcare leadership.

But before embarking on an examination of COVID-19's impact on leadership and using my personal belief as a foundation for the chapter, I felt I should reach out to a number of healthcare leaders to garner their opinion. In late 2021, I sent a brief e-mail survey to more than 350 leaders asking them if they felt that leadership had changed as a result of COVID-19. Essentially the question was: Are the actions and behaviors of effective leadership different post-COVID? Is what makes an effective leader the same now as it was in 2019? 2000? 1990? And so on?

I felt that some would posit that "leadership is leadership; no matter the situation or circumstance," while others (perhaps those who ascribe to the contingency view of leadership) would say that COVID did require different actions for leaders to be effective. Is it possible that this question is akin to the old question of "how many angels can dance on the head of a pin?"

I would ask readers to ponder the question and answer it before reviewing the results provided in the appendix of this chapter.

VIEWPOINTS OF VARIOUS HEALTHCARE LEADERS

While the statistical results may be of interest to many, the specific comments received provide more insight and counsel for leaders to ponder.

> "The key to the question is 'highly effective leaders.' I believe highly effective leaders are ones who have and adhere to a solid foundation on how to lead people to accomplish the

THOUGHTS FROM THE FIELD

The Survey:

The actions and behaviors of highly effective leaders are the same now as they were prior to COVID.

Strongly Disagree	Disagree	Neither Disagree nor Agree	Agree	Strongly Agree
1	2	3	4	5

Briefly explain your answer
Identify yourself:
Leader with a clinical background
Leader without a clinical background
Male
Female
Over 50
50 or under

desired mission. That solid foundation doesn't change as circumstances change. In fact, just the opposite is true. The effective leader's solid foundation is key to bringing people and, therefore, the organization through a crisis such as our current pandemic."

"Most leaders in health care came into leadership when care and business models were relatively static and stable. Over the past 20 years health care has grown more complex and disrupted. That was true before COVID, and the leadership of organizations and communities that had been particularly disrupted pre-COVID was already showing the stress and strain of overmatched leadership. COVID accelerated and amplified the ways in which leadership, built for execution at scale, is ill suited to a turbulent, dynamic, complex and disrupted context. Leadership must be agile, adaptive, purpose oriented and must account for human complexity—specifically the loss or fear of loss humans experience amidst change and transformation—like never before."

"It has always been important to get out and round in frontline areas and talk with providers, nurses, staff. I think a lot of that pulled back with Covid due to much more work being remote/webex compounded by the 'busy' nature of the last 18 months. We initially found rounding was the first thing to come off our schedules to make room to do the 'real work.'. We realized what a mistake that was and ramped up/revised our senior leader rounding. You need to be in-person to develop relationships and also to hear what is working well/not working well with covid protocols and other work. Also just connecting with others and hearing the impact of the stress on their personal lives and how that is impacting the work as well. Bottom line—rounding/getting out is always important but more so now!"

"I have watched leaders across my organization increase their effectiveness working together as a team, as we had to prepare and constantly introduce change to keep the organization moving forward through the pandemic."

"While the challenges that we as healthcare leaders have faced over the past two years have been unprecedented, the skills that we had to employ to navigate through the challenges are not novel. Healthcare is, at its core, still about relationships and communication. Leadership visibility, effective listening, ethical management, and critical thinking were fundamental success factors in leading through the crisis of Covid and will still be the foundation for effective leadership beyond the pandemic."

"I believe the actions and behaviors of highly effective leaders don't change with the circumstance (COVID), their DNA stays true given any issue."

"Highly effective leaders have the ability to adapt to new situations and crises. Poor leaders will be exposed in times of stress."

"COVID served to shine the light on the weakest of leaders but accelerated change management/nimbleness higher in the rankings."

"I truly believe the actions of highly effective leaders are the same now with the caveat that some have become more highlighted or even reprioritized, for lack of a better word. The resilience and well-being of employees as well as communication have been some of the highest needed traits to work through Covid of which I think leaders know, but are not always good at. I have found that truly giving employees the autonomy to be creative and come up with solutions has been greatly highlighted in my opinion and an action/behavior we many times speak of, but do not always give total permission for. It is amazing what teams can create when given a goal and guardrails without overseeing every aspect of their work."

"The pandemic stretched & challenged leaders in a new way. Those who were highly effective gained new insights and were flexible and resilient in their response, making them better and more effective leaders. Others we thought were effective leaders often failed to rise to the demand, and we determined the true highly effective leaders."

"Dealing with and motivating in ambiguity and the willingness to adapt rapidly to the environment have always been critical. Now these two leadership traits are laid bare as the unequivocal top two."

"The crisis has caused good leaders to reflect on how they lead and what are those practices that support pursuit of high reliability. Practices include: articulate values, model professionalism themselves, communicate communicate communicate, continue to expect excellence, care for the caregivers and harvest innovation. Crisis can cause good leaders to get better."

"Leadership today demands more wholehearted relationships with your people. You have to show them vulnerability, while also instilling confidence through trustful actions. We can't show up with just our Good to Great books anymore—we have to also have a touch of Brené Brown and Simon Sinek. Authenticity and the courage to show up and lead, even when you may admittedly not have all the answers (because, who does their first time living through a pandemic!?)."

"I think COVID highlighted the difference in leadership styles and competencies. The most effective leaders had many of the skills and philosophies prior to COVID . . . such as remaining calm in the face of uncertainty, communication, being visible, listening to the needs of the staff and establishing operational plans. These skills and competencies were not new but an effective leader recognized the situation and stepped into the gap to lead their teams."

"I don't think any of us can act exactly the same now as before. But I do think that there are distinct differences between clinical and non-clinical leaders and the behaviors and attitudes that have changed. And I think the acuity of change is also different. In a non-clinical setting, I think we have been forced to learn how to develop remote accountability on a larger scale. I think we are expected to be more flexible and accommodating in our scheduling of hours and our expectations for engagement during the entire work day. I also think we must be more sympathetic and patient as the pandemic has affected (and continues to affect) different families in different ways. I also think that we now have competing managerial styles when we have a more traditional leader who thinks that things can 'return to normal.' Even for those of us who value face to face contact, perspectives on the effectiveness of remote leadership (even at the most senior levels) have changed and for senior leaders who value flexibility over loyalty, there is a greater likelihood of turnover."

"Actions and behaviors needed during COVID have been long term crisis management with a perspective on population health. For many traditional leaders this has made their weaknesses highly visible. The traditional focus on just profits doesn't work now."

"Not having the right skills is causing a significant turnover in tenured leadership in our organization."

"The focus must shift from the boardroom to front line employees and clinicians. The successful leader must be out and about on the front lines for part of EVERY day, including beyond normal work hours."

"I think you have to be more agile and resilient post COVID."

"The critical leadership call is to care deeply for all your people and those they care for. The challenges for them have intensified, but their need for a thoughtful, compassionate, listening leader has never been greater. It is not a different challenge, but just amplified."

"The actions and behaviors that make a leader highly effective aren't as prone to change over time—even with the challenges of a global pandemic. On the other hand, the required skill set to effectively lead and operate a healthcare enterprise were changed by COVID with labor expenses/shortages and supply costs spiraling out of control during a sustained surge while payments are fixed or shrinking."

"I think highly effective leaders have changed somewhat after the pandemic, meaning, highly effective leaders possess flexibility, innovation, and effective listening skills—high emotional intelligence, along with their IQ. Post pandemic, highly effective medical leaders additionally [have] become even more agile and adaptive innovators. They [have] also been effective and successful if, along with their EI and IQ, they have been practicing appreciative inquiry in listening to and working with their teams."

"I don't know that I like the question Carson. I struggle with answering 'complete agree' vs 'totally disagree.' I think it's two different questions. I think the characteristics/behaviors that made a leader effective before COVID are the same as during and probably after, whenever that might be. The actions aren't the same because the decisions needing to be made in the timeframe that was required weren't the same. While still seeking input from others, I found myself making decisions quicker and oftentimes with less information than was desired or could be obtained because that was usually what the situation required."

DISCUSSION

People worldwide have made significant changes in their work styles, habits, and locations as a result of the COVID pandemic. Many of these changes related to significant ways in which people work while others related to their feelings. Consider how remote work; lockdowns; disruption of commerce; "screen time" (giving way to "Zoom fatigue"); fears about health and safety; supply chain disruptions; and stockpiling food, equipment, medicine, and more have all served to alter life. These all have had a direct bearing on the practice of leadership. To say the least, leaders have been exceedingly challenged. It seems evident from the responses to the survey that there is no consensus regarding the effect of COVID-19 on leadership. The one obvious message, however, is that these leaders have been significantly affected by COVID-19. As a result, the demand for strong values-driven leadership is more important than ever. Therefore, I will drop the question posed in the survey and move on to a focused discussion of what healthcare leaders should be doing.

Perhaps it is a worn-out cliché, but healthcare is different. And COVID-19 battered healthcare more than it did any other field. The most serious outcomes—life-threatening situations, death, family separated from loved ones—were felt in the healthcare setting more than in others. As in a few other fields, most healthcare work must be done in person. Remote work, adopted by many other businesses and fields, is simply not feasible for most workers in healthcare.

As the pandemic continued, pictures and descriptions of harried healthcare workers filled the news. Yong (2021) writes about a nurse who described her experiences in a COVID unit as "death on a scale I had never seen before." He continues to report that "[the] U.S. Bureau of Labor Statistics estimates that the health-care sector has lost nearly half a million workers since February 2020."

Challenges leaders must grapple with include complex aspects of human behavior and incorporate issues of psychology and sociology. COVID-19 pushed many leaders to serve as therapists and grief counselors. It was no longer "work as usual." Mukherjee and Krish (2021) suggest five ways leaders can reframe their approach in a post-pandemic world.

1. The individual as a whole
2. The leader as a sociologist
3. Psychological safety, well-being, and motivation
4. Equitable experiences
5. Insight over data

Note that the first four of these relate to the psychosocial aspects of leadership.

Prior to COVID many strongly believed there was a definite separation between work and outside life. Now those lines are blurred as video meetings give a glimpse of workers' home life, children, pets, and other personal aspects of reality. Leaders also found themselves having to think more about sociology and psychology. Supporting employees' well-being became something far more important than simply offering employee assistance programs. Discussions about burnout and resiliency mushroomed from clinical workers to the entire healthcare workforce.

Equity also became a key challenge, and one that affected women more than men. Mehta and colleagues (2021) note the following:

> COVID-19 has also had a disproportionate effect on women health-care workers. Women comprise 70 percent of the global health and social care workforce, putting them at risk of infection and the range of physical and mental health problems associated with their role as health professionals and careers in the context of a pandemic. The pandemic exacerbated gender inequities in formal and informal work, and in the distribution of home responsibilities, and increased the risk of unemployment and domestic violence. While trying to fulfill their professional responsibilities, women had to meet their families' needs, including childcare, home schooling, care for older people, and home care.

Clearly COVID-19 has made leadership more complex. Although it was important before, leaders must be even more aware of the more subtle and delicate aspects of managing the issues that impact the culture. Mukherjee and Krish (2021) state, "A remarkable feature of the pandemic has been the focus on these intangible assets, that are by definition harder to measure. These will be key when it comes to acquiring and retaining talent, and account for as much as 85 percent of the total business value across industries."

As mentioned earlier in this chapter, COVID-19 had a profound effect on healthcare workers. Despite society hailing them as "heroes," many have left the field. Vanhaecht and colleagues (2021) write, "The toll of the crisis has been heavy on health-care workers. Those who carry leadership positions at an organizational or system level should take this opportunity to develop targeted strategies to mitigate key stressors of health-care workers' mental well-being." Berlin and colleagues (2022) present recent survey research done by McKinsey which shows that "Thirty-two percent of registered nurses (RNs) surveyed in the United States in November [2021] said they may leave their current direct-patient-care role." This represented an increase of ten percentage points in under ten months.

According to research done by Norman and colleagues (2021), "the majority of the sample (52.7 percent–87.8 percent) endorsed moral distress. Factor analyses revealed three dimensions of COVID-19 moral distress: negative impact on family, fear of infecting others, and work-related concerns. All three factors were significantly associated with severity and positive screen for COVID-19-related PTSD symptoms, burnout, and work and interpersonal difficulties. Relative importance analyses revealed that concerns about work competencies and personal relationships were most strongly related to all outcomes." Furthermore, a study by d'Ettorre and colleagues (2021) indicates "the need for urgent interventions aimed at protecting healthcare workers from the psychological impact of traumatic events related to the pandemic and leading to Post Traumatic Stress Syndrome is increasingly a key issue in the management of [the] COVID-19 pandemic."

HOPE

One aspect of values-driven leadership relates to helping sustain a culture in the workplace where hope can thrive. This often-used word can carry many meanings, but it is incumbent on strong leaders to understand how to apply the concept of hope in practice. Maak, Pless, and Wohlgezogen (2021) suggest that "it is the role of leaders to instill in people a sense of hope for 'future goodness' and dignity, to be guardians of radical hope and *see into the future.*" Royal (2020) writes in a Gallup Blog that "a Gallup study of over 10,000 employees found that followers have four primary needs of their leaders: trust, compassion, stability and hope. They're all critical, all the time. But since the outbreak of COVID-19, hope is more valuable than it's ever been. Because hope is what will get us through this." He continues to report that "employees who strongly agree that their leader makes them feel enthusiastic about the future (Gallup's measure of hope in the workplace) are 69 times more likely to be engaged in their work compared with employees who disagree with that statement."

LEADER "TO-DO" LIST

The pandemic has placed an enormous focus on the importance of healthcare leadership. Highly effective leaders have had to step up their efforts to support a very tired and stressed workforce. Looking at some of the key areas that helped workers during the pandemic, Adeyemo, Tu, and Keene (2021) write, "We identified 6 main themes related to leadership response and support of healthcare workers during the pandemic, namely: (1) Effective communication and transparency; (2) Prioritizing their health and safety; (3) Employee scheduling considerations: autonomy, assignment support and respite; (4) Appreciation—financial and nonfinancial; (5) Showing up and listening; and (6) Stepping up with resources."

Groysberg, Abrahams, and Connolly Baden (2021) write that "leaders must be honest and vulnerable with their teams, present-ing themselves as fully human and recognizing their employees' humanity as well. Intimacy means closeness, and while social dis-tancing remains important to mitigating the spread of COVID-19, psychological proximity—interpersonal trust, alignment on values and strategy, shared understanding of key facts—has never been more crucial. Psychological proximity requires gaining trust, listening well, and getting personal."

Ahern and Loh (2021) stress that leaders must be both visible and responsible:

> In order to build trust and the confidence of followers, leaders need to make decisions and provide a sense of control. Crises require leaders to take responsibility and do this visibly. By being visible and responsible, they are showing accountability and sharing risks with their followers, an important sign of solidarity with the many health workers and others who face personal risks during the pandemic. By being responsible, they show and model personal vulnerability. Taking responsibility also means that leaders exhibit constancy and resilience, that they are in this for the long haul and can be relied on to continue to persevere on behalf of their followers.

CONCLUSION

Whether COVID-19 *changed the definition of* leadership is likely not as relevant as recognizing that it *has had a significant impact on* leadership. The values espoused in this book all serve to undergird the interactions leaders have with their followers prior to, during, and after crisis situations such as COVID-19. What better values to drive effective leadership during these kinds of situations than respect, ethics, interpersonal connection, servant leadership, drive to make positive change, and emotional intelligence? And working effectively in teams during very trying times certainly requires cooperation and sharing, cohesiveness and collaboration, trust, and skills at managing conflict. Effective leaders must use these values as a foundation in dealing with all types of catastrophes.

Exercises

Exercise 24.1

Review one of the following articles. What are the key takeaways from the article you reviewed?

Geerts, J. M., D. Kinnair, P. Taheri P, A. Abraham, J. Ahn, R. Atun, L. Barberia, N. J. Best, R. Dandona, A. A. Dhahri, L. Emilsson, J. R. Free, M. Gardam, W. H. Geerts, C. Ihekweazu, S. Johnson, A. Kooijman, A. T. Lafontaine, E. Leshem, C. Lidstone-Jones, E. Loh, O. Lyons, K. A. F. Neel, P. S. Nyasulu, O. Razum, H. Sabourin, J. S. Taylor, H. Sharifi, V. Stergiopoulos, B. Sutton, Z. Wu, and Marc Bilodeau. 2021. "Guidance for Health Care Leaders During the Recovery Stage of the COVID-19 Pandemic: A Consensus Statement." *JAMA Network Open* 4 (7).

Maak, T., N. M. Pless, and F. Wohlgezogen, F. 2021. "The Fault Lines of Leadership: Lessons from the Global Covid-19 Crisis." *Journal of Change Management* 21 (1): 66–86.

Mehendale, R., and J. Radin. 2021. "COVID Forever Changed the Way we Work . . . Maybe for the Better." Deloitte Health Forward, August 26, 2021. https://www2.deloitte.com/us/en/blog/health-care-blog/2021/covid-forever-changed-the-way-we-work-maybe-for-the-better.html?id=us:2em:3na:hf:awa:hs:092121:mkid-K0150368&ctr=cta1hc&sfid=0033000000ZVrEiAAL.

Royal, K. 2020 "Leading Your Workplace with Hope Through COVID-19." Gallup Workplace, April 20, 2020. https://www.gallup.com/workplace/308459/lead-workplace-hope-covid.aspx.

Young, E. 2021. "Why Health-care Workers Are Quitting in Droves." *The Atlantic*, November 16, 2021. https://www.theatlantic.com/health/archive/2021/11/the-mass-exodus-of-americas-health-care-workers/620713/.

APPENDIX

Results of the Survey Discussed in the Chapter

Of the 183 respondents who participated in the survey, 40 percent had clinical backgrounds. Sixty percent of respondents were male, 40 percent were female, and 90 percent were over the age of 50.

The following graphic illustrates their response to the following statement: The actions and behaviors of highly effective leaders are the same now as they were prior to COVID.

Survey Response
The actions and behaviors of highly effective leaders are the same now as they were prior to COVID.

Totally Disagree	Strongly Disagree	Disagree Somewhat	Modestly Disagree	Slightly Agree	Agree	Strongly Agree	Completely Agree
5	45	35	10	3	25	35	25

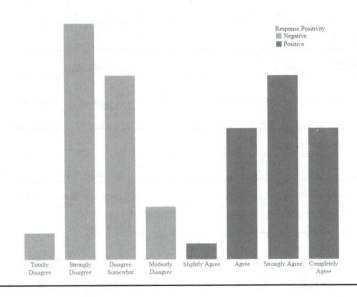

Response Positivity
▨ Negative
▩ Positive

REFERENCES

Adeyemo, O. O., S. Tu, and D. Keene. 2021. "How to Lead Health Care Workers During Unprecedented Crises: A Qualitative Study of the COVID-19 Pandemic in Connecticut, USA." *PLoS ONE* 16 (9): e0257423.

Ahern, S., and E. Loh. 2021. "Leadership During the COVID-19 Pandemic: Building and Sustaining Trust in Times of Uncertainty." *BMJ Leader* 5: 266–69.

Berlin, G., M. Lapointe, and M. Murphy. 2022. "Surveyed Nurses Consider Leaving Direct Patient Care at Elevated Rates." McKinsey, February 17. https://www.mckinsey.com/industries /healthcare-systems-and-services/our-insights/surveyed -nurses-consider-leaving-direct-patient-care-at-elevated-rates

d'Ettorre, G., G. Ceccarelli, L. Santinelli, P. Vassalini, G. P. Innocenti, F. Alessandri, A. E. Koukopoulos, A. Russo, G. d'Ettorre, and L. Tarsitani. 2021. "Post-Traumatic Stress Symptoms in Healthcare Workers Dealing with the COVID-19 Pandemic: A Systematic Review." *International Journal of Environmental Research and Public Health* 18 (2): 601.

Groysberg, B., R. Abrahams, and K. Connolly Baden. 2021. "The Pandemic Conversations That Leaders Need to Have Now." Harvard Business School Working Knowledge, April 21. https://hbswk.hbs.edu/item/the-pandemic-conversations -that-leaders-need-to-have-now.

Levine, D. 2021. "U.S. Faces Crisis of Burned-Out Health Care Workers." *U.S. News & World Report*, November 15. https:// www.usnews.com/news/health-news/articles/2021-11-15 /us-faces-crisis-of-burned-out-health-care-workers.

Maak, T., N. Pless, and F. Wohlgezogen. 2021. "The Fault Lines of Leadership: Lessons from the Global Covid-19 Crisis." *Journal of Change Management* 21 (11): 1–21.

Mehendale, R., and J. Radin. 2021. "COVID Forever Changed the Way We Work . . . Maybe for the Better." Deloitte Health Forward, August 26. https://www2.deloitte.com/us/en/blog /health-care-blog/2021/covid-forever-changed-the-way-we -work-maybe-for-the-better.html?id=us:2em:3na:hf:awa:hs:0 92121:mkid-K0150368&ctr=cta1hc&sfid=0033000000ZVrEi AAL.

Mehta, S., F. Machado, A. Kwizera, L. Papazian, M. Moss, É. Azoulay, and M. Herridge. 2021. "COVID-19: A Heavy Toll on Health-care Workers." *Lancet Respiratory Medicine* 9 (3): 226–28.

Mukherjee, R. B., and A. Krish. 2021. "5 Ways the COVID-19 Pandemic Is Changing the Role of Leaders." World Economic Forum, October 4. https://www.weforum.org/agenda /2021/10/5-ways-the-pandemic-is-changing-the-role-of -leaders/.

Norman, S. B., J. H. Feingold, H. Kaye-Kauderer, C. A. Kaplan, A. Hurtado, L. Kachadourian, A. Feder, J. W. Murrough, D. Charney, S. M. Southwick, J. Ripp, L. Peccoralo, and R. H. Pietrzak. 2021. "Moral Distress in Frontline Healthcare Workers in the Initial Epicenter of the COVID-19 Pandemic in the United States: Relationship to PTSD Symptoms, Burnout, and Psychosocial Functioning." *Depression and Anxiety* 38 (10): 1007–1017.

Prosser, D. 2020. "The Impact of the COVID-19 Pandemic on the Future of Healthcare Leadership." *HealthManagement* 20 (4). https://healthmanagement.org/c/healthmanagement /issuearticle/the-impact-of-the-covid-19-pandemic-on-the -future-of-healthcare-leadership.

Royal, K. 2020. "Leading Your Workplace with Hope Through COVID-19." Gallup Workplace, April 20. https://www.gallup .com/workplace/308459/lead-workplace-hope-covid.aspx.

Vanhaecht, K., D. Seys, L. Bruyneel, B. Cox, G. Kaesemans, M. Cloet, K. Van Den Broeck, O. Cools, A. De Witte, K. Lowet, J. Hellings, J. Bilsen, G. Lemmens, and S. Claes. 2021. "COVID-19 Is Having a Destructive Impact on Health-care Workers' Mental Well-being." *International Journal for Quality in Health Care* 33 (1): mzaa158.

Yong, E. 2021. "Why Healthcare Workers Are Quitting in Droves." *The Atlantic*, November 16. https://www.theatlantic .com/health/archive/2021/11/the-mass-exodus-of-americas -health-care-workers/620713/.

SUGGESTED READINGS

Kaushik, D. 2021. "Medical Burnout: Breaking Bad." Association of American Medical Colleges (AAMC) Insights, June 4. https:// www.aamc.org/news-insights/medical-burnout-breaking-bad.

Rose, S., J. Hartnett, and S. Pillai. 2021. "Healthcare Worker's Emotions, Perceived Stressors and Coping Mechanisms During the COVID-19 Pandemic." *PLoS ONE* 16 (7): e0254252.

Professional and Personal Values Evaluation Form

OUR BEHAVIORS REVEAL our values more clearly than our words do. Civility often prevents us from saying what we truly think, but it does not always prevent us from reacting with our body. As a result, we give out two varying reactions to one scenario.

This questionnaire assesses your values on the basis of your perception and others' perceptions. It contains two tools—Self-Perception and Others' Perception.

Directions: After you complete the Self-Perception questionnaire, ask four to five fellow team members whom you think know you well to complete the Others' Perception questionnaire. Ideally, a neutral third party should collect the completed questionnaires and compile averages and ranges for the answers. This process might encourage others to be more honest when evaluating you. Following discussions with the neutral third party about the responses, you may meet with the individuals who evaluated you to compare and contrast all perceptions. Use the following scoring Likert scale for the assessment:

Strongly Disagree	Disagree	Neither Disagree nor Agree	Agree	Strongly Agree
1	2	3	4	5

SELF-PERCEPTION OF VALUES

1. I respect other people.
2. I serve as a good steward of the talent, authority, resources, and position I hold.
3. I am an ethical person.
4. I keep my word.
5. I seek to develop positive and wholesome relationships with others.
6. I desire to serve others.
7. I want to make a difference and effect positive changes and contributions.
8. I am committed to the vision and goals of my organization.
9. I work hard.
10. I am a highly dedicated person.
11. I am emotionally mature.
12. I value the contributions of a team.
13. I cooperate with fellow team members.
14. I share information and other resources with fellow team members.
15. I try to build trust with others.
16. I am willing to trust others.
17. I affirmatively try to bring conflict to the surface to manage it effectively.

OTHERS' PERCEPTION OF ___(Insert Name Here)___ 'S VALUES

1. Your colleague respects other people.
2. Your colleague serves as a good steward of the talent, authority, resources, and position she/he holds.
3. Your colleague is an ethical person.
4. Your colleague keeps her/his word.
5. Your colleague seeks to develop positive and wholesome relationships with others.
6. Your colleague desires to serve others.
7. Your colleague wishes to make a difference and effect positive changes and contributions.
8. Your colleague is committed to the vision and goals of your organization.
9. Your colleague works hard.
10. Your colleague is a highly dedicated person.
11. Your colleague is emotionally mature.
12. Your colleague values the contributions of a team.
13. Your colleague cooperates with fellow team members.
14. Your colleague shares information and other resources with fellow team members.
15. Your colleague tries to build trust with others.
16. Your colleague is willing to trust others.
17. Your colleague affirmatively tries to bring conflict to the surface to manage it effectively.

Emotional Intelligence Evaluation Form

EMOTIONAL INTELLIGENCE IS a person's maturity quotient. Maturity is the ability to manage emotions, make sound decisions, positively influence others, and be self-aware. The questions in this instrument assess the emotional intelligence of a person in the workplace on the basis of the perception of those she/he works with directly or has worked with directly in the past.

Directions: Read each question carefully and circle the answer that most appropriately describes the person being evaluated. There are no right or wrong answers, but carefully reflect on each question and answer.

You have been asked to evaluate _____(insert name here)_____ along several interpersonal dimensions. Five or more individuals—peers and subordinates—are completing this questionnaire. When you are finished, please return your questionnaire to ___(name of third party)___, who will compile the results and provide summary averages to the person named above. Because the questionnaire does not require your name, your participation is anonymous; please do not share your responses with anyone.

What is your relationship to the person being evaluated? Please check one.

_____ Peer (work at same organization)
_____ Peer (work elsewhere)
_____ Subordinate
_____ Superior (full-time paid boss)
_____ Superior (voluntary board member)
_____ Other

Use this Likert scale for the assessment:

Strongly Disagree	Disagree	Neither Disagree nor Agree	Agree	Strongly Agree
1	2	3	4	5

1. This leader creates the feeling that she/he looks forward to each day with positive anticipation.
2. This leader truly believes that her/his work really makes a difference in her/his organization.
3. This leader has an even temper.
4. This leader rarely gets frustrated.
5. This leader has the creative ability to solve problems among people.
6. This leader truly enjoys being with other people.
7. This leader has strong control over her/his emotions.
8. When times get tough in the work setting, others can turn to this leader for guidance.
9. When mistakes are made, this leader's first instinct is to take corrective action (rather than place blame).

10. Other people would describe this leader as a person who does not "fall apart" under pressure.

11. This leader is well suited for her/his career.

12. If this leader had the chance to start her/his career all over again, she/he would still choose a leadership position.

13. This leader respects other people.

14. This leader is highly motivated.

15. Others would say this leader has her/his ego under control.

16. This leader has an appropriately high level of self-esteem.

17. Although this leader may at times get upset or angry, she/he has the ability to control emotions.

18. This leader has an appropriately high level of motivation.

19. This leader always seeks win-win solutions in conflict situations.

20. This leader would be the last person I would describe as a hopeless individual.

21. Although impatient for positive results, this leader does not allow her/his impatience to create a negative working environment.

22. This leader is a person whom others trust.

23. This leader is appropriately self-confident without being overbearing.

24. This leader is sensitive to others' feelings.

25. This leader listens well.

26. The last description you would expect to hear of this leader is "flies off the handle a lot."

27. This leader maintains a good balance in life.

28. This leader is emotionally stable and healthy.

29. This leader faces setbacks and adversity well.

30. This leader would not be described as hostile.

31. This leader has developed good mechanisms to get feedback from others.

Leadership Team Evaluation Form

ALTHOUGH THIS QUESTIONNAIRE has not been validated (i.e., no study has been performed to determine the correlation between the results of this questionnaire and performance outcome, such as profitability, patient satisfaction, physician satisfaction, or employee satisfaction), it provides the team with an initial tool for assessing the components of team effectiveness.

Because each component contributes to the overall efficiencies and inefficiencies of the team, each must be independently evaluated. To ensure comprehensive representation, all team members must complete the questionnaire. To ensure confidentiality of the responses, the team must select a neutral third party to collect the questionnaires; tally the ratings; and write a report, which must be distributed to the team for discussion.

Directions: Rate the following statements as correctly as possible. Please submit your completed questionnaire to _____(name of third party)_____ by __(date)__ . Please do not share your responses with others.

Use this Likert scale for the assessment:

Strongly Disagree	Disagree	Neither Disagree nor Agree	Agree	Strongly Agree
1	2	3	4	5

TEAM LEADERSHIP

1. The CEO or leader is not autocratic.
2. The CEO or leader does not make team decisions outside meetings.
3. The CEO or leader develops an atmosphere that encourages openness.
4. The CEO or leader is not afraid to be a full and equal participant in team processes.
5. In establishing the team, the CEO or leader ensures that all team members understand the decisions that should be made within the team setting and the decisions that should be made outside the team setting.
6. The CEO or leader ensures that time is set aside to occasionally discuss roles and decision-making rules and protocols.

TEAM COMPATIBILITY

7. Members share common values and goals.
8. Members have personal compatibility.
9. Members have professional compatibility.

TEAM INTERACTION

10. Members have camaraderie.
11. Members occasionally socialize outside of the workplace.
12. Members have frequent communication.
13. Members have open and candid conversations.
14. Members exchange accurate and timely information, prohibit or limit exaggeration, and discourage information hiding.

TEAM MIND-SET AND STRUCTURE

15. Members are committed to the same goals.
16. Each member understands her/his role within the team.
17. Members have actively and openly discussed team roles.
18. Members have mutually agreed to the assignment of team roles.
19. Members are highly interdependent.
20. The team has a high energy level.
21. Members acknowledge, discuss, and manage conflict.
22. Members are frank with each other and engage in little politics.
23. The size of the team is between 6 and 11.
24. There is a proper balance of titles among members.

TEAM MEETINGS

25. Meetings are well organized.
26. Meetings have objectives.
27. The agenda is followed closely during meetings.

28. Members show appropriate courtesy to each other during meetings.

29. All members actively participate in meetings.

30. Meetings have an appropriate level of formality but are not stiff.

31. Meetings end with an understood conclusion.

TEAM DECISIONS

32. The team observes decision-making protocols.

33. The entire team is responsible for decision-making.

34. The entire team has been trained in decision-making techniques.

35. The team has openly discussed its decision-making styles and processes.

36. The entire team realizes the danger of using compromise as the only end result of a decision-making process.

Grading Healthcare Team Effectiveness

THE FOLLOWING ASSESSMENTS are meant in the spirit of continuous improvement. They follow the outline provided in chapter 18, "Evaluating Team Effectiveness." A review of that chapter can be helpful in better understanding the nature of this analysis. A fictional evaluation of a poorly performing team is presented here first. It is followed by a blank form for you to use in conducting a similar evaluation of your team.

SAMPLE LEADERSHIP TEAM: STRUCTURE SIZE

The team comprises 20 or more individuals—far too large to be truly effective.

Grade = D–

Hierarchy

There is very little proper balance among the leadership team members. For a variety of reasons, some individuals simply carry more weight. As one CEO is known to say, "In some teams, you count votes, but in many others, you weigh the votes."

Grade = F

MEMBERSHIP

The senior team comprises some members whose position cannot possibly be linked to any logical reason to be a member.

Grade = C

SAMPLE LEADERSHIP TEAM: ACTIVITIES

Decision-Making

The team has no defined rationale for decision-making. Few team members have ever taken a course in decision-making. The team members simply kick ideas around until the leader (usually the CEO) calls for a decision—or, worse yet, indicates her own decision.

Grade = D–

Meetings

Typical meetings are the source of wasted time, rudeness, passive-aggressive behavior, and frequent sneaky looks at the smartphone by all in attendance. Few meetings are well planned, and fewer still provide any logical flow regarding topics. Tactical matters compete with strategic matters, and most participants secretly view the entire event as an enormous time waster.

Grade = F

Necessity

The team has far too many meetings, and those it holds usually last far too long.

Grade = C–

Objectives, Agendas, and Handouts

Although agendas are used much more than in the past, the effectiveness stops there. Minutes are characteristically a huge waste of effort. The traditional rule requiring that handouts be provided in advance is among the most violated.

Grade = D

Roles and Norms

Roles are played and norms exist—but they are rarely, if ever, discussed.

Grade = D–

Time

"Talk, talk, talk, when do we eat?" Because the meetings are not managed in a timely manner, the team finds it must often order in for food when important and weighty topics are discussed (and of course, all topics are important and weighty for this team).

Grade = D

Format

The team has used the same meeting format for decades. They rarely mix up methods or approaches.

Grade = C

Etiquette

Smartphones, administrative assistants entering the room to pass notes to some higher-level team members, sidebar conversations, late arrivals, early departures, doodling, lots of talk but very little frankness, breaking up the flow of conversation by getting up for a coffee refill—have we said enough?

Grade = D–

Participation

Some members are highly participative, some rarely participate, and some fall in the middle. The team leader is rarely effective in using techniques to draw all members out. Moreover, the power imbalance means that much goes unsaid for fear of retribution.

Grade = C

Wrap-Up

The team does poorly in wrapping up its meetings. Although it has adopted some of the agenda-tracking minutes that are used in quality improvement work groups, the agendas are rarely followed.

Grade = C

Protocol Development

There are no set ground rules and guidelines for team interaction, meeting management, and decision-making.

Grade = D

Hearing the Famous Statement

A vast majority of the time, the following statement can be heard at the end of the typical leadership meeting: "Meeting's over, let's get back to work."

Grade = A

YOUR TEAM: STRUCTURE SIZE

Grade =

Hierarchy

Grade =

Membership

Grade =

YOUR TEAM: ACTIVITIES

Decision-Making

Grade =

Meetings

Grade =

Necessity

Grade =

Objectives, Agendas, and Handouts

Grade =

Roles and Norms

Grade =

Time

Grade =

Format

Grade =

Etiquette

Grade =

Participation

Grade =

Wrap-Up

Grade =

Protocol Development

Grade =

Hearing the Famous Statement

Grade =

Index

Note: Italicized page locators refer to exhibits.

in, xviii; micro and macro view of, vignette, 113–14; self-evaluation questions, 122

Ethics statements, 116

Etiquette: meetings, 302–3

Eulogy virtues, 106

"Evidence-Based Management" (Pfeffer & Sutton), 48

Evidence-based practice: definition of, 24

Exaggerating: avoiding, 118–19

Exceptional Leadership (Garman & Dye), 36, 105, 204

Executive leadership styles, *361*

Executive search process: haphazard, 84–85

Executive teams: rebuilding, 217

Exercise, 206; regular, *185*

Expectancy theory of leadership, 33

Expense accounts: judicious management of, 121

External behavior: internal values as driver for, 69

Extraversion, 38

Eye contact, 133

Facebook, xix

Facial cues, 188

Failure: reframing as learning agility, 365–66

Fairness: inclusive leadership and, 335

Fallacy, solid evidence *vs.,* 48

Fatigue, 184

"Fault Lines of Leadership, The: Lessons from the Global Covid-19 Crisis" (Maak, Pless, & Wohlgezogen), 426

Favoritism, 256, 364

Fayol, Henri, 24, 91

Fear: driving out, 252–53

Federations, 83

Feedback: establishing system for, 103–4; seeking, 202–3, *207*

Festinger, Leon, 352

Few Good Men, A (film), 224

Fiedler, F. E., 27

Financial margin, 381

Financial sustainability: challenges with, 374

Finesse, using, 255

Fisher, R., 276

Five Dysfunctions of a Team, The: A Leadership Fable (Lencioni), 47, 252

Five-factor model of personality, 38–39, *39*

Followers: focusing on needs of, 134; four primary needs of, from their leaders, 424; in interactive framework of leadership, 27, *28*; leadership's dependence on, 29; personal values and, 62; respect and, 98; servant leadership and, 146, 148; transformational leadership and, 31. *See also* Leaders

Following through: integrity and, 119

Food, stockpiling, 420

Force for Change, A (Kotter), 35

Forcing, 272

Forecasts: leadership imperative and, 5

Forman, H., 104

Forming, storming, norming, and performing stages (Tuckman), 218

Forrestal, Elizabeth J., 71, 161

Foster, Mary, 283

Franklin, Ben, 136

Fraud, 136

Freedman, Joshua, *359*

Frontline staff: servant leaders and, 151–52

Frost, Robert, 58, 59

Fulghum, Robert: "golden rules" of, 136; my take on kindergarten lessons of, *137*

Functions of the Executive, The (Barnard), 26

Gabor, A., 27

Gallup, 48, 138, 165

Gandhi, Mahatma, 187, *188*

Garber, Peter, 103

Garman, Andrew N., xxii, 28, 50, 135, 154, 167, 181, 293

Gaslighting: definition of, 349

Gawande, Atul, 8, 14

Geerts, J. M., xxiii, 426

Gender inequities: COVID-19 and exacerbation of, 422

Generosity, 398

About the Author

CARSON F. DYE, FACHE, president and CEO of Exceptional Leadership, LLC, is a seasoned leadership consultant with more than 40 years of leadership and management experience. Over the past 20 years, he has conducted hundreds of leadership searches for healthcare organizations, helping to fill chief executive officer, chief operating officer, chief financial officer, and physician executive roles in health systems, academic medical centers, universities, and freestanding hospitals.

Mr. Dye has provided clients with extensive counsel in succession planning, leadership assessment, CEO evaluation, coaching, and retreat facilitation. He is certified to use the Hogan Leadership Assessment tests for evaluation, coaching, and leadership development. He also has extensive experience working with physician leaders and has helped organizations establish physician leadership development programs.

Mr. Dye has served as an executive search consultant and partner with Witt/Kieffer, TMP Worldwide, and LAI/Lamalie Associates. Prior to these roles, he was partner and director of Findley Davies's healthcare consulting division in Toledo, Ohio. Dye has 20 years of experience in healthcare administration, serving in executive-level positions at St. Vincent Mercy Medical Center in Toledo, the Ohio State University Wexner Medical Center in Columbus, and Cincinnati Children's Hospital Medical Center and Clermont Mercy Hospital—both in Cincinnati.

Mr. Dye has been a regular faculty member for the American College of Healthcare Executives (ACHE) since 1987 and has presented workshops for 48 state and local hospital associations. He also teaches in the ACHE Board of Governors Examination preparation course. In addition, Dye is a faculty member of The Governance Institute and has held faculty appointments at the University of Alabama at Birmingham in its executive MBA program and at the Ohio State University in its Health Services Management program.

Mr. Dye has written 12 previous books, all with Health Administration Press, including three James A. Hamilton Book of the Year winners: *The Healthcare Leader's Guide to Actions, Awareness, and Perception* (2016); *Developing Physician Leaders for Successful Clinical Integration* (2013); and *Leadership in Healthcare: Values at the Top* (2000). His other titles include *Enhanced Physician Engagement Volume 1: What It Is, Why You Need It, and Where to Begin* (2022); *Enhanced Physician Engagement Volume 2: Tools and Tactics for Success* (2022); *Exceptional Leadership: 16 Critical Competencies for Healthcare Executives* (2015); *Winning the Talent War* (2002); and *Protocols for Healthcare Executive Behavior* (1993). The Dye-Garman Leadership Competency Model, found in *Exceptional Leadership*, has been used by many healthcare organizations as a competency model for assessment, executive selection, development, and succession planning. He has served on the boards of Lourdes University; The Sight Center / Toledo Society for the Blind, where he served as board chair; and the Visiting Nurses Association. Mr. Dye earned his BA from Marietta College and his MBA from Xavier University.

About the
Contributors

KATHERINE A. MEESE, PhD, is an assistant professor in the Department of Health Services Administration at the University of Alabama at Birmingham (UAB). She also serves as the director of Wellness Research in the UAB Medicine Office of Wellness, director for the Center for Healthcare Management and Leadership, and program director for the Graduate Certificate in Healthcare Leadership. She also serves as the chair of the Well-Being Council for the National Center for Healthcare Leadership. She earned her PhD in Health Services Administration with a specialization in strategic management from UAB and joined the faculty in 2020. Dr. Meese has several years of industry experience, which encompassed work in ten countries on four continents, including finance, venture capital, and management within a large academic medical center. She has cowritten two textbooks for organizational behavior in healthcare with Dr. Nancy Borkowski that are used in healthcare management programs across the country, and has written several book chapters. Her research has been published in *Anesthesia & Analgesia, Journal of Healthcare Management, Health Services Management Research, Journal of Health Administration Education, Health Care Management Review*, and a variety of other journals. Her research interests include organizational behavior, leadership, well-being, and delivery models that enhance organizational learning.

DAVID A. ROGERS, MD, MPHE, is a professor in the Department of Surgery at the University of Alabama at Birmingham (UAB), with secondary appointments in the Departments of Medical Education and Pediatrics and an adjunct appointment in the Collat School of Business. He served as the senior associate dean of Faculty Affairs and Professional Development at the UAB Heersink School of Medicine from 2012 until 2021 and continues to serve as the codirector of the UAB Healthcare Leadership Academy. He was named the UAB Medicine Chief Wellness Officer (CWO) and was appointed to the ProAssurance Chair of Physician Wellness in 2018. His approach in this role is to promote team well-being by working collaboratively with many groups at UAB and UAB Medicine to provide appropriate support programs and reduce work-associated demands. While affecting positive change at UAB Medicine, he aspires to facilitate original scholarship related to workplace wellness.

Dr. Rogers received his medical degree from the University of South Florida and completed his general surgery training at the Medical College of Georgia. He subsequently completed his pediatric general surgery training at the University of Tennessee and a pediatric surgery oncology fellowship at St. Jude Children's Research Hospital. He received a Master of Health Professions Education degree from the University of Illinois at Chicago and completed the Surgical Education Research Fellowship program sponsored by the Association for Surgical Education.

Dr. Rogers's initial administrative role was as the surgery clerkship director, and he continues to be involved in surgical education by serving as a faculty member of the American College of Surgeons Educators' course. He is also the past chair of the American College of Surgeons' Residents as Teachers and Leaders program. He serves as a codirector of the Association for Surgical Education Surgical Education Research Fellowship. A recipient of numerous departmental and institutional teaching awards, Dr. Rogers is a 2012 recipient of the Association for Surgical Education Distinguished Educator Award.

CARLA JACKIE SAMPSON, PhD, FACHE, is a clinical associate professor and director of the Health Policy and Management program and online Master of Health Administration program at New York University's Robert F. Wagner Graduate School of Public Service. Dr. Sampson is board certified in healthcare management and is a Fellow of the American College of Healthcare Executives. Previously, Dr. Sampson was assistant professor and director of Healthcare Management Programs in the Department of Risk, Insurance, and Healthcare Management Programs in the Fox School of Business, Temple University. Research interests include healthcare workforce policy, social determinants of health, and anchor mission strategy development. Dr. Sampson was a research assistant for the Florida Center for Nursing and was lead author for the report "Emerging & Evolving Roles and Occupations Within the Healthcare Industry: Florida's Perspective." Dr. Sampson has extensive experience in the online and traditional classroom setting. Areas of teaching experience include organizational strategy, executive leadership, human resources management, and healthcare policy.

Prior to her appointment at Temple, Dr. Sampson was the vice president of the Commission on Accreditation of Healthcare Management Education (CAHME). Her role was to assure excellence in the educational preparation of future leaders in the healthcare industry through the management of CAHME's accreditation program. With her planning and under her direction, CAHME launched several initiatives to implement and improve the quality of competency-based education, streamline the accreditation process, improve the consistency of site visits, increase transparency in the accreditation process, and develop workshops on CAHME's accreditation criteria for program directors and site visitors. While at CAHME, Dr. Sampson also served as a consultant to all programs seeking initial CAHME accreditation and oversaw the design and implementation of an electronic accreditation system. As an independent consultant, Dr. Sampson has successfully assisted healthcare management education programs in becoming accredited and in preparing for reaccreditation.

Dr. Sampson was awarded a Doctor of Philosophy in Public Affairs—Health Services Management and Research from the

University of Central Florida, Orlando. She earned an MBA in Healthcare Management and a Master of Science in Healthcare Financial Management from the Fox School of Business.

Margot Savoy, MD, FAAFP, FABC, FAAPL, CPE, CMQ, is senior vice president, Education, for the American Academy of Family Physicians. She was formerly the department chair and associate professor for the Department of Family and Community Medicine at the Lewis Katz School of Medicine at Temple University and Temple University Hospital, and also served as the chief quality officer for the Temple Faculty Practice Plan. She graduated from the University of Maryland School of Medicine in 2002; completed the Family Medicine Residency program at the Crozer-Keystone Family Medicine Residency Program in Springfield, Pennsylvania, in 2005; and graduated from the University of North Carolina at Chapel Hill Gillings School of Global Public Health in 2008 with an MPH in public health leadership with a focus on public health practice. She is certified by the American Board of Family Medicine and the Certifying Commission in Medical Management and is a Fellow of the Advisory Board Company.

Patrick D. Shay, PhD, is an associate professor in the Department of Health Care Administration at Trinity University in San Antonio, Texas, where he teaches graduate courses on such topics as health services organization and policy, healthcare innovation, population health management, and healthcare organization theory and behavior. His research applies organization theory to healthcare organization phenomena, including the activities and configurations of local multihospital systems as well as the impact of regulation on post-acute care providers, among others. Prior to his doctoral studies, he worked as a healthcare administrator for a post-acute care system in south Texas. Dr. Shay received his BS in business administration and MS in healthcare administration from Trinity University and his PhD in health services organization and research from Virginia Commonwealth University.